NASTRAGULL

—— BOOK TWO ——

HUNTED

ERIK MARTIN WILLÉN

ASC PUBLISHING

NASTRAGULL: HUNTED
Copyright © 2022 Erik Martin Willén

All rights reserved. No part of this publication may be reproduced, distributed, or transmitted in any form or by any means, including photocopying, recording, or other electronic or mechanical methods, without the prior written permission of the publisher, except in the case of brief quotations embodied in critical reviews and certain other noncommercial uses permitted by copyright law. For permission requests, please write to the publisher.

This book is a work of fiction. The characters, incidents, and dialogue are drawn from the author's imagination and are not to be construed as real. Any resemblance to actual events or persons, living or dead, is entirely coincidental.

Published by ASC Publishing

ISBN: 978-91-988090-1-5

ALSO BY ERIK MARTIN WILLÉN

NASTRAGULL

PIRATES
BOOK 1

DAWN SETS IN HELL
BOOK 3

SECTION TWENTY-ONE
BOOK 4

THE BEAST
BOOK 5

OTHER NOVELS

THE LUMBERJACK

*For my older brother Magnus,
who never gave up believing in me and always stood by my side.*

*Discrimination and segregation are evidence of lower
intelligence and lack of common sense.*

ERIK MARTIN WILLÉN

ONE

THE guests moved into the grand ballroom after the fifteen-course dinner, and found a live band playing on a disk-shaped platform hovering above the center of the vast dance floor. The arched roof overhead was currently de-opaqued, displaying the stars of the local galaxy in all their splendor. Some guests began dancing, while others investigated the various bars and lounges scattered along the walls. After everyone had settled in, a rather famous celebrity joined the band and started to sing.

Admiral Busch gallantly escorted Nina to the dance floor, while Alec joined with Tara. Since the two young women had no clue what they were doing, their dancing experiment soon came to an end, and both of them turned disappointed expressions on their escorts. "Sorry," Nina muttered. "Pirates don't dance much."

Busch patted her hand comfortingly. "No worries, dear. You'll learn someday."

Alec leaned toward Tara and whispered, "Stay close."

Tara nodded, and reached out to take Nina's arm. She gestured to a servant for more cocktails.

The Admiral reluctantly relinquished his hold on Nina and murmured to Alec, "This is a little too much, even for me. I'm sorry, Alec, but I must insist that we return to the fleet immediately." He raised his right hand, motioning to Alec to keep his mouth shut. "It's my final decision. I must obey my orders—and you must obey yours."

"Mr. Horn!" Zala interrupted as she approached, escorting a military officer dressed in a white uniform offset by black boots. Like Busch, he bore an Admiral's stars. The fruit salad on his chest included several medals, along with a ribbon over his breast with an order of some sort attached to it. His uniform stood out in the crowd, and Alec was rather surprised he hadn't noticed it before. Then again, there were literally thousands of guests attending the ball.

The uniform was standard issue for the Florencian Federation Space Navy. *Fish Fucker,* Alec thought distastefully.

Zala fluted, "I hear you will soon leave us, Mr. Horn, and I was hoping we could get to know each other better first."

"Why, Ms. Zala, I'm sure we'll meet again someday."

"That would be nice, young man," she said, smoothing her blouse fussily. She looked like a pig playing dress-up. "Do make sure you let us know how to reach you."

"Of course I will."

"I almost forgot...here is Admiral Jonas Nass of the Florencian Federation. I promised him I would introduce the two of you. Jonas, this is Mr. Alec Horn."

"Pleasure to meet you, sir," said Nass, extending his hand.

Alec smiled uneasily as he shook hands with one of Florencia's most feared military officers. "To what do we owe the pleasure, sir?" Alec asked.

"I've heard rumors that you're looking for good investments."

"I was under the impression that your federation didn't care much for capitalistic investors. Isn't it against your cultural philosophy?"

Nass smiled cheerfully. "Oh, we're not as totalitarian as all that."

"They're always looking for money," Busch snapped.

"And whenever the bastards run out, they steal it." He cut his eyes toward Alec. "Be careful, Master Horn. I have had the dubious pleasure of bearing witness to their piratical actions myself, on several occasions."

"Ah, Admiral Busch. Never quite got over the loss at Bazzira, I take it," Nass observed with a hint of a sneer. "What was that, ten years ago?"

"Gentlemen, no hostility here, I beg you both," Zala said quickly. "Please be civilized. It would be bad for business if you two were to start something here." She gestured at the crowd.

The two admirals glared at one another, until Busch broke the silence. "I'm surprised that the commander of the Florencian 9th Galactic would leave his fleet for a simple dinner party."

"I see your intel is lacking, as usual."

Busch frowned, then opened his mouth to say something, but was interrupted by Lady Fuzza. "Oh look, finally, fireworks!" she exclaimed loudly.

They looked up through the ceiling; the starscape outside was lit up with hundreds of colorful explosions.

Alec gazed at the remarkable display with an impressed expression...though when he glanced at the girls, they seemed a bit frightened. "I've never seen anything like this before," he admitted to Zala. "It's beautiful."

"It *is* highly unusual to have fireworks in space, given the expense," Zala said primly, looking pleased.

Admirals Nass and Busch viewed the display with much less enthusiasm. "I take it old Cook is nearby?" Nass murmured to his rival.

"You never know." Busch muttered back through clenched teeth.

Alec glimpsed movement from the corner of his eye, and lowered his gaze to see a tall figure draped loosely in black stand up from a nearby table and turn in their direction. Zala noticed him looking. "That is Zoris af Sun, our guest of honor and the host of tonight's art auction," she explained.

An effeminate-looking man hurried up to Zoris and started whispering urgently to her. She emitted a strange sound from behind her veil, a piercing keen that sent chills down Alec's backbone. He was pretty sure she was upset, and equally sure he knew why. He casually turned away from her and decided to focus on the remarkable fireworks display overhead.

He noted, with alarm, that one of the rockets seemed to have gone a bit off course; it was zooming straight toward the station at a high rate of speed. Thousands of guests and servants gasped as the rocket hit the force dome and exploded into a huge fireball above them, shaking the station and bathing them in a wash of hot colors.

"Lovely!" a stout matron cried.

"More, more!" another guest shouted, clapping her many tiny hands.

There was another explosion, immediately followed by another. The first explosion made the station shudder like a building in an earthquake. The next wasn't as bad, but it caused the lights to flicker.

"Shit!" Nina shouted into the sudden silence. She knew what was happening, if no one else did yet; and a glance at Tara confirmed that she did, too.

By now Lady Zala's expression had morphed into something more concerned, as Admirals Nass and Busch looked at each other, both suddenly knowing exactly what was happening. They folded up the sleeves on their respective uniform jackets and peered at the displays on their wristcomps.

"Not ours," Busch said quickly.

Nass replied, "Not ours, either."

They exchanged puzzled looks as several explosions in succession rocked the ballroom, accompanied by hundreds more lighting up the Big Dark outside. With the exception of their huddled group and a few others, the other guests were still oohing and ahhing over the colorful display, though some of them voiced their concern as the floor shook and the lights flickered again. The hosts and servants scurried about, trying to calm them by making up answers to their wondering questions; but their temporary lies were interrupted by the alarm that suddenly sounded from hidden speakers, drowning the music from the orchestra and a certain very upset celebrity, who was singing louder than ever, trying vainly to be heard over the din.

The alarm was followed by a calm female voice—Coco Cabelle's, though few in the ballroom were aware of that—who delivered one of the most terrifying messages anyone in space could hear: "Attention! Attention! New Frontier 16 is under attack, apparently by pirates. Civilians, take cover and remain where you are for the duration. DO NOT try to return home or otherwise leave your current locations; we need the passageways clear. Station personnel, secure all stations. All security personal prepare for battle. Attention! Attention! New Frontier 16 is under attack..." The warning looped continuously against a backdrop of a high-pitched alarm.

"Only a complete fool would attack one of these fortresses," Nass growled. "Unless they already have..."

Both Admirals finished Nass's sentence: "...troops on the inside!"

Their theory was soon confirmed by another, more desperate voice from the intercom: "Security personnel, report to sectors A-6 through A-12 to repel borders! Report to repel bord—" The voice was cut short by the loud crackle of a blaster shot followed by an explosion; and the intercom fell silent.

Tobbis scurried up to Zala, sputtering something indecipherable, and the two Key Administrators hustled over to Admirals Nass and Busch, demanding that their two fleets immediately assist New Frontier against the pirate threat. Neither of the Admirals paid them much attention, instead dividing their attention between their wristcomps and the massive fleet heaving into view in the far distance. Hundreds of large ships were already visible, moving in fast, steady and confidently opening fire on their prey with laser cannons, particle beams, and missiles. Most of the weapons fire was intercepted by NF16's point defense, but a few shots got through to chew at the station's armor. As they watched, a flight of offensive missiles reached out and turned a score of the oncoming ships into glowing dust.

Bush gritted his teeth and said, "Two hundred, at least."

"More like five hundred," Nass countered. "Look, whoever it is, they're mad to attack a station like this while our fleets are nearby!"

"Maybe they don't know about our fleets. Or maybe they think they can beat us." Busch gestured toward the other side of the force dome, where a second huge flotilla was flicking into view, arranging itself into attack formation. By the looks of things, it was neither Nastasturan nor Florencian.

Two naval officers appeared suddenly and joined their respective Admirals. A captain reported to Busch, while a commander reported to Nass. After the junior officers had completed their reports, telling them nothing they didn't already know, Nass broke the silence. "I take it that the piracy laws demand that we put our own interests aside?"

"They make us allies, for the moment," Busch replied.

The two Admirals turned and saluted each other.

"We need to get the hell of this tin can," Busch declared.

"Yeah, but they brought us here in their own ships—"

"There they go," Busch exclaimed, gesturing toward several dozen corvettes flying in formation away from the station, on a mission to intercept the oncoming threat.

One of the corvettes exploded into a shrapnel as a missile struck it dead center; another rammed some of the debris from the destroyed corvette, leaving a gaping hole in its hull that spewed vapor and bodies. Fires and minor explosions flickered inside the corvette as it careened out of control, veering back the way it had come and, seconds later, flattening itself against the station's deflector shields. A few escape pods managed to launch; one bounced off the ballroom's force dome.

The automatic defense system having decided that the electromagnetic shield had taken enough damage, a metal shield irised into place over the dome, casting the ballroom briefly into pitch dark. Panic broke out as the guests headed for the nearest exits, even as emergency lighting flickered to life.

Admiral Busch had to shout to be heard: "Alec, what about your ship?"

"It's on its way!" Alec shouted over the screams from the panicked crowd. "Follow me! Clear a path for us to that exit!" Alec ordered the Grisamm monks, pointing at a hatch in the far distance.

The monks had their cloaks slide into backpack devices on their backs, revealing their body armor and armaments. Cursing their girly outfits, Nina and Tara crowded up against Alec, grim expressions on their faces.

Admiral Nass looked hesitantly at Busch, who snapped, "Would you rather command your fleet from here, Nass? Or is the admiral in charge competent to do the job?"

"My fleet admiral isn't even with the damned fleet."

"Please, gentlemen, discuss that later. You need to hurry if you want to leave!" Alec shouted.

Nass and Busch signaled to their respective aides to clear a path through the terrified people blocking the exit in front of them. The others followed him out, but just as Alec reached the exit, he immediately realized that it would be impossible to get through the crowd to the ship. Realizing the same, one of the Grisamm charged up his weapon and lifted it grimly, ready to clear a bloody road for them.

Alec placed his hand on the large gun and shouted over the alarm, "No, no shooting! Just get rid of all these people!"

"How?" The monk demanded.

Alec looked around for a moment, and then smiled savagely. He grabbed Nina roughly and yanked the bodice of her dress. "*What the fuck are you doing!*" Nina shrieked as thousands of pearls scattered across the floor. Hands on her hips, she yelled, "All you had to do was ask, big fella! I've already seen your equipment, after all!" Clad only in sheer panties and footwear, she bent down and removed a shock-stick from one boot.

"Oh no, I can do it myself, thank you!" Tara assured one of the Grisamm monks, when she saw that he was ready to give her the same treatment. She yanked on the front of her dress, and thousands more pearls cascaded to the deck. All around them, people were treading on the pearls, slipping and falling with terrified cries.

"Shuffle your feet so you don't fall!" Alec shouted, and led the way as people fell around them left and right. Enough of the other guests slipped on the pearls that they were able to push their way through and into the foyer outside, which led directly to a covered exit to the VIP docking bay. A dark shape hovered at the end of the bay, mated directly to the atmospheric shield: the *Predator*. Amid the crowd of smaller shuttles and limos, it looked like a bull among sheep.

As Alec and his companions approached, running full-out now that the danger of stepping on the pearls was gone, Pier charged out of the airlock, followed by a stream of personnel, mostly former pirate women—who, to Alec's dismay, were kitted out in their full pirate regalia, which was to say that no two were dressed alike, and certainly none were wearing their shipsuits.

True to form, the panicked ballroom crowd (which hadn't so much as blinked at the sight of two nearly-nude women in their midst) took the women for what they had been but no longer were: cries of "Pirates! The pirates are here!" flashed through the crowd, causing even more panic. When Alec glanced back, he saw that the people who had managed to get through the exit were now trying to get back into the ballroom, and were jamming up against the crowd still trying to get out. Several fights started, and soon it turned into a general melee. "I don't have time for this," he growled, as he turned and sprinted toward his ship.

To make matters worse, his erstwhile crew thought it was all good fun, and started singing one of their notorious pirate ballads. Alec grabbed Pier and skidded to a halt. "Dammit, man, get them to shut the hell up! Holy Gull, this is *not* helping at all!"

Pier grinned puckishly, then placed his index finger to his mouth while making an soft ssshing sound. Alec shouted, "Do you want to keep this job?"

Grin widening, Pier tapped in a recall order on his wristcomp, and the wristcomps of the various *Predator* personnel scattered down the corridor started braying like deranged mules.

AFTER what had seemed like an eternity but was, in fact, less than five minutes, everyone who belonged on the *Predator* was aboard, along with a smattering of military guests. Alec was bent over, hands on knees, gasping for breath. Somehow, the much older Admiral Busch had found his way to the bridge already, and was shouting into his wristcomp, telling Tobbis and Zala to for Gull's sake lock themselves into their own command bridge already. They babbled back, and he assured them that his fleet and Nass's would do everything they could to assist New Frontier.

Predator began to accelerate away from the station, followed by dozens of private civilian shuttles and limousines. It was no safer in near-space: missiles and rockets of all sizes probed through the area, while particle and laser beams lit up the debris clouds like neon, and magma bursts and chemical explosions bloomed all around. It just got worse as thousands of small, unmanned fighters launched from the space station, descending on the pirate flotillas like angry wasps.

Dozens of the rebuilt civilian transport and cargo ships that the pirates were using as gunboats were vaporized in the opening seconds of the skirmish; hundreds more were damaged, some critically. But the defenders' initial victory was short-lived: there were still hundreds of pirate vessels left to face, and the survivors started picking off the drones one by one with forcelances and point-defense missiles. Several large battle cruisers, previously hidden in the holds of cloaked super-transports, waded into the fray, directing magma blasts at weapons and shield platforms on New Frontier 16 and slagging the drone fighters with lasers.

Few of the weapons were directed at the station itself, as it was too great a prize to risk, and the protective forceshields remained intact in most areas. In those areas not already taken by infiltrated pirates, it was easier and safer to force their way in via mechanical means. Within moments, ships equipped with ramming arms, just like those on Zuzack's *Bitch*, converged on the station, ramming their way inside. Other ships descended on the two large docking bays that were, by then, controlled by the pirates.

The situation was complicated by the hundreds, if not thousands, of civilian transports and cargo ships that were scrambling to get themselves as far from the battle as possible. As with any battle, there was collateral damage; here and there, civilian ships flashed into vapor as they passed through particle beams or laser fire, and took various levels of damage as their paths intersected with those of missiles fired at other targets. There were unexpected acts of heroism as well: without prompting or deputization by the NF16 security forces, some of the larger civilian vessels turned and fired upon their aggressors, who wisely avoided them in favor of easier prey. Some of the civilian vessels took the battle to the pirates: one in particular, a yacht emblazoned with a stylized sunburst, leaped eagerly into the fight, disabling and destroying every marauder it encountered. Diving into a cluster of converted supertankers, it released a spray of sprinter missiles that latched onto their targets in an instant, before detonating in a series of white-hot nuclear blasts that left the retreating yacht shaken but unscathed.

ZORIS af Sun paced the corridors of her yacht, snarling. She kicked aside the body of one of her security guards, but otherwise ignored it; the cyan blood that spread over the cold, hard deck like thick syrup was more interesting to her, but she had little time to dwell on it. Her hand was still squeezing the man's pulped heart. She stumbled as the ship corkscrewed through another cluster of pirate ships, the inertial compensators unable to entirely handle the quick movement, and dropped the heart to clutch the wall.

She stalked over to the ship's captain, who was huddled against the bulkhead near what remained of his men, and thrust a blood-stained finger into his face. "Captain. Take us away from this mess and find out who stole my property."

"Aye aye, milady." The Captain trembled as he hurried back to the bridge.

None since the betrayers have shown such an appalling lack of respect for me and my property, she fumed as she made her way to her private quarters and towards her giant bed. It tore her up, it really did. Zoris lay down and cried. The sense of injustice she felt at the moment was simply more than she could bear. She hated the universe and everything in it. She hated her own parents, even, who had had the audacity to give her life; she cursed them and the day she was born, her gaunt face awash with a purulent mixture of tears and gore. She didn't care; it was comforting, in fact. All she cared about now was getting her property back in time for her next masterpiece. Nothing else mattered to her, except perhaps finding the thieves…and having them over for dinner.

THE battle for New Frontier 16 wasn't going well for the defenders. As the little fighter/interceptors ran low on ammo, they re-armed when they could; but when the supplies of missiles and power modules ran out, there was nothing to do but turn the little darts themselves into kinetic weapons. Many were directed to fly straight into the pirate ships by their pilots, all of whom were sitting safe aboard NF16. The drones couldn't easily destroy one the larger vessels, but when properly placed could disable them, especially when one or more attacked simultaneously. For more than an hour, the defender drones delayed the main onslaught; by then, there were fewer than two hundred of the little ships left. That was the signal for just over a hundred heavy corvettes and missile boats to press the attack.

Zuzack stood with his arms thrust up to his elbows in a hologram that represented local space. The battle for NF16 was a colorful fireworks display in the lower left quadrant; at the moment, his attention was engaged by a large group of ships that was approaching his battle group. He twisted one hand just so, and the cluster of ships he was peering at magnified to a point of near uselessness, the images blurry and indistinct. "Who are they, Zuzack?" a low voice demanded.

He glanced at his brother sidelong. "They're too far away to tell right now. But I'd guess they're almost as numerous as we are."

"Sir!" shouted the flagship's captain from behind them. "Our third column reports that it's engaging a very large fleet of Florencian warships, supported by a smaller group of Nastasturan capital ships! They're asking for help!"

Horsa snarled, "Tell them to get away from there and join us here." To his brother, he muttered, "Neither federation is powerful enough to stop us, not this deep into the neutral zone."

Zuzack drew in a sharp breath. "Brother. Another fleet." He thrust his hand into the image and pulled that sector into the center, twisting up the magnification with one hand, focusing with the other. According to the counter, there were nearly a thousand ships in the fleet, some of them outmassing the Walsatures supertankers. "Captain," Zuzack called distractedly, "can you see them on your display, or are they too far out? Coordinates Red 03, Blue 27, Green 08. More or less."

"Yessir, the computer's running a diagnostic right now." After a long moment the Captain said grimly, "Looks like it's composed of ships from the Night-Hunter and Red Knight clans."

"That cow Ogstafa!" Horsa bellowed. "Bitch must have followed us, and now she's waiting for us to be done so she can come in to pick the carcass. Or finish us off!"

"The woman has no honor," muttered Zuzack ironically. He ran his own diagnostic on the display. "Right, confirmed...I'm also seeing some Sunray markings." He pulled his arms out of the holo-display said, "Not even we can take on three or more clans, brother. Not if a third of us are fighting two Federation fleets more than three hours away."

"Thinking of quitting?" Horsa taunted.

"Me? Hell no. Let's kill them all. We just have to find a way." He tapped a booted foot on the deck, and stroked the dark fuzz that had finally begun to sprout on his wrecked chin. "We must make a deal with Ogstafa and her friends."

Horsa looked like he'd rather swallow broken glass, but he eventually admitted, "I suppose you're right. Captain, get us in range and establish a link with the old bitch's flagship. Zuzack, take command of the battle while I make contact with Ogstafa. Remember the main reason we're here."

Zuzack gave his brother a strange smile. It was difficult for Horsa—or anyone for that matter—to read Zuzack's expression since that Oman had stolen his face, but Horsa could recognize the disappointment in his brother's eyes. Grudgingly Horsa said, "Well, revenge too, of course. We'll find the little coward who did that to you."

Zuzack nodded sharply. "I'll return to the *Bitch*, then."

"Do that, and remember: you must keep our clan together in the process. And let's make sure this attack soon ends, or we'll likely have some deserters on our hands."

Zuzack nodded to his brother, and they embraced before Zuzack left the command bridge and headed toward the docking bay where the *Bitch* waited.

All Zuzack wanted was revenge; getting the map back was now a secondary motive. He burned with a desire to find the little Oman who had disfigured him—not to kill him, no, but to take him to the Black Lady so she could turn him into an art piece, just as she had done to the traitor Alexa. *I do so look forward meeting Alexa the next time the Black Lady invites all the clan leaders for her next dinner extravaganza*, he thought, licking his lips with anticipation.

Horsa's battle cruiser, the *Rapacious*, changed course abruptly, and part of the main column followed. The *Bitch* joined in the melee in the space around New Frontier 16 with the rest of the main column—though Zuzack held his beloved ship out of range of the space station's weapons arrays, preferring to batter it with long-range missiles and protect it against the few remaining fighter/interceptors by remaining behind a shield comprised of lesser ships. It wasn't that he was a coward as such; rather, it was easier for him to control his forces from a distance. Like most pirates, he preferred easy prey and quick, merciless strikes that limited his own damage. The only reason that the Wulsatures kept attacking in the face of the current stiff resistance was the knowledge of the incredible wealth that would soon be theirs if they could win through. But if the main onslaught failed, then it wouldn't be long until most of the clan sounded retreat.

"Captain, we've taken two of the larger docking bays, and almost fifty levels on the southern and eastern quadrants of the station," Hughes reported. Zuzack glanced at him and sneered; the rat-man was dressed in his ragged white Florencian admiral's uniform.

"Make sure we keep those sectors at any cost," Zuzack ordered. "If we fail to take the rest of the station, we can always barter our way out. Have there been any new developments with our third column?"

"Nossir. Apparently they can't punch through all the subspace jamming."

Zuzack eyed Hughes' uniform. "You were in the Florencian military. Do you think the federations will send any reinforcements?"

"Florencia certainly would," Hughes said confidently. "We're close to Handover, but it would still take days, perhaps weeks, before they could easily mobilize an Intergalactic fleet, which is the type they'd send for an action of this size. On the other hand, if there are any ships or smaller fleets available nearby, they'll certainly send them here. The Nasties have no bases as near as the Florencians, but they would send any galactic fleet ships they can scramble in response to a distress call. Those could be here in a matter of days, or even hours."

Zuzack nodded sharply and eased into his command seat, observing the various sectors of the battle in a scatter of monitors and holodisplays ranged before him. He tried to focus on all the glorious mayhem, but had difficulty doing so, as his mind drifted whenever he thought about the thief who had stolen his face.

―――――――――oOo―――――――――

THE Nastasturan 11th Galactic fleet lay concealed among the drifting mountains of a minor asteroid belt in the outer fringes of the system New Frontier currently occupied, electronic shields and countermeasures fully deployed. Admiral Cook paced the length of his flagship's bridge, worrying about Alistair Busch. On his latest return leg, he noticed Commander Ezim waiting patiently for him, saluting stiffly.

When he returned the salute, the young man launched into his spiel. "The situation at New Frontier is confusing at best, sir. We've received reports from Admiral Busch's fleet and several civilian vessels that two convoys of civilian ships have attacked the primary station, New Frontier 16, and have engaged both Admiral Busch's fleet group and the Florencian 9th Galactic. And sir, we have received confirmation from Admiral Busch that Admiral Jonas Nass commands the Florencians, and that for the moment they are cooperating against the attackers."

Ezim pressed a button on his wristcomp, and a sparkling holographic sitrep map flashed up between them. The commander pointed toward the center of the display. "As you can see, sir, Admiral Busch's second, Commander Kelab, has moved her ships into a defensive position here. Meanwhile, Admiral Nass sent a third of his capital ships—that's about a hundred vessels—to investigate the battle at New Frontier, apparently, and they were attacked here, by the civilian convoys." The Commander tapped his wristcomp, re-centering the display on a clot of red and blue symbols that were snarled together into a confusing knot. "An hour into the fight, one of the civilian convoys withdrew, and is now heading directly for the New Frontier 16."

The Captain of the *Unity 1*, Greenlaw Adnil, joined them at the logistics map. "I take it Commander Kelab can't reach Admiral Busch and wants to know what she should do?"

Cook looked at the holographic map for a moment and then began pacing again, thinking over what should be done. After traversing the bridge and returning, he said to Ezim and Adnil, "If I send Busch's column toward the station, Florencia's 9th and some pissed-off civilians will be behind them, while another group of pissed-off civilians will be between the station and his second group. If I withdraw Kelab's group to join us here, then they'll still have the 9th behind them." Admiral Cook scowled. "This sector is supposed to be free of any significant pirate activity. But who else could these 'civilians' be?"

The two officers exchanged glances. "It seems likely, sir, given their aggression. Why else would a large civilian convoy attack a mercantile outpost?"

"Exactly," Cook growled. "If they *are* pirates, then things are easier than they might otherwise be—or so it seems to me. We and the 9th could extend the accord that Busch seems to have forged with Admiral Nass, and take them on together."

"Has that ever happened, Admiral?" the Captain asked.

"Yes, several times, but you never hear about it in our news media or from the politicos...idiots think it's bad for voter morale to discover that we do, on rare occasions, fight side-by-side with a totalitarian power."

"I had the impression Florencia was backing these pirates," said Ezim.

Cook shrugged. "Some they do and some they don't, but of course they call their groups 'freedom fighters against the exploitative imperialists'. Apparently, this batch isn't one of theirs." He addressed Adnil. "Captain, send Captain Copola on the *Crusher 5* my compliments, and direct him to proceed to New Frontier 16 to pick up Admiral Busch. The admiral is then to take command of the *Crusher*, and rejoin his own battle group. Meanwhile, we'll leave this position and advance towards a rendezvous with Kelab's battle group. Dismissed."

THE Battle of New Frontier was in something of a lull as all three sides regrouped. The main pirate column had halted its advance, though the pirates already committed, both in space and inside the station, were still fighting with their typical reckless fierceness. Half of the third pirate convoy was kept busy intercepting private civilian ships, though a few managed to escape unharmed. The rest of the third convoy was arrayed in a defense perimeter facing away from New Frontier 16, as if they were waiting for an oncoming threat.

The fiercest melee was taking place on the decks of the New Frontier 16 as security forces and armed civilians—of which there were a surprising number—clashed with the pirates, who had taken full control of several docking bays and many of the enormous space station's levels.

Coco Cabelle peered pensively at the holographic map of the space battle that spread in the air before her. Her elation at having driven back the initial pirate attack—thanks to their heightened sense of preparedness—was long since gone. Things weren't going well for the good guys; pirates controlled most of local space.

Her staff milled about around her, barking orders into headsets and wristcomps and sending groups of fighters, both security forces and ad hoc bands of civilians, into harm's way. Coco Cabelle herself was doing her best to ignore the frightened babbling of the idiots who had ordered her not to prepare fully in the first place, Key Administrators Zala and Tobbis themselves. Sick of hearing them remind her of how important they were, Coco stood up abruptly and snapped, "You've got two choices. Shut up and let me do my job, or leave. Get me?" Zala and Tobbis looked like they were ready to protest at her outburst, so she said pointed to the sitrep map and shouted, "Most of this is your doing, you bloody fools! If you'd let me do my job right in the first place, *this might not have happened!*"

Without a word, the Key Administrators nodded in unison and retreated to a quiet corner of the room.

"How many times have I said I told you so?" Tobbis whispered fiercely.

"Shut up! You never complained whenever you got your piece of the action, now did you?"

But Tobbis wasn't going to be silent. "You've gone too far this time, Zala!"

"You think I'm in on this madness?" Zala demanded, eyes wide. "Are you insane?"

"I don't know what you're about anymore," replied Tobbis, grabbing her pudgy arm. "Don't you understand that our dream of owning our own system is all but ruined now? The Brakks and the insurance companies will send out their police and investigators, and then we'll both have had it. Assuming we survive this."

She yanked her arm out of his grasp. "Of course we'll survive. All we need to do is make some kind of deal with the pirates, and then we can start to rebuild."

"How can even *you* be so naïve?" he spat. "That will just send a message to every pirate and mad warlord in the universe that if you need loot, just attack New Frontier and the Key Administrators will pay you off!"

———o〇o———

𝖥𝖨𝖭𝖠𝖫𝖫𝖸, Coco thought, as she deactivated the nano-bug she'd planted on Zala's robe earlier. *Unassailable evidence.* When would they learn to stop underestimating her? A white-hot mixture of triumph and fury rose in her at this final proof of their corruption and perfidy. Billions of credits of property lost or destroyed, thousands murdered, tens of thousands enslaved...just so a couple of miserable executives could line their pockets illicitly. With a supreme effort, she quashed the surge of emotion, and turned toward the corner where Zala and Tobbis were still having their quiet squabble. She called out blandly, "Instead of counting your money and coming up with more problems, perhaps the two of you can give me a hand calming our citizens?" she suggested. "Do either of you have any idea why pirates should suddenly attack us, in a sector that both of your organizations have certified to be pirate-free?"

"Why should we know anything about this?" snapped Tobbis.

"If you're referring to the enormous amount of tritonium silver and crystal-silver that has been deposited in our vaults lately, then you know the answer to that question," added Zala. "It was transported to a more secure location a month ago."

"No, I wasn't thinking about that. I doubt even that would be reason enough for an entire pirate clan to attack us. This entire enterprise is madness, frankly, and I would encourage the two of you to inform me about anything that might help our situation."

Zala looked her over as if she were some particularly rare and hideous species of bug. "We will inform you of what we care to, when we care to," she said haughtily. "Remember your place, Coco Cabelle."

Coco stood up and stalked over to the Key Administrators, looking down at Zala with a contemptuous expression. "My *place*, Key Administrator Zala, is to protect New Frontier 16 from enemies both foreign and domestic, no matter how highly they may be placed or however much they may think of themselves." She gestured toward the sitrep map, trying to control her emotions so she wouldn't give too much away—only as much as it took to get the corrupt officials before her to tip their hands. "Allow me to give you a quick update here, my Queen," she sneered. "We have over eighty thousand pirates inside the station alone. At the moment they have been stopped, thanks to the efforts and blood sacrificed by my people and the civilians you seem to have such contempt for. Civilians who, might I add, are *ostensibly* the very reason you have the wealth and position you currently enjoy. These people are dying for you out there, and more will die yet. It's only a matter of time before the pirates start advancing again, and they're sure to receive reinforcements when their main force returns."

"What do you mean, when they return?" Tobbis said fearfully.

"I'm assuming they will. At the very least, they need to return to claim their people."

"We do all the assuming here," Zala pronounced arrogantly. "Incidentally, you have a great deal to answer for. How could these scum possibly get inside our station? We do have the best sensors money can buy—and supposedly the best security personnel." She glared at Coco.

Coco returned her glare coolly, and when she spoke, her tone was so cold it practically frosted the air. "Apparently the initial contingent of approximately 1,800 pirates infiltrated the station as part of a large shipment of chattel slaves that arrived a few weeks ago. A shipment you signed for, Key Administrator Zala."

The diminutive woman stared up at Coco, speechless.

"Oddly enough," Coco murmured, "only a few of those slaves were placed for sale, whereupon they were snapped up by your young friend, Master Alec Horn. The rest were...misplaced. Somehow, they were accidently released *en masse* a few hours ago, due to what appears to be a computer malfunction. Somehow, they acquired weapons that they then used to massacre the personnel manning one of our larger private docking bays. By the time we were onto them, they had docked half-a-dozen large civilian trade vessels that happened to be filled with tens of thousands of their friends. Needless to say, that entry point is closed now." It had taken a nuke to close it, but she wasn't prepared to tell them that at the moment.

The Key Administrators has been shocked into silence, so Coco pressed on. In a gesture of condescension, she bent over and placed her hands on her knees to bring her face that much closer to Zala's—like one might do with a little child. "As to how they escaped our sensors, I have two points I'd like to make. First of all, they used large general fluid tankers with double hulls. Between the hulls, there was a layer of water or oil. Our sensors picked that up, and treated them as regular cargo ships."

"That doesn't explain why your sensors didn't pick up the amount of fluid!" Tobbis shouted desperately. "Their ships should not have been allowed to dock!"

"That was my second point, Mr. Tobbis. The sensors would indeed have been able to detect the ruse, had they been able to perform the standard deep scans they were programmed to do. However, last week, someone very skillful managed to slip a Trojan into the system that quietly disabled that feature, while masking that fact to the system's autocheck features."

Zala found her voice. "Trojan, my ass!" she shrilled. "Excuses, all excuses! Your incompetence exceeds you!"

"Perhaps you would like to fire me," said Coco. "But of course, I don't work for *you*. I work for the Brakks who actually own this station—and rest assured, at the moment I'm the least of your problems. The Brakks themselves are aware of everything I've just told you and more—and as you know, there is no organization more tenacious in righting the wrongs done to it than the Brakks. As for the pirates...you do realize that the odds are very good that we will all die here, or worse, become their captives?" Coco's words hit home, and Tobbis and Zala shifted uncomfortably. "Now," Coco continued, "The best thing we can do is to work as a team. Whatever happens later is irrelevant for the moment. What do you say?"

Tobbis and Zala looked at each other; and then Tobbis said, "All right, then, let us work with each other."

"I'm in," Zala muttered after a while.

Coco breathed a sigh of relief. "Good, then I recommend that we..." She never finished her sentence; instead, she stared in annoyed disbelief as the two Key Administrators walked away in opposite directions toward their emergency offices, each followed by a cluster of aides and secretaries.

THE *Predator* zigzagged through the panoply of pirate ships darting around Star Dice Station, maneuvering with preternatural precision and leaving clouds of death and destruction behind.

Captain Zlo smiled, knowing he had impressed his new friend Nikko Behl. The erstwhile cargo ship had been restored to its original configuration: a high-tech, ultramodern killing machine. The frigate was small compared to most frigates used by the two federations, but its speed and firepower were impressive, especially given the modifications young Master Hornet had paid for. The pirate vessels that had attempted to take on the *Predator* had paid dearly, and it didn't take long for the word to spread. The only catch was that while the smaller pirate ships retreated, they attracted the larger pirate ships, whose captains had grown curious about why the Star Dice merited such a strong bodyguard.

At the moment, the casino station drifted in loose formation with two similar stations, which happened to be owned by Tota's business competitors. Given the circumstances, Tota and the two owners had been quick to put aside their differences in favor of joining forces against a common enemy. While the stations had not docked with each other, as they might have, they'd maneuvered close enough together to merge and re-strengthen their meteor deflector shields. In combination, those shields worked very well as a defense against missiles, rockets, and particle beams, although they did little more than slow energy weapons down a bit. Similar small alliances were occurring all over New Frontier space, where ships and stations were bunching up into defensive patterns and positions, becoming small fighting islands that frustrated the intentions of the pirate forces, whose casualties were mounting.

The pirates, though, were adapting. As the smaller vessels swung away toward more yielding targets, a dozen larger ships, some of them old battle cruisers, pressed a joint attack on Star Dice Station, accompanied by an entourage of destroyers, frigates, and corvettes.

The *Predator* flashed through space perpendicular to their approach angle, leaving a trail of shield-disrupter mines in its wake. The cruisers and frigates, with their stronger shields, shrugged them aside like any other space debris; but the smaller ships following behind weren't as fortunate. The micro-singularities the mines emitted were more than a match for the weaker shields of the destroyers and the corvettes, so the cluster of mines got through and exploded against their hulls, converting a dozen to pure vapor and leaving all but a bare handful drifting helpless in space. None survived unscathed.

The destruction of their support fleet didn't deter the cruisers, so *Predator* swung about on its gyros and plunged back into the fray, sending a spray of missiles and a bloom of energy beams against the lead ship. Most of the missiles were expended harmlessly against the pirate cruiser's screens, but some chewed their way through to bite huge, flaring chunks out of the ship's flanks, and in combination with the Predator's Class Four forcelances left the big ship as full of holes as a rancid cheese.

The mortal wounds didn't halt the cruiser's advance, but enough shield emitters were lost that the forward shields significantly weakened; so the *Predator* spat out a matched pair of one-man fighters, which happened to be flown by Wolf and Pier. Flanked by a flight of sprinter missiles that passed through what remained of the cruiser's shields and destroyed the last of the emitters, tearing away massive chunks of the ship and spewing twitching bodies into space, the fighters swept joyously into battle. Wolf whooped and aimed his fighter at a vast opening just below the bridge, snapped it onto autopilot, and ejected from the fighter, which was starting to come under crippling fire from the cruiser's remaining weapons platforms. Pier zoomed in, caught his buddy in the green glow of a tractor beam, and scrambled back to the *Predator*.

Meanwhile, Wolf's fighter flew straight into the hull breach and detonated in a blue-white thermonuclear fireball. Several smaller blasts rippled through the length of the ship, escalating into two huge explosions that rent the cruiser into a half-dozen tumbling fragments and a sleet of smaller debris that that slammed into the accompanying pirate ships. Two more cruisers were disabled immediately, while most of the others were damaged. Another cruiser was smacked so hard by a piece of the first vessel's stern that it was shoved into a second, both of which immediately lit off in a very satisfying series of explosions of their own.

The assault on the Star Dice faltered after that, with the remaining pirate ships limping off toward their main column as fast as they were able, desperately trying to avoid the combined firepower of the Star Dice and its allies. Once the attackers had been routed, any of the disabled pirate ships that dared so much as twitch—and some that did not—were laid open to the vacuum with concentrated magma blasts.

The surviving pirate ships regrouped at a safe distance, clearly waiting for reinforcement. Meanwhile, the Star Dice and its companions took advantage of the lull, moving slightly closer together and bringing secondary fusactors online, strengthening their shields. The *Predator* took up picket duty around the stations, orbiting at a safe distance and paying very close attention to their erstwhile attackers.

Organized chaos reigned inside the frigate; it had not escaped entirely unscathed, so damage control teams were scrambling all over the ship, replacing overstressed components, patching holes where debris from the battle had pierced both shield and hull, putting out fires...and handling the dead. Three of the former pirates and one of the Grisamm had been killed when a piece of hull-metal the size of a man's head had ripped into a fire-control room. The emergency bulkheads had slammed down as they were supposed to, saving the rest of the ship from depressurization, but the fire-control team was exposed to vacuum and died within seconds.

Otherwise, some dozen crew had been injured, and were transported carefully to the infirmary, where they were placed under the tender care of Doctor Phalaxor and his nurses, aides and medical androids. Several of the crew were injured badly enough to require full-body autodocs, basically large metallic tubes where they were bathed in healing fluids and radiation. Some were enclosed for a few hours; others, including two rescued from decompressed areas before they could perish, would be there for days or weeks. Smaller autodocs and plain old sutures were used for more minor injuries;

for those suffering permanent damage, like the loss of a limb, stimulated regrowth or cloning surgery was required.

The most expedient method of repairing injured Omans and Oman-related transgenics was, or course, forced regeneration, or stimming; the Ancients had wired regeneration into the Oman genome shortly after leaving the homeworld, and it had bred true throughout all the countless millennia since. Other species, more recently entered into the intergalactic community, required cloned parts. Most of the non-Omans on board were of Lady Fuzza's and Captain Zlo's crested Marengan species, so that made things easier. Fortunately, there were no brain injuries; while brains could, in fact, be cloned, such an act was forbidden on pain of death throughout the inhabited universe.

Alec and Captain Zlo had purchased the equipment for producing surgical clones shortly after purchasing the *Predator*, and pithed full-body clones had been growing for the non-Oman personnel for some time now, particularly the crippled Myra. Most weren't adult-sized yet, so Doctor Phalaxor provided prostheses for the three patients who had major tissue loss. Fortunately, he was well qualified to perform the necessary surgery, which he did with his useful cheerful panache.

He was aided, oddly enough, by a rather unexpected figure: the chief engineer, who usually lorded over a vast chamber tucked toward the stern of the ship. The quiet tri-ocular, mauve-skinned woman, who answered only to the name "Chief," had worked with Captain Zlo for years, and he trusted her implicitly. She was an unusually attractive woman, at least by most standards, and Alec had been rather taken aback when he learned of her appetite for sex.

Both Wolf and Pier had, on several occasions, briefly disappeared before returning in a state of pleased confusion. It didn't take long before Captain Behl realized what was going on, and soon he too took every chance he could to go down to engineering and, ahem, "help out with the engines."

Although Chief was the most popular officer aboard the *Predator*, she had a disadvantage in most polite company: her genetic heritage was somewhat muddled. She was a Marengan citizen, if only because she qualified for membership in no other polity; she had so many different peoples in her ancestry that she was officially branded a "triple-mix," though there were probably more than three species involved. Triple-mixes were generally shunned and considered unfit for citizenship in "civilized" societies, and often ended up as outcasts or pirates.

Chief's sexual specialty was using her unique mental powers to generate multiple orgasms in her partner's brain. At the moment, she had her hands too full with repairs and rewriting AI programs to bother with her usual hobby; however, her talent had other uses. Several of her crew had suffered from agonizing burns when a plasma conduit ruptured, and were currently sheathed in portable healer tubes in an out-of-the-way corner of the engine room. Whenever she had a moment, Chief would open up the gel-bag of an injured crewmember and touch his or her head gently, making them feel less pain and greater comfort.

Phalaxor had agreed to this solution, suggested by Chief herself, with visible relief; the infirmary was already crowded enough as it was.

Except for the Nastasturan captain and the Florencian commander, who served their respective admirals as aides-de-camp, the officers that Busch and Nass had brought aboard were spread out among the crew during the fierce fight, working in the areas of their particular expertise. The admirals and their aides were currently arrayed around a holomap in a small cubby off the command bridge, where Captains Zlo and Behl were directing damage control and maintaining their level of heightened alert. Alec and Frances jointed the officers in the map room after a fast inspection run of the more damaged areas of the *Predator*.

"Can we continue fighting, Mr. Horn?" Busch asked Alec, never taking his eyes from the map.

"Yes sir, we can, but we're running low on some of our armaments." Alec looked a bit embarrassed as he admitted, "We were supposed to pick up more weapons…elsewhere."

Nass grunted. "Can't blame you for that. I'm sure you weren't ready for a full-out assault of a major station...it's not as if it's ever happened before." He reached the map, glancing at Busch. "May I?"

At the Nastasturan Admiral's brisk nod, Nass reached into the holoimage and pulled forward, magnifying it a bit. Then he tweaked it to bring a mass of images to the center. "This make sense to you?"

They launched into a five-minute discussion of ship-strengths and armaments that Alec, with his excellent education but limited experience, was able to follow with difficulty. When they wound down, Busch glanced at Alec and said, "Alec, this is no time to be shy. If you've got some weapons aboard that we'd normally consider less than kosher, just tell us. We're past the point of worrying about petty legalities. I'm sure Admiral Nass would agree."

"Indeed he does," Nass said, nodding his leonine head. "This certainly would be a good time to come clean, young man. As long as we can get rid of the evidence once this situation is dealt with, no harm done."

"Well..." Alec gulped. "I mean, I guess you could say I, but..."

"For the love of Gull, boy! Would you just tell us what kind of extra weapons we have?" Busch shouted.

Alec looked to Frances for help, but the large Grisamm was carefully examining his nails just then. Captains Zlo and Behl, who were making their way into the map room, heard the last comments and decided that it would be far more peaceful back on the bridge.

"Oh no, the two of get your asses back in here!" ordered Busch, who had somehow detected their presence even though his back was turned.

Behl shrugged. "Fine, your Admiralship. If you must know, we've got over two hundred XXX-1 missiles aboard, and..."

Busch spun to face them, his eyeballs almost popping out. "Triple-X! But those are classified!"

"They're not that highly classified," Alec noted, grinning at the sly smiles on the faces of Admiral Nass and his aide, "or if they are, some heads should roll in the military intelligence division. They're hideously expensive, too, but nothing that can't be acquired with several billion credits to spend."

Admiral Busch glared at Alec, who went on for Behl: "We also have about a hundred Florencian T-Star mines, armed with Zed-2 missiles."

This time it was Admiral Nass and his commander who stared at Alec with horror. "How the hell did you get *those*?" Nass demanded.

"Same way I got the Triple X's," Alec replied.

"What were you going to do, start a war?" Admiral Nass barked. He glanced at Busch, who was grinning. "Oh. I see. Well, your classified technology won't make much difference. You'll need a special cybernetic fire control room to control the missiles and mines anyway; fire them off without one, and we might as well get into the escape pods right now."

Busch looked expectantly at Alec, who just smiled tightly and said, "I know."

"You have one?" Admiral Nass asked in a low voice. Alec nodded.

"For each weapon system?" Busch asked him.

Small spots of color appeared in Alec's cheeks. "No, just one. The technologies are surprisingly compatible. It's pretty obvious they all derived from the same source."

Admirals Nass and Busch glared at each other. Heads would surely role for *this*—probably literally, in the case of the Florencians.

Alec tapped a button on his wristcomp, and a nano-wall bulkhead at the back of the map room vanished, revealing a small octagonal chamber with a raised dais in the center. The walls were covered with softly glowing silvery plates. In one corner was a small alcove, in which hung an odd-looking bodysuit covered with what appeared to be electronic sensors. At Alec's gesture, they all entered the room.

"We have two different pairs of hand-control sets, and can change the gloves for respective weapon systems, so we don't need two different rooms. I had to have my people do some reprogramming, but in the tests, everything seemed to work fine, so I'm not too worried about the technologies meshing in battle."

"So that's why you argued with Behl when he decided to sacrifice one of your old fighters," the Florencia commander mused. "You wanted to use this weapon system, didn't you?"

"Other way around," Behl growled. "I thought it was a bad idea to waste a good one-man fighter, no matter how old it was. Still do."

Busch's aide said, "You loaded the fighter down with Triple-X's, right? That's why you were able to kill the cruiser with that final blow."

Alec did his best to look innocent.

"To hell with all the petty rules of engagement...you know what this means, Busch?" Admiral Nass burst out suddenly.

"We can both communicate with our fleets. Well, one at a time."

"This little ship must be worth a small fortune," Nass noted.

"A rather large one, actually." Alec looked at the two admirals in turn. "But does it matter? We're still facing a major battle out there." He gestured widely with one arm. "And for what it's worth, your secret weapon systems were so expensive that I doubt anything smaller than a major government is ever going to able to afford one. I had to spend almost three bars of tritonium silver to get them both."

"Which one was more expensive?" the commander asked. Alec looked at him with a dry expression and said nothing.

Consoled for the moment, Admirals Busch and Nass began working on both separate and joint strategies for their respective fleets. Alec and Frances saw an opportunity to get away, and headed out of the command bridge together.

"Hope we won't get in too much trouble over the weapon systems," Alec muttered as they exited.

"I doubt it," Frances replied calmly.

"Hope so. Anyway, I'll be down at the infirmary checking on our injured. Don't know where I'll be after that, yet. The locator on my comp's active if anyone needs to find me." He waved and started to turn away.

"Sir, hold a moment, if you would." Frances placed a massive hand on Alec's shoulder and said quietly, "Captain Behl filled me in somewhat on what happened between you and the young woman we rescued." Alec focused on the floor as Frances continued, "Master Hornet, I would advise you to be very careful, and never to trust anyone more than you absolutely have to. Most of the former pirates you've taken aboard are a potential risk, and they comprise a good quarter of our crew. I would also suggest that you let them go their own ways as soon as possible. I can replace them with my brothers and sisters as soon as we leave this part of space."

"Thank you, Frances, but I doubt there's any time to do that. And about the person you rescued...I would like to..."

Frances cut him off. "Master Hornet, you are our commander. You should never explain yourself to your subordinates, not even your fellow officers. Perhaps you have forgotten that. You have a very advanced military background; you may be lacking combat experience, but you should keep in mind, at all times, that a commander *never* explains his actions or motives. You do what you decide is best—and rescuing someone from being eaten alive is a more than honorable thing to do. I only hope that we can find all these mad Gormé someday and finish them off, once and for all."

Alec looked at him wordlessly for a moment, before saying, "Well then. I'll go."

Smiling, Francis tilted his head in the general direction of the sick bay. "Go on and see how she's doing. Things should have settled down by now, and Doc should be done scanning her for any bugs, organic or otherwise. For my part, I have some details to go over with some of the crew. I must admit that all of them did a very good job, even the pirate girls. You and Behl did a superb job of recruitment."

"Thanks."

"There *is* one more thing, Master Hornet." Frances gestured to one of his fellow Grisamm monks, who was approaching them. "This is Bax, one of the finest warriors I have ever had the honor to fight next to. Please use him as your personal guard. You are in charge, of course, but as I said before, some of the crew are less reliable than the rest."

"And why should I trust you and your comrades any more than they?" Alec asked lightly.

"Ah, you're learning! Excellent. You shouldn't, at least not yet. But do as you will, and remember that we are on your side, no matter what. Your Uncle Hadrian is an upper-level member of the Grisamm; perhaps he has told you a few things about us?" When Alec nodded, Frances continued, "When Tota told us that you gave hundreds of slaves their freedom, we knew then that we must meet you and offer our services. As I have said, it's your decision as to how long you want us to be a part of your crew. We consider you a brother. You might not consider yourself a Grisamm, but your actions speak otherwise."

Throat tight, unsure what to say, Alec tapped his wristcomp and examined the holo that bloomed in midair between him and the monk. He watched missiles and forcelances stab at New Frontier 16, most dissipating harmlessly on shields but a few penetrating the station's skin in alarming gouts of flame and vapor. After a long moment, he said, "Frances, thank you. That means a great deal to me. I'll keep Bax with me, as you've suggested."

Bax was a tall Saurian man with a serene expression. "Thank you, sir," he said, positioning himself a few steps behind Alec.

"He won't disappoint you, Master Hornet, I give you my word on that." Frances touched Bax's shoulder and walked away, humming some old battle hymn. Alec looked at the huge man behind him, who was half again taller and wider than he, and felt confident that nothing less than a dragon would be able to get by him. When Bax smiled, his grin revealed dozens of sharp teeth. *The smile along ought to scare away most opponents*, thought Alex. Though there was an intelligence in Bax's eyes that belied his frightening appearance, Alec had no doubt that in an instant, those eyes could turn hostile—and the teeth would prove a dangerous weapon against any foe.

The scene that met Alec and Bax at the infirmary was sickening. A half-dozen crew still waited their turns for treatment, meanwhile decorating the corridor with their maimed, bloody, and burned bodies. The sight—and especially the smell—caused Alec's gorge to scald the back of his throat, and it took a supreme effort not to vomit and add to the mess. As he and Bax tried to enter, an officious nurse hurried up and told them to wait outside; when she realized she addressed the ship commander, however, she put her attitude on hold and asked, "Are you injured, sir?"

"No, but I need to talk to Doctor Phalaxor."

"He's in surgery right now. Is it anything I can help you with?"

Alec looked around the sick bay and said, "No, it can wait." He walked away, followed by Bax, leaving the nurse to help a wounded crewmember.

WHEN the Florencian cruiser leading the fight against the pirate convoys was wracked with explosions and twisted in two, its battle group retreated back to their main column. The pirate ships, now relieved of their primary obstacle, set course towards the New Frontier 16 to assist in the battle and coming plunder.

A nervous Commander Jelatha Kelab sat on the bridge of her Admiral's flagship, *Endeavor*, drumming her fingers on the arms of the command chair as she monitored the progress of the battle between a third of the Florencian 9th and several hundred civilian ships. She hated being out of touch with the Boss. Long-range transmission was pointless in the vicinity of the large space battle, because all participants in the fight would as a matter of course jam transmissions and attempt to sabotage the other side's systems with viruses, Trojans, and cyberworms; better just to hang tight and wait.

Moments later, several scout/fighters and courier ships were launched from both Admiral Busch's column and the remaining two-thirds of Florencia's 9th Galactic fleet. When Kelab noticed that her fleet group stood between those ships and the oncoming civilian fleet, she ordered, "Shields up, defensive formation." The twenty-five cruisers took up a globular defensive position, combining their shields into one transparent golden sphere.

The oncoming pirates' only interest, however, was to take part in the plundering of New Frontier 16. They cared nothing about the insignificant little military fleet blocking their way. Normally, they would have run for their lives when they found themselves facing a modern battle cruiser; however, their sheer numbers lent them both the advantage and the courage needed to proceed on their set course, attacking anything in their way.

Lacking Commander Kelab's tactical organization, they launched themselves pell-mell at her little defensive position. Disorganized or not, it was enough to pierce the combined shield in a score of places, killing three of her cruisers and severely damaging two others. Twice as many pirate ships were destroyed or put out of action by the Nastasturan return fire.

Kelab was frustrated and enraged by the loss of the ships under her care, and all her fellow officers on the bridge knew to keep their distance. She decided she had had just about enough of these defensive actions and was just about to order battle formation when a message on her control panel informed her to stand by. The message was from her commanding officer.

But how can he get a message through out here, in this mess? she thought, as another message popped up: "Attack formation Galactic Arrow. Come and get me!" Kelab glared at the message with suspicion, and did nothing until a small light burned green on her computer; the system had detected no false codes. She smiled when she ordered her remaining ships into Arrow formation and gave the order for Galactic assault—the main reason these cruisers had been put into service in the first place.

MEANWHILE, the acting commander of the Florencia 9th, Third Admiral Alaric Luh, saw what was about to happen—and immediately ordered his fleet out of the region.

ZOSSA, commanding Horsa's third column, peered at the goings-on with suspicion, maneuvering the images in his holoview this way and that with quick flicks of his tentacles. Finally, he gave his species' equivalent of a smile and thought, *They are running away.* Aloud, he ordered, "Plot a new course towards New Frontier 16."

But Commander Kelab had no intention of fleeing the battlefield; instead, she turned her ships around and, at full sprint speed, attacked the pirates. They realized too late that they were being attacked; by the time they could react, fourteen of their larger vessels had been destroyed or disabled, and confusion reigned throughout their fleet. Seconds later, the Nastasturan battle group made a second pass through the cluster of pirates at near-relativistic speed, moving so fast that they seemed little more than a bright grayish mass of light. This time, they left behind eight dead ships.

Zossa realized, then, that this was a Galactic fleet attacking at full throttle, making it impossible to see them with the naked eye; even electronic countermeasures were hampered by their great speed. He knew that panic could soon erupt among the other captains, so he ordered his column to scatter and head for safety in the shadow of New Frontier 16. But now they faced another threat: the Florencian 9th Fleet's Third Battle Group had positioned itself between them and huge the station. Zossa felt a tendril of panic, realizing that his position was in jeopardy. Unable to face even a small fleet in Galactic sprint mode, he ordered his fleet to attack the Florencians.

The battle was short and fierce, with both sides inflicting heavy damage. But the Florencians were professional military, and were quick to bind their wounds and regroup; the pirates were bullies, and had soon had enough. Attacking and plundering an easy victim is one thing; fighting in open space against a Galactic fleet that won't easily retreat is something else again. The surviving pirate ships scattered, the smart ones fleeing to close orbits near the New Frontier 16, where neither federation's fleet would dare attack at Galactic speed.

───────oOo───────

ZUZACK cursed fluently and in several languages when he learned that his third column, which was suppose to contain—not attack—the two military forces, had failed in its duties. He sent an encrypted message and a courier to his brother Horsa, requesting his assistance before he was overwhelmed by the unexpected threat from Nastasturan and Florencian forces.

IN the bowels of the New Frontier 16, far from the hoi polloi and the disturbances outside, business was proceeding more or less as usual in the main market and trade halls. After all, all that unpleasantness was located hundreds of levels away, even if a few pirate scum *had* penetrated the interior of the station.

The two Key Administrators sat quietly in a hidden room, staring at a monitor displaying the activities within one of the larger markets. Things were a tiny bit tense, but that was obvious only to the trained eye, and their greed and pleasure exceeded their worry for the things revealed to them earlier in Coco Cabelle's offices.

"I told you so, didn't I?" Zala asked, all but drooling with pecuniary pleasure. "Any time a major conflict erupts in the region, the market shoots through roof."

"Yes, but you never mentioned that *we* would be the center of the conflict," Tobbis muttered.

Zala ignored him and said, "Look, the rates are changing again—and that's just from the trading of representative brokers. I can't wait to see what happens to the market as soon as we can send messages, with our new rates of course, to all the other markets. This is great."

"Only if we survive," Tobbis muttered, with far less enthusiasm. "What if Cabelle has enough evidence to satisfy the Brakks? Then what good will all this mean for the two of us?"

"Don't you worry about her. I've had a contingency plan in place for quite some time, just in case something like that happened."

"May I ask what the plan is?"

"Do you really want to know?"

Tobbis sighed. "No, not really, not now. But I do hope you know what you're doing, since right now we're facing a major catastrophe... especially if the Brakks send one of their insurance investigators."

Zala snorted scornfully. "As long as they get their cut from all our trading, and we make sure they get very large bonuses, I doubt they'll do that. Even this minor incursion will soon be forgotten. Once the federation forces arrive, we will be back in control again." Tobbis looked doubtful as Zala continued. "Nass and Busch demand outrageous prices from us for their services. What do you think?"

Tobbis shook his head, "That's the least of my concerns right know. Did you find out why your friend Horsa is attacking in the first place?"

She scowled. "Idiot, never mention that name again unless we're in a secure location, do you understand?"

———————◦○◦———————

COCO Cabelle cursed aloud. She watched on a holomonitor as her security forces retreated, surrendering yet another level to the bloody pirates. Hundreds of citizens and tourists were unable to escape before the last exits were sealed, and her breath caught as she witnessed their cruel treatment at the hands of the pirates. She cursed the two Key Administrators equally for their incompetence, greed, and idiocy.

A noisily cleared throat behind her commanded her attention. She turned around, faced her adjutant, and barked, "Report."

"Ma'am, our scanners and radars are picking up over one hundred more civilian ships closing on the NF16," Major Lizza reported. "We think that they, too, are pirates."

"Nothing from the two federation fleets?"

"Nothing, ma'am; the communication channels are a hash of jamming static at the moment. But we can see that they're engaging the pirates as they approach the station, and the latest pirate reinforcements are fleeing from those engagements. It's possible that we might not receive any help from either fleet before it's too late… in fact, it could be that the pirate fleet that's just arriving might have destroyed or incapacitated the fleets."

Coco frowned. "If that's the case, Major, we're facing a serious dilemma, and I doubt there will be any kind of happy ending to this mess. When can we receive reinforcements from the Merchants or the Traders?"

The Major answered quietly, "Two or three months, at the earliest."

"And have we been able to contact any Predators?"

"We've launched hundreds of distress beacons into local space, and I'm sure some have made it through the gauntlet and passed through the nearest jumpgates to other sectors. But I doubt that there are enough Predators in this part of the universe to take on over five hundred well-armed pirate ships."

"Five hundred." Coco raised her eyebrows.

Lizza gulped and nodded. "That's our best estimate, ma'am... however, intel suggests there may be over a thousand in all. It's impossible to say at the moment. We've inflicted significant damage on the pirates, and so have both sets of federals, but at the moment... well, if they cooperate, and strike quickly, they could still take New Frontier 16."

"Keeping it is another matter." She tapped on her desk absently. "Then again, we might be able to contain them until reinforcement arrives."

"For several months?" The Major sounded doubtful.

"We don't have much choice in the matter, do we, Major? I don't think there's a single being in this department, or in most of the station for that matter, who will let the pirates have the place without a fight they'll damned well remember. And this is our home; we know it better than they do." She stood. "Has our research section figured out why the pirates are attacking us? It makes no sense."

"We've looked into it," Lizza admitted. "Right now, everything seems to lead back to a wealthy young Oman...a Mr. Horn, I believe." The major looked down at her clipcomp and made a few adjustments, then continued, "Yes, that's his name. There's no proof he deliberately stirred things up, but upon his arrival, he traded in a quantity of high-grade tritonium silver and made enormous deposits in the trade banks of both of the Federated Merchants and the Commercial Traders."

Coco sat down again. She remembered reading a file on young Mr. Horn, of course, and she was acutely aware of all the trouble required to organize several secret shipments of this precious metal to the Brakks' main offices.

The Major continued: "A few weeks later, the first indications of military activity were noticed on the parts of both local Federations. Approximately ten days after that, a small battle group arrived from Nastasturus; two days after *that*, we received a visit from an entire Galactic fleet from Florencia: the 9th from Handover, to be specific. Not to mention that it appears from their interactions at the art function last night that Mr. Horn and an Admiral Busch, from Nastasturus, know each other well. And to top it off, Mr. Horn has resided at Tota's hotel and has had several clandestine meetings with him…and we both know what Tota is."

"Indeed we do, but he assured me he had retired," Coco noted.

"So have we, ma'am."

"Hmmph. Gull help us both if those two greedy space monkeys ever find out." She motioned for the Major to continue.

"We've heard several rumors about Mr. Horn moving some of his fortune, which he never converted or deposited, to a secret location—and as one rumor says, he's planning to go out on a treasure expedition soon. Also, we have to take into consideration Mr. Horn's actions in purchasing and freeing nearly 400 slaves." They both smiled at that; Horn's actions had caused the slave trade to drop precipitously in the last few weeks.

"There are just too many coincidences here," Major Lizza observed, "not to take a closer look at Mr. Horn. And as I was going to mention, most of these rumors point in Tota's direction, too. Of course we don't have any hard evidence we can use to take them into custody, but still…"

"Where are Tota and Horn right now? Do we know?"

"Tota has forted up his station, and he has one Marengan frigate-class ship busy defending it. Ironically enough, its transponder code identifies it as the independent trader *Predator*—though it's remarkably well armed for a cargo ship. As of a matter of fact, thanks to them, we were able to launch the fifth attack with our corvettes and frigates. A large contingent of pirate ships has been attacking

Tota and two other space stations nearby much more viciously than any station other than our own."

"And have you determined who's in charge of that frigate?" Coco asked irritably.

"A moment, please." The Major spoke softly into her wristcomp, and looked startled when she heard the answer. To Coco she said, "Um, the frigate belongs to..."

"Let me guess. Our mysterious Mr. Horn."

By the time Admiral Cook's 11th Galactic arrived to relieve Busch's battle group, he was appalled at the damage: five large cruisers had been destroyed along with all but a tiny portion of their crews, and there were as many more with enough damage to render them useless for battle. The remaining 15 cruisers bore various levels of battle damage, from gaping holes being hastily repaired with massive patches to ablated battle-armor, scorching, melting, and pitting. It hardly resembled the picture-perfect little fleet that had split off from the main fleet a few days before. The entire surrounding region was clouded with debris and decompressed corpses, all of which flashed into vapor when they struck the fully extended EM shields of the surviving ships.

But Commander Kelab had gotten them through the battle, he noted with pride. While she wasn't particularly happy with her own performance—she cursed her own incompetence when admitting her losses—she had inflicted significant damage on the pirate fleet, and was able to provide a wealth of valuable hard-won information. She had determined from an analysis of the wreckage and what little communications traffic was decipherable, for example, that the pirates themselves were from the infamous Wulsatures clan, and she was able to warn Cook about the pirates' use of several illegal weapons, including asteroid mines. She also reported that she and an admiral from the Florencian 9th Galactic fleet were planning a new assault.

Cook belayed that idea, ordering Kelab to use the remaining ships at her disposal for search-and-rescue operations and then, once they were complete, to return to the nearest safe homeport. The Commander made no attempt to conceal her anger at the orders, insisting that she and half of "her" ships were more than capable of continuing their advance on the New Frontier 16, to rescue "their" Admiral, while the other half concentrated on SAR. As much as he admired her spunk, Cook was obliged to get firm with her, and commanded her in no uncertain terms to do exactly as he had ordered.

After breaking off with Kelab, Cook ordered his third-in-command, Lt. Admiral Whit Nelle, to establish contact with the Florencian 9th as soon as possible, and to notify the ships of his fleet to stand to at General Quarters, waiting for battle orders.

———————○O○———————

AN hour later, the 160 capital ships of the 11th Nastasturus Galactic fleet formed up into three loose arrow-shaped configurations, with their points towards New Frontier 16. Two hundred other ships marked in the red and silver of the Florencian Federation Space Navy, all that remained of their 9th Galactic fleet, waited in reserve to their rear, organized into four similar formations.

The acting commander of the Florencian 9th, Rear Admiral Yarps Yrreb, appeared to be the third officer in charge; his fleet's nominal second officer and temporary commander, Jonas Nass, was apparently stuck on New Frontier 16, just as Busch was. Cook had no idea where the Admiral in overall command of the Florencian fleet was; he may well have been a casualty.

After having lost almost a third of his fleet in battle, Yrreb was reluctant to pursue the pirate fleet, and claimed that he had to wait for new orders from his headquarters; meanwhile, he intended to begin SAR forays. Even though Cook reminded him of the intergalactic laws regarding piracy, and urged him to join forces to assist the New Frontier 16 as soon as possible, still the Florencian Admiral refused to advance.

Infuriatingly, that meant Cook couldn't advance either, not knowing what the Florencian 9th might be up to behind him. He found himself in the dilemma of being unable to do anything except wait, while his fleet faced an enemy fleet in the distance.

ZUZACK reached into his holographic battle map and tweaked a sector, magnifying the images of several hundred ships formed up around the New Frontier 16, maintaining a safe distance from its larger weapon systems. The ongoing fighting in the space around the station was petering out, but there was still plenty of fighting going on inside the enormous station itself. Zuzack narrowed his eyes in thought. He had another two hundred ships in reserve; the rest were either attached to conquered ships or smaller space stations, or docked to the New Frontier 16.

Zuzack noted that over two-thirds of the smaller space stations and private ships in the cluster were still available for the taking. All were clustered into small defensive islands; nearly all those that hadn't made common cause with their neighbors had already been destroyed or boarded. Zuzack had ordered some of the ships of the fleet to contain the grouped ships and stations and not attack any, at least not for now. He nervously waited to hear from his brother about the negotiations for a truce and alliance with the other pirate clans led by Ogstafa, who were tracking them now, clearly waiting to pick up any available pieces.

Zuzack frowned when he glanced at the loss tally on the display and realized that nearly 150 ships, some quite large, had been lost to the two federations. He begun to feel sorry—a little—for Zossa when Horsa got hold of him. Then he dismissed the thought. *Nah, more loot for the rest of us.* The smile that bloomed on his deformed countenance made it even uglier.

From time to time, Zuzack glanced at a monitor set for scanning a particular object, which only he and his brother knew anything about: the treasure map. The scanner was also set to detect tritonium silver, which it had in fact found evidence of on New Frontier 16. There was no evidence that the tritonium there was the hoard that the little Oman had stolen, though; and even if it were, the map was far more valuable. Though the bars could buy a whole planetary system, they were just the tip of the iceberg compared to the rest of the grand treasure.

He gritted his teeth, his momentary mirth gone. With the 50 bars Zuzack had picked up, they had thought to purchase their own stellar system and invest in a legitimate mining operation, while building a grand trade port in and around any habitable worlds in the system. It made him sick, knowing that the little Oman had spent or deposited at least ten bars already. The thought of it disgusted him, turning the grotesque smile into an even more grotesque sneer of rage.

The poor crewman who just happened to pass him right about then never understood why his head was suddenly flying through the air, looking at its body on the deck, decorating the floor with a puddle of thick, dark red blood. *Well. More loot to share.* Zuzack retracted his forearm switchblade and leaned on a railing next to his holoimager, peering into the depths of the image, thinking about how much he hated thieves.

"LOOK!" Coco Cabelle peered into her own holoimager as her second pointed. "There must be over a thousand..."

She glanced at a counter in the lower left quadrant of the image; it was still incrementing upward, though the story it told was already frightening enough. "Two thousand," she said curtly. She looked at the counter again. "No, over two thousand ships now. At least a third are large battle cruisers and other capital ships."

Lizza paled, and all around them, silence fell.

Coco took a deep breath as she looked around at her crew. "We have a problem, people, a very big problem. Fetch me the Key Administrators, Major Lizza. If they refuse to come immediately, have them brought by force."

The Major nodded to a Lieutenant, who hurried away, accompanied by two burly non-coms. The rest of the officers converged on the holoimager in the center of the chamber, staring at the new threat closing in on them like a giant steel fist.

"**LAUNCH** *the beacon?*" Key Administrator Tobbis shouted. He was trembling as he continued, "Have you lost your *mind*? Stop all the trading, close down the markets?" He took a breath, and his face turned in interesting shade of mauve as he screamed, "We would lose half our net worth in an instant if we did that, and it would take years before we could recover! You incompetent fool, you were hired to make sure that the trade never would stop, do you hear me? Never! You'll launch the beacon over my dead body!"

"That could be arranged," Coco said coldly. That shut him up, at least for the moment. "It will, in fact, be over your dead body, and Zala's, and mine and everyone else's if we don't," she continued in a calm voice, staring Tobbis in the eyes while pointing at the oncoming threat on the holoimager.

Tobbis opened his mouth to say something, but it died in his throat when he saw the thousands of ships (the counter was up to 2,312) approaching confidently, knowing that the prey before them would very soon be theirs. He looked at Coco in horror and nodded wordlessly. Both turned their gazes to Key Administrator Zala.

"Calm down, the two of you," she said superciliously. "I have everything under control." Coco rolled her eyes and gestured toward Central Control; Tobbis glanced at Zala and followed. Disdaining the use of the silly little hammer on the chain beside it, Coco used her elbow to break the thin glass facing of a box on the wall. She pulled down the simple mechanical handle inside, and a hatch on the floor irised open. A triangular peak rose into view. Both Coco and Tobbis inserted a small computer card into their respective slots, and two openings appeared on the sides of the peak. They put their hands inside, and shot Zala questioning expressions. "We need your hand print for it to work," Tobbis called.

Zala moved towards them confidently as she surreptitiously tapped at her wristcomp. Some of the security personnel present begun to reach for their weapons as she said, "We will not launch the beacon. I said that I have everything under control, if you would only listen to me."

Coco said threateningly, "You either put your hand were it belongs, Zala, or I will remove it myself and place it there..." She trailed off when she felt the cold composite of a gun barrel on her neck. She turned her head and looked icily at her second-in-command, whom she had worked with for years and had trusted above anyone else at all times.

"Sorry, old friend," Lizza said quietly, "but money can be a powerful persuader."

"You were supposed to be untouchable," Coco snapped.

"Well, I was," Lizza said, "but I realized that the time had come for me to retire from all this shit. You should have listened to Zala."

"Quit blithering, idiot," Zala interrupted. "Take them away and lock them up. I'm sure we can get something for them...from the Gormé, perhaps."

"You slimebag. I should never have trusted you," Tobbis said, as two security guards seized him. "The Merchants will find out, and you'll go down history as the one who started a war between us. This is very bad for any future trade, you idiot!"

Coco shouted for her security crew's help, and half of them reached for their weapons—only to see the other half already pointing theirs at them. Scowling, she stood slowly and turned around, her former second gesturing for her sidearm. She took the blaster from the holster on her right hip and handed it to Lizza—just before the Major's head exploded into a gory blossom of blood, bone, and gray matter. Lizza had no way of knowing that for the last few days, Coco had taken the precaution of strapping a tiny single-shot magma blaster to her wrist. Upon casual inspection, it looked like a wristcomp.

Realizing that the frozen moment of shock that followed was her last chance to rectify the situation, she thrust her elbow into the already-bloody face of Zala, who had bone fragments from the Major's head peppering her cheeks. Zala hit the floor hard with a broken nose and several missing teeth. Meanwhile Coco grabbed Tobbis, who was staring at the whole scene in front of him in disbelief, not understanding what just happened.

As they made for safety, Coco heard a firefight break out behind her. She could only hope that her loyal security officers won. As they pounded down the corridor, she heard Zala's shrill voice rise up: "Get them, get them!"

So much for the hope that some of Zala's nasal bones had been shoved up into her scheming brain.

Coco pushed Tobbis headfirst into her office, grabbed a blaster taped to the lintel, and darted back into the corridor. She saw a group of security officers that she recognized as loyals backing toward her as they poured fire into the security command room; she slammed against the wall and provided cover fire. Four of them made it to her office, though one was hit and fell, screaming, to the deck; Ichigo something. She couldn't remember his last name. Strawberry, maybe?

The other officers took up position next to Coco as a contingent of mutineers fought their way toward her office. Coco shouted toward her loyal people to get inside, but just then, one of them fell with a hole burned through his chest, and one of the others was struck in the leg, falling through her open door. She realized that the fight was over, at least for now, so she shouted to the last officer and they helped pull the survivor into the office. Just as the hatch sealed shut, a plasma blast shook it; she could tell that by the electrical discharges that crawled across it.

Thank goodness the hatch was made of condensed hull metal.

So here she was, sealed into her office with three loyal security men, two of whom were gravely injured, and a trembling Key Administrator who may or may not have been one of the people who had gotten them into this mess in the first place.

Outside, the few remaining loyal security officers were forced to surrender by Zala's superior force; it was either that or death. The outraged Zala spat out a tooth fragment and turned to the most senior surviving officer she had suborned. "Get me on a tightbeam signal to Horsa," she hissed.

TWO

A Nastasturan Omega-class battle cruiser, the *Crusher 5*, stationed itself between the Star Dice and the oncoming pirate fleet. The Star Dice couldn't have asked for a better protector: the *Crusher* was quite simply one of the best examples of the most feared class of warships ever constructed, and its crew knew it. Confidently, the *Crusher* issued a demand that the oncoming pirate ships immediately halt their advance, or face the displeasure of the entire Nastasturan military.

The *Crusher* was commanded by one of Admiral Cook's protégés, Carter Copola. He was a naturally large Oman with pale skin, dark, thick hair, and an equally thick beard. He wore the battle fatigues normally worn by front-line troops rather than an officer's uniform, and on his head was a dirty old hat with a black rim. His leaf-green eyes looked on the oncoming threat with a lethal calmness, and a desire that was almost sexual.

Copola loved combat, and any fight would do: in space or hand-to-hand. It didn't bother him in the slightest that he and his people were taking part in the largest gathering of ships most of them had ever seen, and certainly the largest single battle in the last century or so. While most of them had difficulties hiding their trepidation, Copola looked like he'd just had won the lottery. As he gazed at the forward viewscreen, his eyes hungered for battle, and even more so for fresh blood, no matter the color. The thought of losing his crew, ship, and possibly his own life never occurred to him, and wouldn't have bothered him much if it had. *Bingo*, he thought, feeling like the luckiest person in the entire universe.

Copola was as much a mentor to Alec von Hornet as Admirals Busch and Cook, and like them, he loved Alec—though more like a little brother than a son. Hell, he wasn't *that* old. His vocabulary and manner were even less refined than Busch's, but he made up for it by being an extremely cunning diplomat whenever events called for it—quite unlike Busch. His diplomatic skills made Captain Copola a rather eccentric and flamboyant officer, who happened to have an exceptional fetish for his old officer's hat, a hat he had refused repeatedly to exchange for a newer and better one. His excuse for keeping the "rag" was that it brought him luck and clever ideas.

Copola was well known for using musical terms as a metaphor whenever facing danger or battle; he liked to claim that Gull intended him to be a professional singer, but the bastard had forgotten to supply him with the proper voice at birth. The only thing he could do now, before he died, was improvise his skill as the great singer he was—in other words, by wringing it from the sounds from battle.

He had been Alec's personal tutor in the House of Hornet before Alec had gone away to school, and had received his current commission shortly thereafter. He had insisted that his ship should be the one that Admiral Cook sent away to retrieve Lt. Admiral Busch, so that he could learn immediately and firsthand whether or not Busch had found Alec. It was Alec who had came up with his crew slogan for him, just before he took off to the military academy some eight years before. It was the most popular slogan among the entire 11th fleet, and over and over again his fellow captains had tried to talk Admiral Cook into adopting it. Cook had adamantly refused, preferring his own slogan: *"Freedom has a price, and we are the payment."* Meanwhile, the official slogan aboard the *Crusher* remained *"Hack 'em, pack 'em, and sack 'em."* That Alec had come up with the slogan as a very young teen was a fact that only Copola, Busch, and Alec knew. Copola never mentioned that to anyone, as he didn't want his "little brother" ending up in the hands of a bunch of shrinks with no sense, much less any knowledge or understanding of the beauty of battle.

Copola gazed almost with disbelief at the pirate fleet in the far distance, his eyes threatening to fill with tears of joy. Someone said quietly, "Shall we remove to a safer location, Captain?"

Copola glanced down at the ragamuffin standing next to him and growled, "We will do no such thing, Mr. Porthos!" *Shithead*, he thought but didn't say; the Lieutenant Commander came from a highly placed political family. He turned to his bridge crew. "Red alert! Sound General Quarters, Ms. Straithairn." He grinned merrily. "Hack 'em, pack 'em, and sack 'em! The time has come for us to strike up the music, charge all batteries, and stop looking like depressed rodents, people! Look! We have them all to ourselves!" He gestured grandly toward the forward viewscreen, exclaiming, "We don't have to share them with anyone!" He left his officers gaping as he hurried toward his command chair, whistling, giddy as a child who knows he's about to receive a valuable gift that he's desired for a long, long time.

THE *Predator* made a circular sweep around the Star Dice, and its various antennae, weapons systems, and observation blisters either sank into or folded back against its hull. As its form altered and it accelerated to the first level of Galactic speed, new, hardened weapons systems rose out of portals toward the rear of the ship.

Alec and his staff were strapped in their crash couches on the command bridge, with the exception of Alistair Busch, who was locked inside the cyber battle room (CBR). Admiral Nass and the two other officers were strapped into couches in an adjacent chamber, assisting Admiral Busch, who wore the interface suit. It strained over his stocky musculature, but it fit; which was good, since he was the only one aboard with any experience at all with Triple-X missiles. To Busch's eyes, he seemed to be hovering in space, with the battle raging around him. This made it easier for him to coordinate and relate instructions to and from Captain Zlo, Captain Behl, and Alec, and at the same time to control the dangerous smart missiles, which were rather poorly named since they couldn't differentiate between friend and foe unless firmly directed by a dedicated tactician. The plan was that once he had depleted half the missile supply, Nass would take his place and begin the hazardous task of laying the T-Star mines with their built-in Zed-2 sprinters. Each weapon system was configured to destroy a ship up to the size of a battle cruiser, so if they made a single miss-step, they could all end up as radioactive dust.

Needless to say, all the crewmen, from Alec down to the meanest private, wore armored pressure suits. Some of the more experienced crew wore their helmets too, while the less-inexperience made sure theirs were nearby. Alec was one of them.

The *Predator* approached the pirates on their left flank, concealed by the Star Dice and the other two stations in its local group. When they reached the defensive formation, Captain Zlo would alter their course just in time to avoid colliding with its shields, and then fly along the interface between space and shield until they were in range. As soon as Busch had locked onto as many enemy ships as possible and fired, they would turn around and accelerate to second-level Galactic speed, the fastest the Predator could go.

Normally, a frigate of this class could only go as fast as first Galactic speed; but after Busch and Nass had assisted the Chief in making some modifications, they could now cruise at up to twice as fast. The biggest challenges had been programming and plotting a safe course for the *Predator* to travel among the dense traffic near the New Frontier 16. According to the two admirals, it was well nigh impossible, and would most likely lead to the frigate's destruction; but something had to be done. When they had conducted their videoconference with Tota and the other station owners, Tota had suggested that the three space stations remove somewhat farther from the New Frontier 16. It had taken hours before the other owners agreed, and more hours had been wasted as they slowly accelerated away from the main station. Finally, the three stations had reached a distance that Alec and his crew could work with.

When the *Predator* veered away from the stations they were guarding, no pirate ships followed; they apparently intended to avoid tougher prey while there were still much easier targets to pluck. If captain of the sturdy little frigate wanted to make a break for it, more power to him.

The atmosphere on the command bridge of the *Predator* was tense and quiet. It reminded Alec a bit of the frightened anticipation just before the big drop on a rollercoaster ride. *Predator* veered suddenly back toward the space stations, jinking downward at seemingly the last second to pass under the Star Dice; once they were past, Captain Zlo yanked the ship's nose back up and swooped back onto their original course.

"Demon bastard from hell!" Nikko Behl shouted as he and the others looked in horror upon the enormous Nastasturan cruiser that lay dead ahead. Captain Zlo joined in on Behl's cursing and snapped, "Idiots parked everywhere," as he leaned on the throttle, turning the steering globe as far to the left as he could. There was an eerie keening as the *Predator* grazed something on the cruiser; any shields raised on either ship gave no protection at this speed. Tota's voice was heard from a speaker, giving warning too late.

The involuntary shouts were followed by laughter from nearly everyone; the only person not laughing was Alec, who was peering grimly at damage control reports scrolling up the monitor next to his command chair. He breathed a sigh of relief as Lieutenant Brown said precisely, "All clear. No major damage."

———————o○o———————

CAPTAIN Copola sat in the command chair on his own bridge, peering at his own monitors, making sure all stations were ready. He drummed his fingers on his armrest while looking at one monitor, which displayed two large chambers. In one, five crewmen stood on small platforms at their workstations, clad in pressure suits sans helmets and intent on their tasks; in the other, five others floated weightless in zero gravity, wearing both p-suits and helmets. Finally, he received the signal he had been waiting for, informing him that both the Battle-Floor and the CBR were ready for action.

Most of his fellow officers on the command bridge smiled when their captain placed his ragged hat on top of his head, adjusting it carefully, then held his hands high, much as music conductor in front of an orchestra might. His voice carried throughout the bridge: "Listen up, people! When I lower my hands, the only sounds I want to hear are the nice, calming strains of a good, old-fashioned space battle. We'll make one or two attacks and then regroup back here. I realize there are some concerns—*what the hell*?"

The *Crusher 5* trembled and rang like a bell as something zipped out of the space behind Star Dice Station at Galactic speed and scraped along the port side, yanking the cruiser backward five times its own length. Alarm klaxons sounded, and a minor commotion erupted on the command bridge; but Captain Copola and his crew were experienced professionals, and their panic, while justifiable, was short-lived. After a few tense moments, the alarms were history and damage reports and assessments filled the monitors.

"If I catch those bastards I'll keelhaul them all from here to eternity!" Copola roared. His eyes widened as the space before him lit up with a dozen very large explosions.

"Captain, someone's attacking the pirates' left flank," shouted the commander at the Ops station unnecessarily.

Copola looked like someone just had stolen his hat. He muttered, "By all the asteroids in hell, they're stealing our glory!" Scowling, he snapped up a cover on the instrument panel before him and pressed the button under it, giving him full control over the ship's helm. It wasn't exactly legal, and it definitely wasn't standard procedure, but the crew was used to Copola making his own rules—and the fact was that he could handle the ship, as big as it was, better than any of his four helmsmen and half-dozen navigators. Little did Copola or his crew know, then, that they would make history that day, and for two reasons: first of all, Copola proved all the experts on hundreds of worlds wrong when he demonstrated

HUNTED | 59

that a warship could, in fact, travel very precisely at second-level Galactic speed without a preprogrammed AI at the helm, and could take on a large opposing fleet effectively while doing so. Secondly, the very name "Crusher" would become the new term for close battle at any Galactic speed.

THE *Predator* launched a dozen of its Triple-X missiles at carefully selected pirate ships and veered away, out of range of the inevitable debris fields that would soon expand from their targets. Every one of the missiles struck home. Seven cruisers were cut in half, scattering atmosphere, debris, and thousands of bodies across the battlefield; the other five disintegrated into a brilliant, hellish mists of flame and fine particles.

Alistair Busch cursed like the crusty sailor he was at his blasted inability to lock onto more than a dozen targets at a time, not for a second considering the fact that, in a single pass, the *Predator* had taken out more ships than any other ship had accounted for thus far in this forsaken battle. He was preparing for a second pass when the *Predator* was shaken like a rat in a terrier's mouth and tossed aside. Alarms howled throughout the ship as the frigate tumbled off course, all control lost. Emergency gravity control activated inside the CBR, and Busch cursed as he hit the floor hard. It felt like the ship was tumbling along all three of its axes, and from the sound of the din outside, the crew's confusion was turning to panic.

ON the bridge, Alec von Hornet unknowingly did exactly as his mentor Carter Copola had done moments before: he took personal control of the *Predator*, hurriedly typing in a command sequence that locked out Zlo's, Behl's, and Brown's controls; but instead of roaring off into battle at Galactic speed, he shut down and rebooted all the ship's systems, with the exception of secondary maneuvering jets and life support. It was an instinctual thing: he never thought twice about doing it, and didn't second-guess himself. Using the yaw, pitch, and roll thrusters, which were normally only used when docking, he tamed the ship's wild three-dimensional tumble and got it under control. He plotted a new course and steered away from the region of the "spacequake," wondering what the hell had happened.

It was only much later that he learned that the *Predator* had been brushed by the potentiality field of a asteroid mine, a device used to crush asteroids into singularities for power generation and space travel. They were illegal for the purposes of warfare, and for good reason: the one that almost got the *Predator* crushed more than 50 vessels and thousands of sentients into a dense mote smaller than the head of a pin.

Alec pushed the *Predator*'s impulse engines to the limit while sprinting to safety, as the ship's systems came back online and flickered to life. He could hear a sputtering from Admiral Busch in his earbug, protesting the sudden, unexpected return of gravity in the CBR; good, the ship-wide communications were back up. Busch cursed again, even more creatively, when the gravity cut out in the CRB and he cracked his head on a stanchion.

MEANWHILE, the *Crusher 5* was busy making history as it accelerated from Galactic Speed One to Galactic Speed Two, a full 75% of the light speed. They were going almost too fast by then: Copola's crew was able to direct only a few batteries' worth of missiles at the pirate fleet before it flashed past, but those ships died very satisfactorily as the *Crusher* beat the *Predator*'s short-lived in-battle record. Meanwhile, the deflector shields of the huge ship crushed another score of ships of various sizes, including a battle cruiser, as it punched through the pirate fleet. *Crusher 5* found itself in open space, the battle far behind, and Copola eased the ship to a halt and brought it about. The only thing he was interested in right now was finding the bastard who had stolen his most glorious moment away from him. He had little interest in the pirate fleet, instead ordering his staff to locate the glory thief. The bridge crew was secretly relieved; when he'd punched them through the pirate fleet, they were all sure he'd finally lost his last tenuous grip on sanity. The fact that they'd survived the first strike was due more to the famous Copola luck than anything else; a second attack with a single ship would be suicidal, so they were all thankful for the "thief."

Soon enough, his ardor cooled; Captain Copola was, after all, a professional, and knew that his first duty was to establish contact with Lt. Admiral Busch. He ordered his second to launch the two frigates in the main docking bay; the command sighed with relief, but his relief was brief as Copola instructed their pilot to find the "thief" and escort it to them, while the *Crusher 5* would return to the New Frontier 16 in an attempt to locate Busch.

---oOo---

HORSA cursed himself roundly. Given the surprises this day had brought in the form of two large federation fleets, he had been forced to forge an alliance with one of his biggest rivals: the benighted Ogstafa, head of the maggot-eating Night-Hunter clan. He had little choice: Ogstafa and her allies outnumbered his own clan almost two to one, and as things were developing at New Frontier, he needed powerful allies of his own—or all that would be left of the Wulsatures would be pieces. They'd suffered grievous casualties already.

Just then, Horsa received word that his third column had failed to contain the military fleets, and that a Nastasturan Omega-class cruiser had entered the arena. *That's why Ogstafa ordered her armada to halt,* he realized. *She must have suspected that the Omega was on point for a Galactic fleet.* He watched on the holographic battle map as Ogstafa's enormous fleet regrouped from a defensive position, hurrying towards the New Frontier 16.

When they reached the vicinity of the central station, they began attacking relentlessly, showing no mercy and giving no quarter; the only thing they were interested in was loot. Large ramming arms crushed through the unshielded sections of the station, delivering thousands more boarders, while the ones already inside the big station pressed their attack. Thousands more pirates left their ships in pressure suite equipped with jet packs and started attacking the shielded areas on the New Frontier 16, emplacing explosives and disruptor mines in an attempt to destroy the shield generators.

But the attack was unorganized, and most of the pirates were either pursuing solitary aims or working at cross-purposes.

After Horsa had witnessed the onslaught from a safe distance for a while, he set course towards Zuzack's ship. It wasn't long before he received a coded message from the Commercial Traders' Key Administrator, Zala. When he read it, he smiled for the first time in days. "Inform Ogstafa that the New Frontier 16 wants to surrender," he bellowed to his second-in-command as he thought, *All too easy.*

CAPTAIN Behl and Lt. Admiral Busch cursed in counterpoint, not discriminating against any of the crew in their vicinity as they issued their various orders. Alec wondered if they were involved in some type of cursing contest.

It took several hours to repair the *Predator* as they floated, more or less wide open to attack, in the lee of a distant asteroid. The repairs were only temporary, of course, until they could find a spacedock. While the work was being conducted, Alec and Captain Zlo anxiously watched the battle map in the holoimager, their attention glued to the action. They still hadn't determined what had hit them, though Busch and Nass suspected some sort of disrupter mine had warped the space in their immediate vicinity (it had). In any case, they were out of action for the nonce.

In addition to deploying a cloud of small robotic probes around the ship, Alec had launched six of his one-man fighters in a perimeter around the *Predator*, to offer addition warning against any potential threat. Meanwhile, fifty-odd crew members labored in space with twice as many repair androids, sealing up the rents and pits in the ship's hull, and replacing the weapons platforms and communications arrays lost in their collision with the Omega-class cruiser. Two of the larger shuttles brought equipment and materials to them, and also helped scan local space for any threats.

It didn't take long before the alarm came from one of the warning probes launched earlier. Fortunately, most of the ship was battle-ready by then, so the astronauts and maintenance androids closed up shop and scrambled back into the ship. As they made their way to safety, both the Admirals insisted that Alec launch all his one-man fighters, a tactic Alec agreed to. Behl eagerly volunteered to be their wing leader.

So all twelve of the remaining fighters were launched, and *Predator* accelerated toward the oncoming threat. The fighters split into three groups and took up flanking positions on the sides and above the *Predator*. All the ship's copious defense systems were activated, the shields were raised, and three-score members stood ready with pressure-suits and jetpacks if it came down to close quarter hand-to-hand combat in the vacuum. They waited tensely in inside the second and smallest docking bay.

The approaching frigate-class ship stopped at a safe distance as a second frigate approached from below the *Predator* and stopped, waiting to strike if necessary. On the *Predator*'s command bridge, a large monitor displayed the image of gaunt woman in the uniform of a commander in the Nastasturan Space Force, who stared agape at the 11th Galactic fleet's second-in-command, whom they'd already been ordered to locate but certainly hadn't expected to find *here*. The fact that he was flanked by a Florencian admiral and a young man she could have sworn looked just like Marshal Hornet's son didn't help her equilibrium, either. Admiral Busch's orders fell like a meteor shower.

The three frigates set course back towards the New Frontier 16, with the *Predator* at point. When they reached the outskirts of the ongoing battle in the vicinity of the Star Dice, Alec observed that one of the associated stations, another casino/hotel combo, was no longer within the defensive perimeter and was being relentlessly pounded by at least fifty pirate ships. The *Predator* and the two frigates from the 11th Nastasturan fleet positioned themselves in a defensive perimeter orbiting the Star Dice and the other station.

Tota looked very calm on the monitor facing Alec as he explained, "The owners of the *Corfa* wouldn't listen, and decided to make a run for it—don't ask me where. You can clearly see the results." Tota gave them a dry smile.

In the meantime, Captain Copola had managed to pick up transmissions punched through the jamming and interference by the powerful transmitters of New Frontier 16. According to the report he received, thousands of security officers and hundreds of soldiers and officers on leave had fortified themselves in various locations against the pirate hordes pouring into the station. Copola was preparing to launch a rescue when he received a transmission from Admiral Busch. As soon as he was able to open up a holoimage, Busch said curtly, "Regroup with us ASAP. I'm sending you our coordinates."

Mad he might be, but Copola knew better than to question a superior officer, no matter how good a friend. When Busch adjusted the screen resolution to reveal Alec von Hornet standing right beside him, Copola's brows rose. "The missing brat!" he exclaimed, and burst out laughing.

"Good to see you too, old man," Alec smirked.

"Why, you little..."

Busch interrupted. "You too can play later. See you soon." The image winked out.

ON the *Predator*, Admiral Nass leaned over and said to his Nastasturan counterpart, "We need to get into clear space and contact our fleets, Al." Busch nodded his agreement, and they looked at Alec, who just looked back at them. The two Admirals used him as their "liaison" whenever they had a difference of opinion, thus avoiding any arguments in front of the crew. And besides, it was Alec's ship and, according to protocol, he was in charge—no matter the rank or combined experience of the two admirals, their adjutants, and most of Alec's officer staff. Officially, the *Predator* was a civilian ship. Alec had never even contemplated acting as commanding officer as long as the two Admirals were onboard; but the part as liaison had been offered to him and he had accepted it, even as he learned everything he could from the two men in front of him.

The three frigates headed for open space, and Admiral Nass was the first to establish contact with his second-in-command, Admiral Yrreb. He ordered the lanky octopod to advance the entire Florencian 9th Galactic fleet into battle immediately. At first, his second tried to decline, citing their casualties and the presence of the Nastasturan 11th Galactic Fleet as excuses. Lt. Admiral Busch lost his temper at the insubordination, and muttered something to Nass. After a bit more argument and several threats, Yrreb finally agree to send a hundred ships towards Nass' location, while he remained behind with the rest of the fleet, supporting SAR efforts and awaiting the return of their general commander, High Admiral Rimez.

Alec and Admiral Busch noticed a change in Nass when he heard the name *Rimez*. He looked very tired all of a sudden, and his expression was no longer as confident. Anyone nearby could easily determine what Nass thought of his commanding officer, who apparently had taken off on some type of long-term vacation several months before.

Later, when Admiral Cook saw Alec on his own monitor, the older man couldn't hide his relief: he looked like someone had just removed a heavy burden from his shoulders. But when Busch's face popped up next to Alec's, looking innocent, it was clear he no longer felt quite so relieved. Cook observed his second-in-command with suspicion. "Did you start this shit, Lt. Admiral?"

Busch replied, "Who, me? Why, no...but I suspect this one did." He nodded towards Alec.

"I might have something minor to do with this exercise, uncle," Alec admitted. "I suspect it has something to do with the way I made my escape from the Wulsatures."

Cook stared for a pregnant moment before he cleared his throat and said, "I take it you're stuck over there. We're coming in to get you. Dig in. Cook out."

"Wait, Admiral!" Alec shouted.

Cook look at his brother's son, and knew Alec was up to something. And as it turned out, he was indeed—just as he always was. Cook leaned back in his seat and listened intently as Alec outlined his basic battle plan. After a while, they switched Yrreb into the circuit, and he and Cook listened to and argued with both Busch and Nass for another hour.

The primary problem they were now facing was how to coordinate the attack against the pirates. With over 300 cruiser-class ships available, they had a fair chance to contain the pirates, or at least make them scatter. Winning a battle against two or three thousand ships, even make-ready pirate vessels, was nothing any of them even contemplated. In fact, given the odds, both Admirals Cook and Yrreb were both reluctant to initiate a major attack without reinforcements.

Cook made it clear it that could take up to five days before he could expect any reinforcements from Nastasturus, and he firmly believed that the 11th was more than enough to deal with pirate scum when it came to a rescue mission involving Alec and his friends, including Admiral Nass. But a major strike against thousands of pirate ships was out of the question.

Yrreb simply would not attack until Admiral Nass was back with them; the hundred ships on their way were coming to get Nass out, he vowed, and that was that. He had received specific orders of engagement for situations like this from their commanding officer, High Admiral Rimez, and the 9th would deal with the pirates alone once Nass arrived.

As the arguments between the four Admirals descended into absurdity, Alec realized that something had to be done, and he'd have to be the one to do it; but what? The mood on the bridge deteriorated as the crew listened nervously to the argument, weighing the tremendous power and influence of the Admirals.

Fortunately, Frances had just finished his inspection of the repairs and entered the command bridge at that moment, accompanied by a muscular young woman whose raven hair was a snarled mess. She was dressed like an odalisque, and shivered visibly in the frigid air of the bridge, looking nervously around like a shocked puppy.

A murmur rippled across the bridge as the crew noticed the dark-haired beauty. She looked like she wanted to hide from all the eyes aimed at her. Even the arguing Admirals stopped and stared. Frances gestured for her to stop next to Alec's command chair.

Alec stood about ten paces away, next to a railing, propping his chin on his right hand with his elbow resting in his left hand as he stared out into infinity, deep in thought. The shouting game between the four Admirals resumed. Ignoring the hubbub, Francis walked up to Alec and said quietly, "General?"

Alec jumped when he heard Frances speak, still unused to the fact that all the Grisamm monks insisted on using his brevet rank when addressing him.

"I see that our beloved federations are still trying to out-do each other," Frances murmured, his eyes on the starfield visible in the forward viewer. Alec frowned and nodded. Frances continued, "Ah, well, there is someone here to see you."

Alec glanced at the monk. "This isn't a good time."

Frances slid his hand onto the railing and moved closer next to Alec.

"I think you'll want to see this person, sir. And remember, before you see this person, that they are taken against their will as children and are forced to do whatever they are told to do…just like slaves," he finished, gently touching Alec's neck. Then the monk turned and walked away.

Alec looked at his large back, wondering. He wasn't really sure what to think about Frances. For the last few hours, the voice inside his head had been back, babbling at him; was he going insane? He didn't know, but he barely remembered anything from the last few days, which was something he didn't dare to admit to anyone. *Must be post-traumatic stress*, he decided. Eyes downcast in thought, Alec walked back to his command chair…and as he prepared to sit, he noticed a young woman standing there, looking very frightened.

Alexa's attention had been drawn to the tableau of the arguing Admirals behind the open stairs, but even that was little more than a sensory blur to her; she had difficulty focusing on anything. Then she sensed someone close by staring at her, so she turned around—and there was her knight standing in front of her. Her heart tried to jump out of her chest; her mouth went dry, and she began trembling. There they were again: the eyes, the ones that belonged to her knight, hers alone, and pierced to her soul—those deep, dark-blue beautiful eyes.

Suddenly she realized that those eyes weren't looking at her in a loving way *at all*, and instinct took over. She backed away from the glare into the large comfortable chair behind her and fell down into it, crying out.

The bridge crew stopped what they were doing and openly stared at the new event that seemed to be unfolding between their commander and this young woman, and some of their stares were frankly unfriendly, since it was obvious to them that Master Horn had deliberately started this war in order to free her from the Gormé.

Alexa looked around for an escape as Alec said, "I believe you're in my seat."

She jumped up, not realizing that Alec had moved closer; and when she got up, she bumped her mouth hard into his chin, chipping one of her front teeth while leaving Alec with a small cut on his lip.

"By Gull, what's *wrong* with you?" her knight growled. "Do you *like* to inflict pain on people?" Rubbing the oozing cut, he sank down in his command chair.

Meanwhile, Alexa was fingering her chipped tooth with a confused expression. When she realized the damage, she let loose with a hail of curse words that would have impressed Behl, Copola and Busch alike. Alec, who was taken aback by the surprise attack, leaned away while Alexa let him have it. Finally she wound down and sputtered, "Look who's talking, you bastard! Every time we meet you bust my teeth!"

By then, Admirals Busch and Nass had finished their confab with the other two Admirals, and upon approaching Alec's command chair found him beset by a young girl. She was leaning forward most fetchingly and jabbing at him with an index finger, cursing up a storm and giving Alec the lecture of his life. Busch was just about to interfere when Nass placed his hand on his arm and nodded. "Are you married?"

"No," Busch muttered.

"Trust me, then, when I say that we should return to a more peaceful environment."

Alec was completely nonplussed at first; but he finally gathered himself for a counterstrike, jumping up from the seat and forcing

Alexa to take a step back. "How dare you, you lousy little pirate!" What it lacked in articulation it made up in volume.

"Lousy? Who you are you calling lousy? Let me tell you a thing or two, mister...!"

"The Hell I will, you, you..." Alec was at a loss for words. He looked around in desperation, wondering where Bax was, just in time to see the bodyguard's broad back as the double doors to the command bridge closed. "Traitor," he muttered, and then turned back to gaze into the two most beautiful brown eyes he had ever seen. They seemed steeped in sadness and longing, but there was a glint of hope there, too.

Alexa had stopped shouting and was waiting for him to do something...but what? The rest of the crew seemed breathless with anticipation, including the two Admirals—all except Frances, who looked at the forward viewscreen, peacefully contemplating the Big Dark.

Frances smiled as he heard shouts of applause from the people in the room, and knew that they had kissed, just as he and his true love had, once upon a time. He remembered her well...and one day he would avenge her brutal death. His expression changed; and as he stared towards the ongoing battle in the far distance, there was now only pure hatred in his eyes.

Alec and Alexa's first "true" kiss might have been one of the most unromantic in the universe, considering the blood from Alexa's mouth and the blood from Alec's cut, but neither one of them cared; nor did they know or care how long it lasted. The sensation was too overwhelming; Alec embraced Alexa hard, with her arms strapped to her body, not realizing he was hurting her. She didn't care; their love for each other blinded all their senses, and nothing mattered. He was trembling and so was she.

Someone cleared his or her throat behind them. Alec grabbed Alexa by her shoulders and lowered his head to her level, so their eyes met.

"Sir, the Admirals would like a word," the Nastasturan Captain said, rolling his eyes while waiting for a reply.

"Guards," Alec snapped, and Bax returned with two security officers. "Take this pirate below...we still have one or two of the slave blocks left, don't we?"

Alec looked at a confused Bax, who answered, "Captains Behl and Zlo felt we might have use for a few of them, so they're down in one of the cargo bays."

"Good. Put this person in one of them. She is not a part of our crew, and she must be made an example of for her outburst on the command bridge."

Bax nodded to the two security officers, who seized Alexa by her shoulders. She was as surprised as everyone else on the bridge, and didn't realize what was happening until it was too late. She was lifted into the air by two giants back-first, still facing her knight, who smiled at her like stupid boys do whenever they're up to no good. She made some minor resistance, struggling and kicking her legs in the air, insisting that she could walk on her own, so the guards set her down and turned her around. She threw her head back with a concerned expression, trying to catch the eyes of her knight; but he was standing with his back turned, talking to a huge dark man who looked like some type of bodyguard.

"Make sure Doc takes care of her tooth, and guard her with your life," Alec said grimly.

Bax nodded and walked after the security officers escorting Alexa; as he left, another Grisamm guard moved up to shadow Alec. Meanwhile, Behl ordered Nina, Miska, Mohama, Tara, Kirra and Zicci to return with their fighters to be relieved by fresh pilots, and to join Sergeant Bax ASAP in the Deck Five cargo bay.

WHEN the girls received their new orders, they became a bit concerned, and wondered what they'd done wrong *this* time. All of them knew that the Deck Five cargo bay was used for the punishment of the more disobedient crewmembers. About ten of the former pirates had spent a week there, refusing to become part of a half-civilian, half-military operation. Alec had let them go hours before he and the rest had taken off with the *Predator*, not realizing that they would assist Horsa when he attacked. Kirra and Zicci both had already spent a day each on the block when they'd started an argument about not being allowed to go to the ball, and neither wanted to go back.

So they looked like scared rats when they reported to Sergeant Bax, whom all of them had learn to respect very much. He was a friendly fellow, but a very tough drill instructor who maintained strict discipline among the entire crew. None of the girls had ever had a real family, and all of them loved being somewhat free, knowing they no longer had to kill people or be concerned about being forced to pleasure fellow pirates. They looked up to most of the Grisamm monks as if they were parental figures, something they had never had; and more than anyone, Bax was like a father to them.

They lined up perfectly in front of Bax, and Nina gave him a quick report. Bax told them to follow, and none dared ask why. The first things they saw when entering the cargo bay were the two slave blocks, and two guards preparing one of them for a new recipient. They glanced hesitantly at each other, with fearful expressions, but Bax ignored them, ordering the guards to stop what they were doing and to take up posts outside. For the first time they saw Alexa, who sat with her legs folded on a crate, inspecting her teeth in a shining steel pillar next to her. Alexa jumped off the crate when she saw them, and all seven girls embraced wildly while trying to talk at the same time.

After listening in on the girls for a short time, Bax decided to leave them and join the two guards outside, remembering once again why he preferred a nice melee on a calm battlefield to dealing with women in groups.

The girls laughed, giggled, and shouted, asking hundreds of questions and comparing answers. They all told their stories at the same time: what they had learned at the school that two of the Grisamm monks, Nadia and Mikka, had started just for them, and that they were all piloting one-man fighters and that their master instructor, Captain Behl, was the "other guy" who had gotten away from Zuzack.

Alexa told her story about the monstrous woman who bought her, and that Zuzack and his officer staff had intended to eat her at some type of secret function while she acted as some type of art piece...a contradiction that Alexa couldn't explain to her friends since she didn't really understand it herself.

After hearing that, her friends became gloomy and sad, reminded of that other monster, Zuzack, who was still out there—and who, in fact, was bedeviling them at that very moment. Alexa noticed the sudden change in her friends' collective mood, and hastened to move on to another subject. She asked them more questions, and Nina and Tara eagerly told her about the ball, the food, and all the fun they had had and seen...until, of course, they'd been attacked. Kirra and Zicci listened with jealous expressions, while Mohama and Miska acted as if they couldn't care less.

"He took the two of you to a *dance*?" Alexa said disbelievingly, her expression very much like those displayed by Kirra and Zicci. She gave both Nina and Tara a suspicious look; then her friends called her bluff and started laughing again. But whenever Alexa tried to find out more about her "knight," her friends refused to answer, giggling instead like silly girls. Though they *did* give her some personal advice, and soon their discussion turned rather raunchy.

Bax stood outside, listening to one of the two security guards report while simultaneously listening to the girls next door through an earpiece. He listened expressionlessly, not giving away what he was hearing, but frankly he was quite happy for them all, and silently prayed that they would always have joy in their souls. He remembered all too well burying his two daughters, who had been murdered by a terrorist bomb for the sake of some abstruse totalitarian belief system.

He was grateful, at that moment, that his race lacked tear glands, or the two guards in front of him might have witnessed a flood of tears. But they didn't need to know that he had suffered a crippling tragedy in the past; all the Grisamm monks had sad tales that needed telling, but were hardly ever told. Most Grisamm never shared their stories with anyone alive, with the exception of their enemies on a battlefield, as they killed them slowly. It was believed that this made them more effective killing machines. With few exceptions, they were each the end result of someone's perfidy, the scarred products of fanatics, murderers, and totalitarian thinkers in general.

THE *Crusher 5* blasted through the enemy formation, leaving two crippled pirate cruisers in its wake. Escape pods and lifeboats surrounded them in a fragile cloud, most consumed when one of the cruisers blossomed into a fireball as its matter converters cooked off.

Five minutes later, the Omega-class cruiser rendezvoused with the *Predator* and the small group of ships and minor stations that were now clustered around the Star Dice. After a brief flurry of orders, the small convoy set course away from the battle, moving slowly so that the ungainly stations could keep up. The stations flew in the center of the convoy, while the Nastasturan frigates took up flanking positions, and the five battle-ready civilian ships took up the rear with *Crusher 5*. The *Predator* took point. Two hundred auto-piloted drone fighters from the *Crusher 5* surrounded the formation in a steel shield, while Nikko Behl scouted ahead with his attack squadron of 12 one-man fighters.

Needless to say, they drew their share of attention. A few smaller pirate ships investigated them from a safe distance, but were quickly discouraged by the high-bore laser cannons of the *Crusher 5* whenever they got too close. The pirates knew very well that they could wipe out the small convoy that had broken free if they had to, but at the moment they had no interest in attacking, given the level of resistance and the likelihood of destruction. There was easier prey to be had: most of the panicked civilian ships hadn't thought to join a similar defensive alliance, and few who tried to escape alone were able to do so.

Meanwhile, most of the pirate ships had joined in the attack on the central station. More than a thousand ships had already attached themselves to the New Frontier 16, making it look like some mutated metallic monster. It reminded some of those who viewed the tableau of a vast plant under attack by insects.

Two days later, the Star Dice's convoy was joined by six Nastasturan destroyers, sent as reinforcements by Admiral Cook. The destroyers took up protective positions around the convoy as a whole, keeping their electronic eyes peeled for potential attackers. The two primary fleets from the Nastasturan and Florencian federations were approaching, but their nearest outliers were still more than a day away.

As their third day of flight dawned, Alec and his staff gathered at the main holoimager on the command bridge and gazed upon the sad spectacle of the New Frontier 16, which oddly enough seemed to have begun shrinking over the last few hours. They didn't need to be told that many of the pirate captains were casting off, and would soon begin looking for more prey: specifically, them.

During the waning hours of the third day, hundreds of fast transport shuttles from Cook's fleet arrived, and to the relief of all involved were able to evacuate all the civilians onboard the Star Dice and the other stations who wanted to leave. Soon thereafter, four more destroyers joined their column, and escorted the civilian ships along four different courses toward the nearest safe spaceports. Three thousand troops and officers from the Nastasturan fleet boarded Tota's station, though the other stations refused any military help, preferring to defend themselves as necessary with their own security personnel. Most of their civilian guests had remained onboard, trading and gambling; to them it was business as usual, and they weren't especially bothered by the ongoing battle.

MEANWHILE a few hundred pirate ships headed for open space, fully loaded with loot, their captains and crew thinking they'd gotten their fair share. Horsa and Ogstafa begged to differ; they used some of their more loyal captains to intercept these "freelancers." Both Horsa and Ogstafa knew they had to stick together if they were going to be successful. Even at this point, less than a third of the station was under their direct control, and the fighting against the loyal security forces was still ongoing.

Horsa and Ogstafa finally met face-to-face and made arrangements for the next major assault, then started to organize their respective forces into different sections. Several dozen newly arrived independent pirate ships joined the fleet in hope of taking part in the looting; most had heard about the attack from intercepted communications. Like sharks sensing blood from injured pray, these new pirates arrived one-by-one or in small groups. Because Horsa and Ogstafa had both suffered heavy casualties, they welcomed all the newcomers.

LOUD voices and much laughter echoed inside Cargo Bay Five, where Kirra, Nina and Alexa sat with their knees folded on the deck, scrutinizing a variety of dresses and various accessories that Nina and Kirra had either purchased or been given by Tota. They told Alexa about their first shopping tour ever with Sergeants Nadia and Mikka and the other girls aboard Star Dice. It took several minutes before Nina and Kirra could make Alexa understand what the word "shopping" meant and what a "salary" was. When she was a child, she'd never had the opportunity to learn about either; and since becoming a slave, she had known little more than stealing and plundering. Alexa was fascinated by the idea of actually paying for things, and listened intently—and with great envy—as her friends held up their different outfits and jewelry.

Alexa had difficulty believing them when they told her about the many different cinemas, theaters and amusement parks they'd visited so far. Nina looked sad when she explained that all the shows were currently on hiatus because of the battle, but the cute and extremely generous little man called Tota had promised VIP tickets for them all as soon as business was back to normal. He'd also promised them real civilian jobs when their contracts with their present employer had been fulfilled.

Alexa saw an opportunity, and started to ask more about her rude knight. Nina and Kirra glanced at each other and said in unison, "We don't know anything," finishing the sentence with laughter, while Alexa pretended to sulk.

"We can always cheer you up when you get back to your seat," Kirra said, nodding towards the slave block. Alexa got chills down her spine as she remembered her friends attacking her vulnerable naked soles before leaving her just a few nights before.

"Um, no thanks," Alexa answered dryly, and put on a bright smile. "I'm so happy...hell, I can't remember being this bloody happy ever...you shitheads."

Alexa listened with teary eyes and bombarded her friends with questions as they told her everything they could remember since seeing her last. "Has the fighting stopped?" she finally asked.

Kirra glanced at Nina, who replied, "No...well, yes for us right now, but there're still fighting over at New Frontier. Our officers don't think the pirates will bother with us, at least for now."

Kirra eyed her. "You know, you look pretty dirty."

Alexa rolled her eyes as she glanced down at her filthy, torn harem outfit. "Bastard wants to get back at me, I guess."

"You two are *so* meant to be together," Nina laughed, flicking Alexa's nose.

Alexa ducked and flipped back. "What do *you* know?" she sneered, looking mischievous.

"Everyone on board talks about the two of you."

"And on Star Dice, too," Kirra added.

"They do *what*? What do they talk about?" Alexa demanded, looking a bit scared.

"About the secret prince who started a war for his pirate princess," Nina explained, poking Alexa in her stomach. "That's you, toots."

"You don't know what you're saying. If he loves me so much, then why am I here and not with him?"

"Probably because he's training you into submission, like the good little future wife you are," Kirra teased.

"No, I think he's breaking you in," Nina laughed. "You know, for kinky sex."

"But that won't be hard or take too long," Kirra noted.

Alexa poked her tongue out at both of them.

"I know *better* ways to break you in," Nina said, her voice sultry. "Oh yes I do."

"Me too," Kirra added... then both of them shoved their fingers into Alexa's ribs.

She jumped up, shrieking. "Stop it, you villains—and by Gull, if either of you ever tell him I'm ticklish, I'll never forgive you." Alexa tried to look and sound both serious and a little hurt; but Nina and Kirra just looked at each other and called her bluff.

After five breathless minutes of tickling, Alexa caught her breath and pushed them away. "Enough, you sluts! Look at me now! I'm even dirtier than before, so thanks for nothing!"

"Oh," Nina cooed, "I forgot to mention that Sergeant Nadia is going to have a *birthday party* for all of us. You too, I think."

"What the hell's a birthday party?" Alexa wondered.

"Well, I don't really understand what it is, but Tara said she thought it had something to do with celebrating the day you were born or something."

"And you're supposed to celebrate it once a year, either based on the planet you're from or according to the standard calendar. And that tells you how old you are," Kirra added, sounding very proud.

"Why would anyone care about that?" Alexa demanded, looking even more confused. "That sounds stupid. Why would anyone want to be reminded that they're getting older?"

Nina and Kirra shrugged, having no answer. Just then the door opened and one of the Grisamm monks, Sergeant Magg, stuck her head in and said, "He's coming." The girls jumped to their feet, looking around nervously. "Hurry," Magg snapped, sounding a little irritated.

Nina gathered up the many boxes and bags from the shopping tour while Kirra helped Alexa back into the slave block. By the time she was settled in and all the locks were in place, they could hear someone's boot heels clacking on the deck plates outside the corridor. The girls looked at each other with fearful expressions, and Nina and Kirra hurried away to hide. Alexa squirmed in the stocks, sighing and trying to get comfortable.

Magg played her part well, engaging their visitor in conversation as a stalling tactic. Someone laughed shortly, and the door opened, and there *he* was.

Alex nodded to the two Grisamm guards outside Cargo Bay Five, asking them how they were doing, and if they had any questions. They answered him politely but briefly, and he laughed a bit in relief. He placed his hand on the biometrics plate next to the hatch, and as it opened, he thought, *I'm a well-trained officer with over eight years of military school behind me. I have participated in combat on land and in space, and I killed my first enemy with my bare hands. I survived enslavement by pirates, and escaped with an emperor's ransom. I can do this. Yes, I can. She's just a woman. A pirate, yes, but a woman.* He took a deep breath and entered, looking straight ahead.

Alexa shook the hair out of her eyes and cleared her throat, looking down at her lap and ignoring the man who stood in the doorway. *No way I'm going to let this guy, my knight or not, think he can tame me. HA!* She listened as the ironclad heels of his jackboots moved towards her and stopped. She refused to look up, promising herself that her knight was about to learn a lesson in proper manners.

"How are you doing?" The voice trembled, and unfortunately for Alexa all the little bells and whistles inside her went off at the sound of it. *Gulldammit!* she thought, *so much for playing hard to get.* She bit down hard on her lower lip while squeezing her eyes shut, still with her head bent. *Don't look at his eyes. Don't look at those beautiful blue traps.*

Alec repeated the question: "I said, how are you doing?"

She could feel him trembling as he placed his fingers under her chin and forced her head up, facing his. She moved it to the side, away from him, still convinced that she could win this battle.

Alec suspected that Alexa had received much too nice a treatment at the hands of his guards. *I'll have to have a serious talk with my head of security,* he thought, while gazing doubtfully on the beautiful young woman in front of him. No! Not beautiful, but deceptive—and she was *his* prisoner now. Yes, his alone, and according to the laws regarding piracy, he could do pretty much anything he wanted to her. *She will obey; oh yes indeed.* Scenes of Alexa and Nina having sex with the evil Zuzack flashed before his mind's eye; he felt his features clench as he glared down at little monster. *As long as I don't look her in her eyes, then everything will be fine.* He remembered the lectures from Behl, Tota, Frances, Nadia and several others: that girls like this one were victims, and that this fact should mitigate the impact of their actions. He looked at her smudged face, and mistook some of her sweat for tears. His mask calmed, and he felt more confused than ever. "Still going to teach her a thing or two," he muttered to himself.

SERGEANT Bax, being concerned that Alexa might catch a cold, had turned up the heat in the cargo room, not realizing that his own species had a different tolerance for cold than Alexa's. A small white feather from one of Kirra's outrageous outfits was caught in the ventilation flow, and floated aimlessly through the warm, dense air of the cargo bay. The little feather just happened to settle lightly on Alexa's nose as Alec reached out and forced her head up. She glared at it in crossed-eyed irritation, then screwed up her mouth and tried to blow it off her nose. Her erstwhile knight said something to her just then, but her main focus was on the irritating itching sensation from the horrible little white thing stuck on the end of her nose. She sure as hell wasn't going to ask him for any help, so she reached up and removed the annoying feather with her right hand. She held it in front of her and gave it a puzzled look, and then noticed two very confused dark-blue eyes looking at her.

Too late, Alexa realized that Kirra had forgotten to activate the air cushions in the armholes of the stock when she'd locked it down. Without the air cushions inflated, the stock's armholes gaped wide enough to defeat their own purpose. Alexa realized her mistake quickly, and put her arm back through the hole. She looked embarrassed, rolling her eyes sounding like a little mouse as she peeped, "Oops." She raised her eyes carefully, expecting anger.

ALEC looked at her, unable to determine whether he should be confused or amused. The little incident with the feather was so unexpected, and her response so damnably cute, that he was inclined toward the latter. He certainly wasn't angry with her anymore. When their eyes met again, he realized he'd lost his first battle—and hopefully his last. He was about to unlock the stocks, freeing his princess, but before he could but she slid her wrists and ankles out and stood up. They faced each other. It didn't matter how dirty and sweaty she was, and she was indeed both; he was blinded by her beauty.

Alexa wasn't going to wait for the clumsy oaf in front of her to get a move on. She slid out of the stock to give her prince his first lesson in manners and a second face slap... But when their eyes met, her cynicism melted away, and a little voice inside of her shouted out, *I'll be your slave, your bride, your anything, just kiss me...*

And so they kissed.

Both of them were panting hard by the time the giggles of two naughty former pirates caused them to pull apart. Alec looked down at a picture-perfect face; he couldn't see and didn't care about the sweat and dirt. She had the most innocent and questioning expression, framed though it was by her messy dark hair. Alec knew that this was the most beautiful woman in the universe. He had finally completed himself, and at the same time gotten very lost.

Taking a deep breath, he shouted, "Guards!"

Alexa jumped back, wondering, *Gulldammit*, now *what have I done?* as two Grisamm monks hurried in with their weapons drawn. They quickly lowered them when they noticed that there was no danger, and looked a bit embarrassed when Alec ordered, "Have the two of them clean up in here." He nodded his head towards Nina and Kirra, who looked at each other, dumbfounded, and then at Alec's back as he reached out, literally swept Alexa off her feet, and left the cargo bay. She turned her head towards them and poked her tongue out before snuggling her head up against Alec's neck and whispering something that made him walk faster—*much* faster.

Her knight carried Alexa down a long hallway that bent left along the curve of the hull. The big oval windows set into the bulkheads displayed thousands of stars and, in the far distance, the New Frontier 16, which flickered as if with distant lightning. "Wait, let me see..." Alexa whispered.

He set her down gently, and she placed her hands on a railing and looked towards the ongoing conflict in the far distance. She had lived with the Big Dark nearly all her life, and she hated it; she didn't know what drew her to it now. She longed for a life on a clean, peaceful world. She closed her eyes and pictured it in her mind, until she became aware of her knight standing close behind her. She could feel his breath on her neck, sending chills down her spine.

As for Alec, he wanted to come closer, but decided to be a gentleman. Despite not having cleaned herself recently, her odor compelled him; it seemed so natural and somehow fresh. He felt her arms close backward behind his waist, gently forcing him closer. In response, he pushed her up towards the railing with his body, and he felt her muscular back pressing against his chest, causing his heart to pound faster and faster. Alexa leaned her head back towards his neck, and he gave it a soft kiss. She closed her eyes while her skin turned into a sea of goose bumps. He caressed her neck with a soft and gentle touch of his lips, causing her to moan and catch her breath. "Thank you, thank you for bringing out the better in me," he whispered into her left ear while nibbling on it.

With her back still turned to him, she slid her right hand over the front of his trousers with an innocent touch. He was rock-hard already. A strong hand grabbed her hair and forced her neck back. When Alec found her very soft lips with his, he trembled; then their lips parted, and their tongues met. They played softly with each other at first, and when he felt her fingers teasing the tip of his erection, he kissed her hard, forcing his tongue all the way inside her mouth. She met his with hers, and they played their tongues over each other's teeth.

Alexa felt his other hand move up the side of her leg; his grip was firm, but his hand moved with the delicacy of an angel's. It eased towards her hot mons, but to her dismay, changed direction to move up her stomach. His finger made a few circles around her naked belly, working down and round her belly button. He kissed her neck as he started to massage her right breast slowly. His hand moved gently over the soft cloth of her shirt and vest, intensifying the sensation on her erect nipples.

Alexa moaned out loud when he squeezed her nipples. Soon his other hand held her left breast, and she leaned her buttocks towards his groin while holding on to railing, his erection pressed against her back.

"I want you now," she whispered, "now and forever."

She fumbled with his belt, still with her back turned to him, and he pushed her gently away. She was just about to turn around to face him when he pushed up her skirt and mounted her like a bull from behind, filling her to the brim in one single hard thrust. Taken by surprise, she emitted a loud moan of mingled pain and ecstasy; but the initial shock was followed instantly by the wonderful sensation of the two of them becoming one.

He began pounding into her, and like a tornado, he moved faster and faster. Alexa slammed her hands on the viewport as she sensed the electrical sensation of her body reaching toward climax. They came together, screaming out in ecstasy as they lost control, and their climax was punctuated by a massive explosion far away in the background beyond the New Frontier 16.

Neither lover noticed it. She was thrust up against the window on the railing, her feet off the deck. After a long moment, she leaned back, resting on his member inside of her. They were both gasping for air, and the knowledge that anyone might catch them at any moment turned both of them on even more.

He laughed softly and withdrew, and she giggled while looking around. As he zipped his pants, Alexa declared, "Oh no you don't."

She grabbed his somewhat less rampant penis in one hand and set off, with Alec following behind, protesting and trying to get his pants fastened. "Someone might see us," he hissed.

"That didn't stop you before. Now, show me the fastest way to our quarters," Alexa demanded.

"Over there." He gestured towards a lift.

Alexa charged inside, still holding on, and Alec followed with an expression that mixed fright with excitement in equal parts. Alec tried to gain control over his appendage, but as long as she was holding on as hard as she was, it was impossible. Whenever he tried to say anything, she only squeezed harder. So he tried to kiss her again, but she pushed him away, muttering, "I knew the thing was good for something." She looked down at her hand clutching her knight's private joy...well, hers.

The elevator stopped. Several crewmen entered, including Lt. Admiral Busch, who studied a computer pad. "Normally when an Admiral enters a room people stand at attention," he muttered, still reading from the computer pad.

"Oh, he's standing at attention, all right," murmured someone.

Busch, who was used to very strict military discipline, looked in the direction of the cheeky comment and saw a very dirty young woman looking dead ahead...and then, to his horror, he noticed that she was half-naked. It took him a moment to recognize the little vixen from the command bridge. He then saw Alec von Hornet standing behind her, trying to hide in the corner of the elevator. Busch ignored the predicament Alec had gotten himself into, and returned to his computer pad. "Wouldn't let that little mutineer out of my sight if I were you, General," he suggested.

The elevator door opened, and Alec gestured to Alexa to move out. She led the way, maintaining a firm grip on his very useful "handle."

"Will do, Admiral," Alec called painfully as he tried to keep up with the little beauty, or else lose something very important to him.

The elevator doors slammed shut, followed by laughter from the three crewmen, who unlike their admiral had realized their commander's predicament. Busch looked up, confused. "Did I miss something?"

———————o○o———————

ALEC and Alexa reached the last elevator and ducked inside, Alec moaning and protesting over the rough and unfair treatment to his pride and joy. "Does it hurt?" Alexa asked innocently, and gave him a very sad look as she squeezed even harder. "Oh, poor thing, let me see what's wrong." She knelt in front of him and examined the "injured" area. She lifted it and moved it sideways. "I can't see anything wrong, except that it's too soft for my taste."

Alec looked down at her innocent eyes and protested, "Please, you have to give me a breather."

She took the injured body part in her mouth and played her tongue over it. "It's definitely too soft for me."

"Please, wait, someone might come, and..." he cut himself off with a moan as Alexa took him in her mouth and, with cunning fingers, massaged his scrotum. She held his erection up while playing her tongue on and under his scrotum, sucking lusciously on one testicle at a time.

"Please, I must insist we—oh no...that hurt."

Alexa grabbed his crotch hard. She stood up on her tiptoes, while working him faster and faster with her hands. She whispered into his left ear, "The only thing you will insist on is coming inside my mouth."

Alec looked down at the beautiful girl, who was already back down on her knees, her head moving frantically back and forth. She bent her neck back and smiled at him, and he unexpectedly exploded all over her face. She hurriedly placed her lips around his shaft and squeezed hard while gobbling down every drop of his love-juice she could. When she finished, she dried her face off on her sleeve, still milking him with one hand, fully aware she was causing more pain than pleasure. She licked her fingers and said, "Promise you'll never take anyone else to any kind of dance. Ever." She worked her hand faster and faster.

Alec felt like a weak fool as he peeped, "I promise, I promise, please let go..."

"And you have to promise me you'll take me shopping, whatever that means."

Alec looked at the dirty little vixen in disbelief. Alexa took his pride in her mouth again while working him even harder, never taking her eyes from his. Alec was almost kneeling when he cried out, "For the love of Gull, I promise."

She stood up and clapped her hands, making a smacking sound with her mouth. She then leaned forward and kissed him gently on his forehead while she releasing the stop button on the elevator, which Alec had never noticed her push in the first place.

Alec got up from his knees and had just zipped his trousers when the doors opened. Outside were a handful of mechanics and security guards, who wondered if everything was all right. He ignored them and hurried after the little beauty, who stood waiting with her arms crossed, tapping her naked foot impatiently on the cold, hard deck.

I will tame her, oh yes I will, Alec thought, smiling at her.

Alexa smiled back at her knight, thinking, *For Gull's sake, I really need a bathroom, right fucking now!*

---oOo---

COCO Cabelle pushed Key Administrator Tobbis ahead of her down the secret corridor connecting her office to a concealed launch bay, her one remaining loyal security officer following close behind. As they trotted toward the emergency shuttle, she realized that the sounds of magma and laser blasts behind them had stopped, followed by a thumping sound as someone tried to break through a hatch. Her eyes hardened as she thought about the injured security officer, Lieutenant Attis SanDreg, who had volunteered to cover their escape. *His bravery and sacrifice will not be forgotten,* she promised herself.

They hustled through the final hatch into the launch pad, and before closing it, Coco smiled. The act of securing it activated a booby trap inside the cramped corridor—a small device she had installed herself, years ago, just in case something like this happened. Her main duty right now was to shut down trade and to warn the Brakks, her employers, that Key Administrator Zala was in cahoots with pirates. Secondly, she intended to protect Key Administrator Tobbis. There was little more she could do.

Her conscience clawed at her as she thought of the millions of citizens at the mercy of the pirates, and the hundreds of thousands of visitors. What would happen to them? She shook her head in a futile attempt to stop thinking about all her people and their dreams of a new future shattered, and instead focused on the two lives with her, and on her own survival. At least she could save a few.

The only way she could contact the Brakks was to launch and activate the emergency beacon at the apex of the New Frontier 16. Once it was launched, the central computer system on the station would emit a signal that would instantly stop all trade for a half-parsec in all directions. The beacon would then launch hundreds of smaller deep space probes, each taking a warning to every sector within a hundred thousand light years.

Both Tobbis and Lieutenant Uryu looked surprised when they entered the small docking bay and caught sight of the small but well-armed shuttle. Neither had any prior knowledge of Coco's history.

"How is this possible?" Tobbis wondered aloud when he looked around the cramped space and upon all the various types of weapons racked on the walls, along with the crated supplies stacked beneath them. The lieutenant didn't ask any questions. Instead, she began to arm herself while Coco opened a crate filled with half-a-dozen light pressure suits. "Put these on," she ordered, tossing one each toward her companions. As she started slipping into one of her own, she barked, "Hurry. The hatch will hold for a short while, but we have no time to waste. FYI, the Brakks had it installed, and only I knew about it. Not even my former second was privy to the secret." Her eyes darkened as she thought of Lizza's betrayal.

"What are we going to do?" Tobbis gabbled fearfully.

"Well, first we're going for a little ride to the top of the station, and after that we're going on a long cruise."

"What do you mean, a long cruise?"

"Just get dressed. Lieutenant, get those three crates there into the cargo hold, and you," she handed Tobbis his spacesuit, which he had dropped, "put this on, right now."

Tobbis lips moved, but no words left his lips.

"Hurry!" Coco shouted in his face, then turned and stalked toward the shuttle.

"But we can't go out there! There are pirates out there, and they'll have us for lunch!"

Coco slapped the keypad on the shuttle hatch, and as it slid open, she turned to him and snarled, "And they'll have us for dinner in here, probably literally! What do you think will happen to you if your partner finds you alive?"

"She, she is not my partner!"

The security chief glared at him. "Please, you little worm, we both know you're *lying*. If you want to live, we have no other choice. We *must* activate the emergency beacon from the outside; and after that, our best chance is to head for deep space. If we can't, then we might be able to find temporary refuge on the Star Dice."

"You mean Tota's place?"

"Yes, Tota's place, dear. Is there something wrong with that?"

Tobbis looked past Coco's head and frowned. "You think we'll be safe there?"

"No, but at least he and some of his neighbors have built themselves a strong defensive perimeter—and hell, I trust him more than most. Tobbis, I know you had a dream, but your dream is now a nightmare. Forget about profits and trade; that's over for you, at least for now. So for once, do what's right. Help us save lives. Who knows? We might make it."

"Only a miracle can save us." Tobbis sounded sad.

"Then a miracle it is. Now, let's get you onboard and get out of here."

"But what about my wives and daughters?"

"You can't reach them from here, and your personal security should help them. Hell, they might be safer than we are."

Tobbis looked at her for a long moment, then gave her a short nod. Coco saluted ironically as the former Key Administrator of the Federated Merchants made his last and final decision on the New Frontier 16, and without looking back he entered the shuttle, looking more upset than sad.

"All ready," reported the lieutenant.

"I'll be right with you."

After Uryu had entered the shuttle, Coco jimmied opened one of the crates and activated the large mine she found inside. She aimed the laser rangefinder at the closed hatch, and made a final check of the mine's electronics before hurrying back to the shuttle. Just as she was about to enter, she heard brief cries from behind the hatch as the pirates activated her booby-trap: eight thick laser beams criss-crossing the cramped corridor, slicing anything inside it to meat scraps. "Hope you were one of them, Zala," she said aloud, and hopped aboard the shuttle.

The shuttle launched with Coco at the helm, while Lieutenant Uryu navigated. Behind them sat Tobbis, typing into a keyboard. Writing his last official report, Coco suspected, but she didn't have time to worry about that. She had to keep the shuttle as close to the NF16's hull as she dared, given the desperate situation in near space. A great deal of debris and more than one decompressed body bounced off the shields as she maneuvered around weapons platforms and gashes in the hull.

At one point soon after exiting the station, what felt like a giant's hand smacked the shuttle's rear end, trying to shove it out into the fray. Coco managed to retain control, and glanced at her display to see a huge fireball erupting from the security pad behind them. Shortly thereafter, they cruised past a large glass dome sealing one of the trading floors, and she noticed that the trade seemed to be going on as usual. Tobbis remarked, "Now that's what I call determined trading, don't you?"

Coco and Uryu glanced at each other and rolled their eyes.

Another explosion shook the small craft, and warning lights flickered on the nav panel, followed by the soft hoot of an alarm. A check of the sensors indicated that two one-manned fighters were on their tail, lashing out with particle beams. The lieutenant activated a control on her helmet to provide a heads-up display, and used the HUD to target the fighters with a pair of heavy blasters mounted to the hull. One blast struck a fighter, shredding it into debris; the other dodged, and continued to attack relentlessly. Coco hit her retrorockets, and the fighter zoomed past. This time, the lieutenant didn't miss, and the fighter blossomed into a ball of hot gas and debris.

By then they'd just about reached the upper part of the station, but there was more bad news: there were hundreds of pirates on the hull in pressure suits, fighting a like number of security officers. "I'll bet Zala sent them here," Coco snarled.

"You are right, Ms. Cabelle," Tobbis observed. "Look, some of our security people are fighting alongside the pirates." He pointed at the melee below. Many of the loyal forces took cover behind anything that could shelter them, while others were entangled in hand-to-hand combat. The pirates and mutineers outnumbered the loyal security force by more than three to one, and attacked from all directions.

"Let's even the score, shall we?" Coco's face was grim.

Gyros spun and retros huffed as the shuttle made a quick turn to face the battle directly. Without being told, the lieutenant set the particle beams to fire on any lifeform lacking the recognition signal woven into the fabric of the security force spacesuits. It wouldn't kill the mutineers, but it took out the pirates most effectively. "Shit, I can't get the mutineers," the lieutenant snarled.

"Lock onto any suit emitting a Commercial Traders signal," Tobbis said quietly, still looking at the monitor of his computer as he typed. "I would guess most of the mutineers are Zala's people." Coco nodded consent as Uryu reset the autofire sequence using the HUD, and seconds later a series of bright lances licked out, taking out at least a score of individuals wearing security p-suits. "Hope you're right, or I just killed a bunch of friendlies," Lieutenant Uryu muttered, while selected a new set of targets and triggering the autofire sequence. Coco spun the ship for another pass.

"You have to set down right here?" Tobbis protested. "Isn't there anywhere else we can launch it from?"

"No, this is the only place, and Zala knows it," Coco answered harshly.

———o〇o———

TEN minutes later, Coco was skimming through space wearing a heavily armed jet pack. She landed among the twenty survivors of her loyal security forces, and immediately, they all saluted her. A captain bowed, and thanked her for saving their lives. "Can you take us with you?" he asked, glancing at the shuttle.

"Eight of you can fit inside, and that's all. The rest can attach themselves to the exterior, but of course, that all assumes we're able to launch the beacon. I'm glad you received my message, captain."

"Me too. What can we do to help you, ma'am?"

"Just cover me. I'm sure they'll soon be back."

Coco knelt and opened a small hatch on the hull. The captain ordered perimeter defenses and ten guards took up position, while the others activated their jet packs and covered them from above. "Hurry, they're coming," Lieutenant Uryu said through her earbug.

Coco tapped a few keys, and a much larger circular hatch appeared. Inside was a large, blunt-nosed missile. "That's it. Let's get out of here," she ordered.

They launched themselves into space in a staggered column, and began jetting towards the waiting shuttle in erratic broken-field patterns. Nonetheless, the space around them lit up with laser and magma fire, and more than half were hit. For those who were hit, death came suddenly: no pressure suit could withstand a wide-bore laser lance, much less a magma blast.

"They'll pay for this, I swear," Coco muttered, aware of how melodramatic that sounded but not caring in the least. She shifted the heavy blaster in her right hand and squeezed off a few shots at the nearest pirate ship. She doubted she did much damage, but hell, it was the principle of the thing. The captain positioned himself to her left and shouted for her to go. The fire kept coming, and only six of them made it inside the shuttle; the captain and one sergeant secured themselves at the base of one of the weapons pods on the exterior.

Almost a hundred pirates and mutineers wearing jet packs converged on the location where the beacon was about to deploy, while two large destroyers approached the station, firing torpedoes against the beacon bay in an attempt to destroy it. They weren't picky about where they placed their shots: the torpedoes missed their target, but slammed into the cluster of their allies, killing half of them in one fell swoop.

All Coco could do now was hope. She didn't have to order Lieutenant Uryu to accelerate away as she clambered out of the airlock;

she could feel and hear when the engines charged up and the shuttle started to zigzag through space. She removed her helmet and tossed it to one of the surviving security guards. "Strap down and get ready for the ride of your life," she ordered, dashing into the cockpit.

Just as she strapped herself into her seat, space turned brilliant white and, an instant later, a massive shockwave sent the shuttle tumbling end over end. But the explosion was a mere prelude: from the beacon bay launched a missile several hundred meters long, arrowing into the deep toward the nearest Brakk outpost. The two pirate destroyers initiated pursuit, unleashing every available weapon after it; but that was their undoing. When the rocket reached its preprogrammed distance from the station, half of it dropped away and, as soon as the destroyers were upon it, exploded in a nova of light that vaporized the destroyers and blinded anyone who happened to be looking in that direction. The other half immediately splintered into hundreds of smaller missiles that took off in as many directions; one was the emergency beacon, but which?

―――――――○○○―――――――

THE flare of the explosion was noted with interest on the flagships of both the Nastasturan and Florencian fleets, which were still hours from New Frontier 16. Admirals Cook and Nass both realized what it meant: the station's emergency beacon had been released, and trade between the Commercial Traders and the Federated Merchants would immediately stop in this sector. Until they knew what had happened, confusion might trigger a war between the two trading empires; and that would cause economic damage to everyone.

Cook shook his head. What was never suppose to happen just had, and in the middle of it all was his own nephew. In fact, his nephew had probably caused it, more or less. He could see the headlines now. He imagined his brother, Marshal Guss Von Hornet, erupting like a volcano, and smiled.

"Find out if Admiral Rimez has joined his column," he snapped to the Captain of the *Unity*, "and send an alert to High Command requesting immediate reinforcement." Cook scowled; he had hoped that his fleet would be enough to bring about a glorious victory here. They certainly needed it. The temporary peace—or more realistically, the ceasefire—between Nastasturus and Florencia had made the citizens of Nastasturus forget the true danger posed by Florencia, and over the past few years several fleets had been mothballed and a number of military bases had closed.

He received the report on Rimez faster than he'd expected. "Their First Admiral has not yet arrived, and that's all they told us, sir," reported the Captain. "However, our scouts report that a large private yacht has docked with their flagship."

Admiral Cook tore out his earbug and threw it at the monitor in front of him. Normally he didn't lose his temper, but he'd just about had it with the idiots traveling several dozen kilometers to his fleet's port flank. He itched to advance faster, but didn't dare; he'd never let them get behind him. He suspected that Florencia was allied with several of the larger pirate clans; and even though that hadn't been proven, he could never take the chance that it wasn't true. He smiled when he thought about the report Busch had sent him, and knew that the old dog had probably only scratched the surface. That was something they'd both learned from many years of experience. All their communications would be reviewed by military and civilian intelligence at a later date; no reason to provide them with too much information. After all, most of them *were* civilians.

Cook turned his attention towards his battle plan, stalking to his ready room and peering at the holoimage that floated over his desk. The New Frontier 16 hovered in the center, clotted with hundreds, possibly thousands, of pirate ships clinging to its surface. A small blue pip marked Busch's present position: two space stations accompanied by a cloud of ships. The other space station that had started out with their convoy was a good distance away, and was now marred by its own retinue of clinging pirate ships. "Fools," Cook muttered when he looked at it.

The picture was a live feed from a series of recon satellites, some dropped by the 11th and some already orbiting the big station. It had taken very little time to hack through their encryption codes and take control. Cook picked up a small remote and tapped a few controls; several ships representing the Nastasturan 11th and Florencian 9th fleets were manipulated into possible scenarios, positions, and formations.

By then, Admirals Cook and Nass had finally established contact, and decided that the lead ship for the attack on the pirate incursion should be the *Predator*. Both Nass and Busch would advise the fleets from their position.

A message appeared on the holographic map. Rimez had arrived. Finally, the real battle could begin.

THREE

NEAR the center of the Herica galaxy, in a binary system located just outside the great whirl of the supermassive black hole at the galactic center, lay the world of Tallas. Tallas was the capital world of the Nastasturus Federation, where the elected and appointed leaders of every class of citizen—from Elite right down to Fifth—met in assembly.

In a deep valley, surrounded by an enormous waterfall that fell straight down for a thousand meters, lay a huge hall constructed of dark glass and marble pillars. When the cascade from the waterfall struck the rocky lake at the bottom of the torrent, it generated a wall of foam that hid the goings-on inside the hall from spying eyes; the black glass conspired to further shield the activities within. The inner walls were lined with electromagnetic shields that muffled sound, keeping the noise of the waterfall out and the discussions inside in.

The stone seats were hewn from one giant stone outcropping, golden in color and very impressive. The large stone pillars were composed of dark blue marble with gold and black veins. The huge round hall itself seated ten thousand appointed officials or their representatives; at the center, on a circular dais, sat, stood, or lounged (according to species requirements) the fifty Vice Presidents, one for each sector of Nastasturan space, arrayed in a semi-circle around their highest-ranking leaders. The assembled officials and representatives represented many different races, though Omans and Oman-related species dominated. Regardless of race, all wore the same light blue tunic over their respective civilian or military clothing. Each bore a bright ribbon decorated with various ornaments and patches over their left shoulder or shoulder-equivalent, indicating how important that individual was. On the opposite shoulder was a colored plaque; the color represented their political affiliation, and the engraved symbol the system or world of their origin.

Although the hall was a babble of voices, everyone spoke Nadjarish, the artificial language created for Federation commerce thousands of years before. While translator devices were available, they were rarely used except by visitors from outside the Federation. The one thousand pillars scattered among them soared two hundred meters in height; each was surrounded by Marines in old-fashioned pre-Space military dress, more for show than anything else. At the moment, voices echoed from the top level all the way down to the floor, followed by scattered applause directed toward the large woman at the central podium.

"And in conclusion," she said, "I must add that we must...we *will* no longer allow these colony worlds to continue their insubordination, preventing us from liberating them and saving them from their own unintelligent mistakes. Their freedom depends on us, and no one else. After all, they are ruining their own planets. We must save those planets. I propose a police action, one that will immediately take control and possession over these three colonial resources." The speaker nodded her head to indicate she was finished.

Unlike most of the delegates, the speaker was a non-Oman; at the moment she held her head high while stretching her back in a superior pose, looking displeased. Her last words were followed by applause and shouts from all directions. She bowed her head towards the podium bearing the various Cabinet secretaries and Joint Chiefs, and with great dignity ambulated back to her seat behind them. As was proper and polite, the rest of the delegates ignored the shiny track of slime her one great snail-like belly-foot left behind.

The top officials were seated in levels, with of course the highest-ranking individuals seated toward the top; but even the lowest ranking of the central leaders sat five meters above the hoi polloi. They watched the speaker quietly as she made her slow way to her pit, their expressions blank and serious. The central seating area was built so that anyone at the podium should feel small and insecure; or at least, that had been the intent when it was built, some six thousand years ago.

As the lady went back to her seat, she glanced repeatedly at the man who was ostensibly the Federation's most powerful individual, President Alexander Petrius III of the house of Petrius. Two generations ago, his house had been merely First Class citizenry; now, of course, they had risen to the Elite ranks. Petrius was a striking man of Oman descent. His long face combined with calm eyes and neat features made him look much softer than he was.

He motioned his head toward the Speaker of the Hall, First Lady Móhatta, in a gesture for her to proceed. The Speaker sat in the center on the top level, with only two people flanking her: President Petrius to her right, and Marshal Guss Von Hornet to her left. Hornet was obviously bored; he paid little attention to the individual speakers, as he'd heard it all before. His thoughts were back home; immediately before he'd left the palace, he'd argued with his wife, Lady Beala. The woman he adored like a goddess had threatened to leave him if her only son and heir wasn't returned immediately in one piece. He sighed deeply.

A woman in an Army general's uniform emerged from an opening in the wall behind them, and hurried up the long, wide steps to the Marshal's chair. He was deep in thought, so the woman had to clear her throat more than once, prompting disturbed expressions from both President Petrius and the Speaker. When Hornet noticed, he gestured to her and leaned forward slightly. Her words galvanized him. "Marshal, it appears that Admiral Cook has a major battle on his hands," she whispered quietly, concealing her mouth from the President and Speaker with one hand.

Refusing to let his emotions show, Hornet stared straight ahead as he whispered, "Florencia?"

"No, my lord. Pirates."

Still looking straight ahead, he snapped, "Nothing the 11th can't handle, Valenz. Don't interrupt me unless it's important."

The general closed her eyes and took a deep breath, and when she spoke again her voice was just a bit louder. "Sir, Admiral Cook reports thousands of enemy ships. It appears that four large clans have allied to attack the 11th, as well as the New Frontier community in one of the disputed zones...along with a large Florencian fleet."

The Marshal blinked. "You said the Florencians weren't involved."

"I'm sorry, sir, I suppose I should have been more specific. The Florencians on our side, sir, against the pirates."

For the first time, Marshal Hornet faced his aide. "You said there were thousands of pirate ships?"

The general nodded, and handed a note to her Commander-in-Chief. "Sir, I hard-copied Admiral Cook's last message for you, just so there would be no mistake. The encryption codes match, as you can see from the header."

Hornet nodded as he took the small note, unfolded it and read:

Guss:

Space is lit up!

New Frontier 16 outpost. Coordinates follow.

Thousands of hostile ships, apparent pirate invasion. We are engaging with assistance from Florencian 9th.

Please send reinforcements immediately.

Admiral Hadrian Cook af Hornet, Commanding
11th Galactic Fleet Space Navy
Grand Federation of Nastasturus

The first sentence was the most important part of the message. What it meant, in simple military terms, was war; previously, it had been used only whenever Florencia had broken the truce, and never during a civilian conflict—not revolutions or acts of terrorism, or even pirate incursions. That told Marshal Hornet a great deal, despite Cook's assertion that the Fish Fuckers were their allies now. Cook would never use it lightly, and never for something like this, unless there was Florencian perfidy involved. The implementation invariably moved the entire Nastasturus military to the first level of war preparedness, and the consequences that followed could be disastrous—not just politically for those in power, but also financially and socially for every citizen of Nastasturus.

Hornet gestured to the general, who backed away while he neatly folded the note. He looked straight at the assembly, and when he sensed someone staring at him he turned his head to his right to meet the calm gaze of President Petrius, who was leaning back, looking over the spine of the Speaker of the Hall.

After two full ten-year terms in office and most of a third, Petrius knew from experience when something was wrong; he was an expert at reading his old friend's eyes. Guss had been by his side from his first day in office, so Petrius he was quite aware that something momentous had just occurred.

Hornet handed the note to the nervously waiting general, and had her convey it to the president. Petrius read the note, then closed his eyes glumly as he crumpled it in his fist. He stood and walked over to his Marshal, oblivious of the disturbance his sudden interruption caused. The Senator currently speaking stopped talking and looked irritably towards his elected superiors, as Lady Móhatta turned her own elegant head toward the two men.

A grumble echoed through the large chamber. "Order, order," the Speaker barked into a microphone. "Point of order, gentlebeings. My apologies for the interruption, but we beg your forbearance for a few moments." She pressed a large triangular button, wrapping the upper tier in a shroud of silence.

His face pale, his aplomb completely compromised, the President demanded, "Where has Florencia invaded?"

Marshal Hornet motioned to the general, who whispered urgently to Petrius. The Speaker rose and joined them, looking none too happy. The President passed the message to her; she smoothed it out and looked it over, then lifted her head, expression unreadable.

"He can't sound the war alarm over a bunch of pirates, can he?" the President demanded of no one in particular.

Lady Móhatta, who in addition to being the Speaker of the Hall was the elected leader of the loyal opposition, answered curtly, "Actually he can, Mr. President. Should the report be accurate and not some type of joke, then it is his duty." Marshall Hornet cast her an irritated glance, which she ignored. She continued, "A pirate incursion of this size can be compared with the one approximately five hundred years ago, when a fleet started at Marengo and worked its way through half of Florencia and on into our territory, whereupon they scattered and..."

"Spare me the history lesson," the President snapped.

"Admiral Cook would never ring the war-bell unless he had to," Hornet pointed out, "and he would absolute never call for reinforcements unless it was urgent, not even if he were facing a larger Galactic fleet from Florencia." The three looked at each other for a long moment in silence; all of them knew what this meant.

"Speaker of the Hall, perform your duty, if you would please," President Petrius ordered, perhaps more harshly than he intended.

Nodding silently, Móhatta glided back to her seat, dropped the silence field, and called "Order! Order!" into the din of voices that resulted. It took five minutes before the people in the room finally quieted down and leaned forward, eagerly awaiting news. Most, Hornet noted with distaste, looked like greedy children longing for candy.

"I do not address you now as a government official or leader of the loyal opposition, but as a citizen of the Nastasturus Federation," Lady Móhatta proclaimed. As whispers rustled through the chamber, she called, "Your attention, please." It took a few moments before she got the complete silence she demanded. When she continued, it was in a softer voice. "Fellow Nastasturans, it is with great regret that I must inform you of a major pirate incursion in one of the disputed regions between our Federation and Florencia's."

At that moment, the fall of a needle would have sounded like an explosion. She continued into the silence: "Space is lit up."

The needle hit the ground then, as a roar of outrage tore its way out of thousands of throats simultaneously. It was impossible for her to continue.

"YOU failed, you incompetent fool," Key Administrator Zala shouted angrily, poking a long finger into Zuzack's chest with a look of consummate disgust. "You'd better find and kill both Tobbis and Cabelle, and no mistake. If they get away, we've had it."

Zuzack smiled at Zala, making his already ugly mug even uglier.

"What was I thinking," she railed, "working with a bunch of pirate scum?"

"We both work for the same employer," Zuzack noted.

"We did until you attacked one of their fleets, you stupid, stupid man!" Zala started pacing the deck, shaking her head in disdain. "What were you idiots thinking, attacking New Frontier? You must realize that such an attack would attract every military fleet from here to eternity, idiot!"

"If you had helped us earlier in locating the Oman we were looking for, this would never have happened."

"And you think you're going to find him now, here? You should never have come here in the first place to fence your spoils. And why the hell did you bring that civilian transport here? Did you think changing the name on the ship would be enough of a disguise? Great Gull, you didn't even change all the transponders! The ship's been broadcasting its true identity for thousands of light years! There have been *hundreds* of questions raised about the ship already; we've even had high ranking officers from both federations here asking questions!"

"I didn't—"

"Aren't there any neurons in that thick skull of yours? You should have fenced it *somewhere else*, over in another sector, as you used to."

She snorted. "Why do I have to tell you this? You must be completely brain-dead. You and your idiot friends have ruined trillions of credits worth of capital investment, not to mention the fact that the bloody beacon has shut off all the trade in the sector. Soon, all trade *everywhere* between the Traders and Merchants will stop until they know what's going on. So you'd better catch or kill the Merchants' Key Administrator, or he'll surely testify against us."

"Against you, and only you," Zuzack corrected. "Now give me the information about the Oman."

"Not until I know you've killed or captured Tobbis and my former head of security."

Zuzack moved his right hand to his gun holster. Zala looked at him and raised her eyebrows. "Don't be a fool, idiot. You still need me, and I'm sure as hell not going to end up dead as a result of your stupidity."

Zuzack calmed down and smiled. "Don't worry, my fellow pirate," he boomed. He'd hoped Zala would say something about his insult, but instead she just gave him a cold stare, saying nothing. *Well, then. She's under no illusions as to what she's about.* Aloud, Zuzack continued, "We'll find them, never fear. Just make sure you have the information about the Oman when we do—and he'd better still be in this region." The *or else* went unspoken as he turned and stalked away.

After Zuzack was gone, Zala sat down heavily in the nearest chair, breathing hard. Bravado aside, she'd never been so scared in her entire life. She knew that if she had shown Zuzack any hesitation or weakness, she would have been done for. There was still hope; she could still come out on top, as long as Tobbis was removed. Whatever message he might have transmitted through the emergency probe could be easily manipulated before the Brakks. It was her word against his, in any case; besides, as long as she could present a reasonable profit, they wouldn't be too concerned, so she shouldn't be. As for Cabelle, she could easily twist the facts to make the Brakks believe the security chief had been working with the Wulsatures.

The plan was a little rough around the edges at the moment, but after some fine adjustment, her scenario would definitely work.

But she had to meet with Horsa first. His younger brother's competence was highly overrated; Horsa at least had class, and understood the importance of trade and profit. After all, they had worked together for more than fifty years.

WHEN the federal fleets finally arrived and positioned themselves at a safe distance from the New Frontier 16, the pirates were waiting for them. The pirate crews cheered when they realized they outnumbered the oncoming fleets almost ten to one; but the older pirates knew it wouldn't be so easy.

Horsa and Ogstafa, both old hands as high-stakes space battle, carefully deployed frigates, destroyers, and cruisers, and released a cloud of thousands of unmanned fighters as skirmishers. As expected, some of the independent pirate captains with smaller, faster ships thought this would be a great time to head out with the loot they'd already captured, but their perfidy had already been foreseen by the savvy clan leaders; the deserters were immobilized within seconds. Thus disciplined, the pirate horde tightened around the New Frontier 16, digging in prior to the final assault.

The exterior of the massive space station, as well as near space, was firmly under pirate control. Meanwhile, some fighting was still going on inside, but it had diminished to minor skirmishes.

HADRIAN Cook grimly surveyed the situation in the holo-image before him. There wasn't enough room this close to New Frontier 16 for either fleet to accelerate to Galactic battle speed; however, despite the imbalance of forces, there was still hope. The Federation fleets had far more advanced technology than the pirates, and no pirate he'd ever seen had cared for long, drawn-out space battles. They preferred blitzkrieg attacks on easy targets.

Admiral Cook's fleet began engaging the pirate contingent harrying the starboard flank of New Frontier 16, on the side between the big station and the distant Star Dice convoy. The convoy itself would stay well back from the battle, with the military and civilian ships remaining in reserve, just in case they were needed to either press the attack or protect the casino stations. Meanwhile, the Florencian 9th would attack the pirate forces on the opposite side of the main station. Both forces would engage with only half their ships, leaving the remainder in reserve at the fringes of the battle, where, ideally, they would also be able to intercept any fleeing pirate ships. It would be a simple standoff battle.

On the Nastasturan side, thousands of fighters and many of the larger carriers and cruisers formed up into several formations and accelerated to attack speed, Cook's flagship *Unity 1* positioned at the center. They opened up long-range with missiles, torpedoes, and sprinter rockets; as they got within effective range, particle cannons, magma lances, and laser beams were brought into play. Simple kinetic rounds followed the energy weapons. Not unexpectedly, the massive attack ripped great swathes out of the pirate fleet. The Florencian attack was similarly effective, forcing the pirates to fall back to new positions.

As planned, both Lt. Admiral Busch and Rear Admiral Nass ordered their respective fleets to advance with the remaining reserves. As a result, panic spread among the decentralized pirate fleet, and ships began to scatter. Several rammed each other in the general confusion, scattering debris and body parts into a section of space already oversaturated with both.

―――――――⸰O⸰―――――――

HORSA glared at Zuzack in the holodisplay and growled, "You are sure it will work?"

"It will work, brother, but only for a short time. It worked for me on one of their frigates, in any case."

"That's all we need. Anything from Zala about you-know-who?"

"Nothing. She refuses to talk unless we bring the other Key Administrator to her dead or alive, along with some woman—Coco something."

"Cabelle. She's the head of security for New Frontier 16, a former Predator. Zuzack, we don't have time for this. Make her talk. Use whatever means necessary, do you hear me?" Horsa flicked off the holoimage with a wave of his hand, and smiled as he confidently keyed in his new battle instructions to his captains. An image bloomed in the air before him, and he watched it with great interest, lifting an eyebrow at the extent of the carnage thus far. He cared little for the heavy losses they had already suffered, considering that this next strike ought to end it once and for all. He tapped his fingers on the armrests of his throne while he waited for the enemy's main column to enter the circular perimeter on his screen; then he pressed a button, sending the attack order to his captains.

EVERYONE on the command bridge of the *Predator* watched in disbelief as the *Unity 1*, Admiral Cook's flagship, took a score of missiles, magma lances and laser blasts simultaneously from as many pirate vessels. It seemed to dissolve rather than explode; one minute it was there, the next it was a glowing cloud of dust. It was followed into oblivion within seconds by at least two dozen more Nastasturan cruisers.

First Officer Brown shouted, "They have your shield configurations, sir!"

As the senior surviving Nastasturan officer—or so he had to assume—Admiral Busch immediately ordered the entire fleet to reconfigure their shields; meanwhile, he dashed back to the CBR and hastily donned the full-body VR suit. By then his fleet's individual ships had altered their shields, but a dozen more ships were lost before the process could be completed. The damage was done, and the Nastasturan reserves had already fully engaged. What had been intended as a standard by-the-numbers battle had turned into a disorganized melee, a state of affairs the pirates were far more used to than the Federation fleets.

Into the confusion the pirates released their next surprise: hundreds of cruisers and frigates launched from the docking bays of the New Frontier 16, directly into the thick of battle. It seemed that Ogstafa and Horsa had maintained a reserve of their own. Fireballs, kinetic rounds, missiles, and energy beams filled near space in every direction.

As Admirals Nass and Busch argued over who was best qualified to use the CBR at the moment, Alec gazed thoughtfully at the utter chaos clouding the main holoimage. After a long moment he glanced at Alexa, who stood next to him; she smiled at him confidently, but her eyes told a different story. *Something's wrong,* he thought, *very wrong indeed.* A slight headache, followed by a dizzy sensation, presaged the return of the voice in his head. He wanted to turn to Busch or Behl for advice, but no, he couldn't tell anyone. They would think him mad.

Was he?

Shaking his head fiercely, Alec turned back toward the holoimage, and gazed into its hypnotic depths. After a while, he felt someone squeezing his arm; it was Alexa, still smiling confidently, still looking scared. He looked around at his bridge crew; they were all performing their duties diligently, yet they all seemed to be waiting for something; and they all glanced at him whenever they thought he wasn't looking. He met Frances' calm and friendly gaze, as he too smiled. *Do they know?* Alec wondered.

Things seemed to ease into slow motion. He could hear, from a far distance it seemed, Captain Copola reporting crisply, "Have located Admiral Cook's lifepod. Attempting rescue." Alec blinked and settled his earbug firmly in place, relief flooding his every cell. Somehow, Uncle Hadrian might have escaped. He closed his eyes, hoping he would wake up from this nightmare, back in his bed at home...home? What was his home...? Would it all end here, today, with him dying and never knowing?

It seemed to Alec that he awakened at that moment—or at least, some subtle part of him did. Everything remained in slow motion, his vision and hearing bell-clear, but the sights and sound seeming kilometers distant. He couldn't focus on anything in particular, though he was vaguely aware that someone was talking to him...or perhaps over him. It was there, the entire battle, inside of him; he didn't know how, but it was all there. The battle and the solution.

The *Predator* cruised confidently into the melee, following Alec's unstated will. The *Crusher 5*, having successfully completed its rescue mission, followed close behind, flanked by six destroyers.

His mind awhirl, Alec von Hornet left his station and walked straight to the CBR, ignoring all the people around him, not caring in the least about their worried stares. His presence, followed by his vacant stare and an extended right hand, put an end to the non-productive argument between the two Admirals. They looked at each other and shrugged. At his distant command, Busch began stripping out of the control suit, and Nass handed Alex his own command glove. They both helped him don the suit. Once he was helmeted, Alec said firmly, "Admirals, please take command on the bridge. Pay special attention to the primary battle map, report all flanking movements to me, and move the *Predator* to a central position. Your battle cards, please."

Both Admirals reluctantly handed him their respective battle cards, the rectangles of memory plastic that, when inserted into the glove-computers of the control suit, allowed the user to communicate with and give orders to their respective fleets.

"Cyberspace, or..." Nass started to ask.

"No, I'll stand on the platform."

"But you need to be in cyberspace to control the..." Busch began, but shut his mouth with a snap when he saw the expression on his protégé's face. Both Nass and Busch were used to taking orders, and they knew when someone else was in charge. Both of them left Alec, and he watched them through the control link as Busch settled into the command chair, while Nass positioned himself before the battle map. "You two in here," Alec said, naming their aides; moments later, they had taken position inside the cramped CBR.

Alec activated the control system, and the battle appeared before him in its full three-dimensional glory, painted onto his retinas by tiny, clever lasers. He nodded and the helmet visor slid down, intensifying his vision. A sixth-level front appeared, with every ship in the region depicted. The Nastasturan ships were picked out in blue, Florencians in red, the pirates in yellow, and the civilians in white. Ships of unknown provenance were colored green, while the various stations were bulky blocks of magenta. Alphanumeric keypads appeared in front of him, one blue and one red; each pad represented a fleet, the individual keys—and there were hundreds—a squadron or, in the case of the capital ships, individual vessels. A distressing number of keys on each pad were grayed out, indicating that the ships or battle groups they represented were disabled or destroyed.

Brain humming, Alec raised his hands and started tapping the holographic keys, issuing orders to regroup, integrating the data he received from the ship captains as it flooded in to him. Although the shields on the Federation ships had only been down for a few minutes, the casualties were very high—high enough for Admiral Rimez to decide to go for reinforcements rather than take the fight to the enemy, taking over half his fleet with him as escort. Rolling his eyes, Alec issued a command for Nass to take control of the remaining Florencian forces. Under his patient care, the ships regrouped carefully on New Frontier 16's starboard flank, between it and the Star Dice convoy. The ships that received the order but were unable to leave the melee received assistance from ships directly controlled by Alec; this resulted in some losses, but most made it to the rendezvous.

Alec had no idea how long it took him organize and regroup the fleets, but he managed it, to everyone's surprise but his own. By the time he was done, sweat was sleeting down his body, but he showed no evidence of disengaging. He was completely focused on the battle. The pirates made a new, better-organized attack on the two Federation fleets, and Alec quickly positioned the ships in a covering position while retreating.

Meanwhile, Nass gave orders to several of his captains to take up a defensive position around the *Predator*. Admiral Busch did the same, and soon over twenty cruisers englobed the frigate, Nastasturan ships intermingling with Florencians. After running a brief simulation, Alec sent all his fighters to the rears of their respective motherships, while ranking all the associated frigates and destroyers to the sides in a looser, larger globe around the inner convoy. He sent the most damaged ships, amounting to about a third of the frigates and destroyers, to the Star Dice to act as a reserve. By then, the civilian convoy had swelled by another half-dozen smaller stations and dozens of ships.

Once the crippled ships were well away, Alec ordered his fleets to split into two mixed groups for safety, and to position themselves as far away from each other as possible in case the pirates struck again. Ultimately, that maneuver saved the federation fleets. The pirates realized that something strange was about to happen; they became hesitant, stopped pursuing stragglers, and regrouped in the vicinity of the New Frontier 16. As far as they and their leaders were concerned, the shredded galactic fleets posed no major threat for now. There was looting to be done, after all.

"**WHAT** the hell's happening?" Ogstafa bellowed to Horsa from her monitor.

"You idiot whore, you should never have allowed them to regroup!"

"We never realized they had regrouped until it was too late. I've never seen the Nasties and the Fish Fuckers cooperate like this before! We didn't expect this shit, and don't tell me you did!"

Horsa calmed himself. "I will not lie to you," he admitted. "This was unexpected. The two Federations cooperating... Well, it doesn't matter now. You take the port wing, Ogstafa, if you will. Zuzack, you take the starboard." He glanced at his brother, whose image occupied the right half of the split screen. "I will attack their center. They are weak and beaten. Let us crush them once and for all. Outflank them, and I will divide their center—and this time, you fucking hag, your ships will pursue them no matter what, or our deal is off, and you will have to answer to me. Now attack."

ALEC, still ensconced in the cybernetic world of the CBR control suit, saw immediately what the pirates had planned. What appeared to be a swarm of disorganized ships flinging themselves at the two mingled fleets was in fact a façade; a closer examination revealed three organized columns, poised to attach on the flanks and in the center, pinching the fleets together, with no apparent reserve at all. They approached like a swarm of angry wasps, seeking to trigger even more disorder and confusion. Without thinking, he ordered his two fleets back together, a maneuver that caused both Nass and Busch to turn pale. The two prongs snapped shut on the pirate flanks in a move much like they'd intended to pull on him, crushing them between. Meanwhile, he directed his convoy back toward the reserve waiting with the Star Dice.

HORSA ignored the warning shouts from his staff officers; he knew a victory when he saw one, and ordered his main column to follow through to destroy the command ship at the center of the small globular formation of ships. Why a frigate was leading the battle was something that never crossed his mind; his blind rage to destroy this enemy, to snatch something from the jaws of defeat, urge him on. Even more urgent was the fact that he had detected his brother's escape shuttle aboard the damnable frigate. If the shuttle was there, his treasure map and half a galaxy's ransom of loot probably was too.

He growled like a mad dog, oblivious of the stares his crew cast in his direction. He must capture that ship, intact, at all costs. Even if the thief had figured out how the map worked and had already reprogrammed it somehow, he could make the bastard talk, one way or the other.

Nearly blind with fury, Horsa transmitted a strict order to all his surviving ships not to destroy the frigate, but to capture it intact. He sent the frigate's transponder codes and image to all his captains, including its puzzling ensign: two lines to the left of an Oman eye and one to the right, with a triangle in the background. With the order, he issued a bounty of one billion credits. It didn't take long before every pirate ship that could manage it pulled out of its position and started chasing the frigate. Ultimately, though it put hundreds of ships on his tail, their disorganization helped Alec. They were no longer a fleet, merely a collection of disparate, ineffective ships.

OGSTAFA'S flank was on the verge of being obliterated. As she watched one ship after another explode into vapor or spiral out of control, she cursed Horsa for placing a bounty on a single ship. What the hell was he thinking? She knew all too well, and he should, that most of the captains and certainly the other clan leaders would now focus their attention on the frigate. Reluctantly, she ordered her entire clan—those who would respond—to regroup at New Frontier 16. Most of the ships that had survived rejoined her flagship, *The Lucky Lady*, but a bit less than half decided to take their chances at capturing the frigate.

She spat at the holoimage before her. At least now she knew why Horsa had attacked the New Frontier outpost: the answer, whatever it was, could be found inside the frigate. To hell with that; Horsa and Zuzack were on their own against the enemy. Her clan was standing down...or at least as much of it as she still controlled.

The combined Federation fleet that had been harrying her ships allowed her to withdraw, refocusing their attack on Zuzack's flank. They proceeded to crush the now-divided pirates, who were leaderless since Zuzack himself had left his battle group in the lurch after receiving his brother's instructions. Left to their own devices, they were no match for the disciplined military ships, who dismantled the pirate force, often quite literally. Those that still could scattered as their resolve failed, and suddenly they were no longer a threat.

---oOo---

HORSA himself had cause to regret his unthinking decision to place the bounty on the frigate. On his flanks were two stations pouring fire into what was left of his column, while the Federation reserve of damaged ships had limped into his path and were shoving missiles, mines and energy beams directly at him, hindering his pursuit of the little frigate. As it vanished into the distance, he snarled and called for ramming speed. He could still end this. With over a thousand ships left, he felt confident; he smiled, already smelling victory.

His smile faded to horror when a hundred new and undamaged ships appeared from behind the screen of reserves, and an implacable voice flooded the communications channels: *"Pirate vessels: stand down and heave to immediately, or be destroyed. This is your one and only warning."* The lead ship transmitted a code that every pirate in the known universe knew and feared: *By order of the Commissioned Pirate Hunter Forces.*

Predators.

A vast bay yawned open on Star Dice station, and an ancient juggernaut emerged, moving into the field of battle ponderously but inexorably. It bore the typical Predator ensign, as did the hundred smaller ships: a pointed fang inside a circle. The juggernaut took up position as support for the newly arrived Predators.

The voice again swamped the communications channels. *"Pirate ships. The sterilization process will commence in one standard minute."* The voice of the Predator admiral was matter of fact, and there was no further mention of surrender. Seconds later, the voice continued: *"Predators: from the least to the leader, wipe out the Wulsatures clan. Standard protocol. Take no prisoners."*

Horsa knew victory when he saw it, but he also recognized defeat. Of course, he refused to merely surrender, instead transmitting a code that told his ships to scatter. The order was hardly necessary: most were already going their own ways. There was still much to be looted in the region, and truly their enemy was too weak to follow through with any significant counteraction. "Little frigate, I know you, and I will find you soon," he vowed quietly, as his own cruiser veered off on an erratic course into the Big Dark, followed by several stragglers. Brilliant lights winked across the battle map as the Predators made good their threat, taking out dozens of his ships before they could get underway.

Predators be damned, a goodly number of pirates dug in and faced the attack, especially those already riddling New Frontier 16; after all, there was still much to be plundered, and those ships attached to the station couldn't easily leave anyway. Better to go down fighting than just give up; the Predators would find a reason to kill them whether they surrendered or not. The remaining pirates took up a defensive perimeter around the central station, sending in shuttles full of crew to take part in the rape of New Frontier.

Horsa's ship returned to the station hours later, after leading several Predator ships on a merry chase through the outer reaches of the system. He docked next to Ogstafa's flagship, which was battened onto the bay nearest the station's primary control center. Horsa stood for a while before the battle map, glaring at the distant sector where the battle was still raging, thinking, *You'll be back soon; the taste of victory always brings people like you back. If I must, I will set the largest bounty in history on your head, thief!*

---oOo---

ALEC recognized the voice that made the grim pronouncement: it was, of all people, Mr. Tota. A glance around him revealed that Behl had also made the connection; he was looking at Alec with a cocked eyebrow and a dry smile. "Little pants-pissing alien, ha!" he muttered. So Tota had been a Predator this whole time.

For his part, Alec had no intention of giving the pirates any second chances. Back in the control suit in the *Predator*'s CBR, he began rearranging his forces— Nastasturan, Florencian, and civilian—into a single gigantic front, and respectfully requested that Tota withdraw with his 101 ships and hold them in reserve. Admirals Busch and Nass tried to catch his attention several times, but he ignored them. There wasn't time.

Several hours later, as Alec was tweaking his arrangements and was about to give the orders for a strategic advance, his cyber-vision blurred suddenly and he sagged. Too long in the suit. He was barely able to transmit his orders to Admiral Busch before he collapsed.

Busch cursed up a storm and relayed the orders to everyone in the fleet.

Alec missed most of the battle that he had set into motion, though he watched endless recordings of it later. By the time he came to, it was all but over, and he was unable to enjoy even the mopping-up. He staggered into the command bridge and collapsed into his seat, utterly exhausted even after five hours unconscious, sweat pouring down his face. He stared vacantly at the battle map, ignoring the shouts and cheers that erupted among the bridge crew as each pirate ship died. He massaged his temples in a feeble attempt deal with his headache. The voice was gone for now, but he knew it would come back.

When he sat back up he staggered again, and someone provided a shoulder to lean on. He looked up, panting, and saw Alexa, his angel. More astonishing, he was just in time to see Nass and Busch embrace each other as the bridge crew cheered them on.

After that, it was all over but the crying. The last few pirate ships were destroyed, with the exception of the very few that the Predators allowed to surrender. In the hours after, the surviving capital ships from the Nastasturan, Florencian, and Predator fleets flew across the bow of the *Predator* one by one, tipping their own bows in a gesture of respect. Many of the larger civilian ships joined in the salute.

Everyone involved was quite aware that they had made history: never had a battle like this one ever taken place, and never had the two Federations joined forces on such a large scale. The pirates had been nearly obliterated. But the price was high; silence fell as the bridge crew of the *Predator* gazed upon viewports, viewscreens, and battle maps, at the carnage clogging the space around them. Corpses, whole and fragmentary, wheeled aimlessly through the fleet formations, dangerous new meteors than would haunt this space for eternity. Worse was the debris of the destroyed ships, ranging from monoatomic specks to chunks the size of mountains. And enough air had been vented to space to make the Big Dark almost breathable.

As the somber mood spread across the crew, they turned, one after the other, to face their commander. He sat in his command chair in silence, attended by his dark-haired beauty—the defiant woman that most believed was the main reason for this battle. Only Horsa, Zuzack, Alec, and a few others knew the complete truth. Towering behind Alec stood Frances and Bax, like two dark war-gods. The dim red lighting, in combination with the sharp flashes of dying ships from the battle maps, combined to lend the scene an unreal quality, as if all the occupants were dipped in blood.

―――――――○○○―――――――

ADMIRAL Jonas Nass had seen many victories in his long life, and nearly as many defeats. All of them had sent chills down his spine, but after this particular victory he thought he had seen it all—until he looked at the young man he knew as Alec Horn. The goose bumps crawling across Nass' skin weren't from the joy of victory; at least, not any more. He wasn't afraid to admit to himself that he was frightened of the young man slumped in the chair, and of what he was capable of.

Though he had never seen it before, not even in the eyes of his own ruling council, he could tell when he was looking into the eyes of a conqueror. "Gull save us all," he whispered. He felt that they stood on the edge of a precipice, and that this young man would have a primary role in whatever events conspired to push them off. What nearly made him piss his pants in fear was the fact that he knew, somehow knew, that he was looking at the man who would bring Florencia to ruin. Perhaps not next year or next decade, but someday; a person with this kind of martial ability, with this kind of charismatic hold over the hearts and minds of his followers, couldn't help but conquer. At that moment, Nass feared Alec Horn more than all the pirates in the universe...and would have feared him even more if he'd known who Alec truly was, and had he recognized those Silver Guard eyes for what they were.

For the moment, though, the young man was more concerned with the dark beauty stroking his hair than with any potential future...or even with victory he had just achieved. Nass glanced at Busch, who nodded and made a gesture. As one, the entire bridge crew, Nastasturan, civilian, and Florencian, stood at attention and saluted Alec. "May we never meet in battle," Nass murmured, and realized too late that Admiral Busch had overheard him.

"Agreed," Busch muttered back, leaving Nass to wonder: did the other admiral mean he never wanted to meet Nass in battle...or the shining young man in front of them?

THE *Gall* held station in a desolate stellar system thousands of light years away from New Frontier, as large as a small moon and just as globular. Named after the secondary god of the primary Oman religion, a demiurge just barely inferior to Gull, the flagship of the Florencian Federation Space Navy measured more than fifty kilometers across and was crewed by more than a million souls. At the moment, it was surrounded by an enormous armada of over a hundred fleets, comprising well over ten thousand ships served by over a billion crew and soldiers. To save supplies and space, most of the sailors were kept in cold sleep, to be revived immediately before battle.

As large as it was, the ship and its armada were dwarfed by three enormous Triton space stations that brought up the rear of the formation. Each station bulked four times the size of the *Gall*, and was designed for nothing less than the invasion and occupation of worlds. Together, they massed nearly as much as a small planet.

A quarter of a light year away, tens of thousands of androids, astronauts, and support ships worked to build the largest expansion of a jumpgate in the history of warfare.

On the main command bridge of the *Gall*, Florencia's supreme military commander, Marquessa De La Hoff, reviewed the commanders of her armada. The creature—she could hardly be called a woman, whatever else she might be—was dressed in a snow-white uniform topped by a silver linen cloak. At the moment she was regarding her armada through the massive duraglass panels that arched across one bulkhead; she glanced in the direction of the jumpgate and licked her pointed teeth. Oh, how eager she was to rip her way into Nastasturan space and fall upon her enemies.

Behind her, all suffering some degree of discomfort or fright, stood twenty officers: each of them an Admiral or General, each with Galactic and InterGalactic insignia on their uniforms. To one side stood a score of hairy, muscular exotics with flattened canine faces; the more superstitious of the officers they shared the deck with thought of them as werewolves, after an ancient Oman legend. The less imaginative just called them Critters, and with their mouthfuls of pointed sharp teeth, that name had stuck. At the moment, several of the Critters hovered around their mistress, making sure she was pleased; from time to time they hissed at the waiting officers in the background, displaying their fangs.

More than one of the officers wished she'd call them off, but none dared say so.

"How much longer before our children can feed?" the Marquessa asked lightly, her back still turned.

The officers glanced uneasily at each other, and it was a long moment before one had the courage to answer, "Less than a month, milady."

"We shall wait. Impatiently," de la Hoff hissed. Just then, two of her Silver Guard entered the bridge and clacked toward her. Her attention now focused on those glittering enigmas, she curtly ordered the assembled group of officers to leave. Before they did, though, one admiral spoke up: "Milady, what about the pirate invasion...should we continue while all the Nastasturan forces are on alert?"

Marquessa De La Hoff's eyes widened, and she turned toward the insubordinate woman, smiling at her in a friendly manner. The other officers lingered to hear what she had to say. After looking at the impertinent admiral for a long moment, the tall woman-thing hissed, "It will be to our advantage, trust me. Now leave."

As the fools filed out, she closed her eyes in another attempt to sense that person who, for a second time now, had invaded her mind. The contact seemed tantalizingly familiar; perhaps it was someone who possessed abilities similar to her own. But who, where, when, and why? Might her natural talents not be as unique as she thought? She decided then that she must find it and meet it, yes she must.

The first time she had sensed it, she had, at first, thought it was her own mind playing tricks on her; but of course, that had never happened before. The next time, the contact lasted longer, and she grew certain that it was not merely her mind playing with her. She trembled now. There was nothing she feared in life, but this new sensation of uncertainty made her doubtful and hesitant; and that alone terrified her.

Still standing, she cast her mind into the realms of sleep, searching for a specific dream about a single soul, somewhere out there in the deep, dark universe, whom she knew as she once had over a thousand years ago.

A meteor shower raged through the New Frontier outpost, Mother Nature doing her best to clear out the tumbling bodies and debris as they passed through the trail of ice and dust left behind by some long-dead comet. Most of the ships that had survived the battle shrugged aside the meteors—after all, their shields were designed to deflect missiles—but a few that had lost shields during battle were struck damaging blows. The Nastasturan Omega-class cruisers crowded close and combined their shields to protect the most vulnerable ships and stations, but some of the larger chunks of space-junk still got through.

Alec's *Predator* was docked on the outer hull of the Star Dice, similarly protecting several of the most damaged ships as their crews and crowds of andies worked feverishly on repairs.

The crews of the intact ships took turns enjoying brief shore-leaves on the Star Dice and the other casino station, the River, much to their great relief. To avoid any tensions between the two forces, the majority of Nastasturan crews were enjoying Tota's hospitality, while the Florencians kept to the River—with the exception of a few hundred officers who had joined with Admiral Nass to convey their respects to Admiral Busch and young Master Horn.

Despite the apocalyptic battle just completed, the pirates weren't entirely beaten; though with the meteor shower and the massive debris field crippling movement and communications, there was little they could do for the moment. But Admiral Busch and his cohort, Nass, seemed unruffled. "Are the two of you sure, Admirals?" Alec looked at Nass and Busch in turn, and they nodded.

"We are," said Nass. "The surviving pirates will remain at New Frontier 16 looting for weeks if they can, or at least as long as the meteor shower gives them cover."

"And we can't continue attacking them without reinforcement, because ship for ship, they still outnumber us," Busch pointed out. "Plus, pirate ships are still arriving."

"Will *we* get any reinforcement?" Alec wondered, as he and the two Admirals studied the holographic battle map.

"Fleets are on their way from both Nastasturus and Florencia, but they'll be here no earlier than a week from now," Busch said.

Nass added, "All we have to do now is contain the pirates until we're strong enough to attack. Al and I can work out a plan to retake New Frontier 16, but in the meantime, let's go down and see what surprises Tota has for us."

Alec nodded decisively and they all trooped off toward a lift, where Frances and Bax were waiting patiently. "So, how much longer will this rock rain continue?" Alec asked the group at large.

"According to our best models, three or four days," Busch answered. "And it's mostly ice, by the way."

They left the *Predator* through a long docking arm attached to the Star Dice, and were met by a cursing Nikko Behl in the airlock. "What's wrong?" Alec asked.

"Look at this!" Behl handed him a clipcomp. "This is worse than a war, I tell you! Just look at the losses!"

Busch and Nass had difficulty hiding their curiosity, and Alec raised his eyebrows as he scrolled through the information on the computer pad. "Mutiny, I tell you, that's what this shit is, and no wonder their old Captain named his ship what he did," grumbled Behl.

Alec shot the Captain a warning expression; he didn't want the officers with him to learn anything significant about the collective past of a quarter of the *Predator*'s crew. Behl nodded, but kept muttering.

"Something wrong, Alec?" asked Busch, while attempting to look over his shoulder.

"Not really, sir. I let Alexa and her friends go shopping with Nadia and Mikka. Apparently Alexa misunderstood me and took all my female crew with her, and Oh. My. Gull!" Alec's eyebrows all but hit the ceiling when he saw the damage to his credit balance. "That's it. I'll have to teach her a thing or two." Alec turned his attention to Behl. "Where are my little ladies now?"

"Well, sir, that's the problem. You, uh, have to see this with your own eyes." Nodding, Alec set off with Behl.

Behind them, Busch called, "All right, then, Master *Horn*. I'll be on the *Crusher 5* checking on Cook, to see if he's fit enough to join us later."

"And I have some things to take care of with some of my staff," Admiral Nass added dryly.

"See you later," Alec called absently, as he, Behl, Frances and Bax took a lift down to another docking area adjacent to the *Predator*'s main cargo bay. He was presented with the sight of mounded piles of boxes and crates covering the deck, and the sound of the excited voices of over a hundred of the crew, who were arguing with Wolf and four more guards who refused to let the women take anything aboard. The women were squawking so loudly that Wolf's voice went unheard; and his desperate expression told Alec that he was in dire need of reinforcement. Myra and several other women had him cornered, all of them poking their index fingers (or reasonable facsimiles thereof) at him, yelling all kinds of nasty things. Wolf motioned with his hands for them to stop, but there was no stopping these outraged harpies.

Alec saw that Nadia was looking on with a smile on her lips, and he shot her a glare that immediately erased the expression. Just then, Wolf also caught sight of Alec, and his eyes pleaded for immediate help. Alec nodded, and Wolf pointed in his boss's direction. Seconds later, the women who'd been badgering Wolf started to converge on Alec.

Behl shouted, "Attention, Gulldammit!"

The women continued towards Alec, Alexa striding determinedly next to the giant Myra, and for a moment Alec wished he was back fighting the pirates. He saw an opportunity and jumped up onto a nearby crate—*To safety*, he thought. "Please, one at a time!" he yelled at the women, all of whom wanted his attention *right now*. The decibel level failed to drop. "You!" he pointed at Alexa. "What the hell's going on? The rest of you shut up!"

Alexa sniffed and gestured in Wolf's direction. "That brute over there refuses to let us bring our purchases aboard. They've passed security inspection, but he's babbling on about regulations and orders, and..."

Alec gestured sharply with one hand and looked at poor Wolf, who was trying to slink out of the cargo bay. "Get back here, Wolf," Alec ordered.

Wolf approached, a resolute expression on his face. "Sir, all due respect, but we don't have the room for all this junk." He gestured to the pile of bags and boxes in front of him. With those words another avalanche from the women fell upon him and all those unfortunate enough to be nearby. Alec could only stand there and shake his head at the commotion. It was a full five minutes before the crew started to calm down.

"We can store it in our own quarters," insisted Myra loudly, as Alexa nodded her head.

Alec sighed. "Myra, dear, that's not the point. Before you do anything with it, I need to talk to you, Alexa, and Nadia for a bit." He smiled tightly, and his dark-haired beauty began to look concerned.

"Ale...sir, this is just the tip of the iceberg," Wolf said, "Look over there."

Alec looked, and saw several dozen large crates. He'd thought they must contain supplies they'd purchased from Tota or received from both Nass and Busch, mostly necessary ammunition and some more weapons. "So there's more?" Alec asked icily.

Alexa spoke up. "Well, yes, but you *did* promise I could go shopping, and since you couldn't come, I, um, invited a few friends." All of a sudden she started studying the floor, making tiny circles with her boot.

Good Gull, she's like a little kid. "A few friends?" Alec looked at her, shaking his head. Myra saw an opportunity and motioned for the girls to start loading; meanwhile, Alec placed his hand gently on Alexa's chin and raised her face towards his.

Tearing up, she whispered, "I'll return all of it, okay? I didn't mean to upset you. I've never done this before, and..." Alexa looked at Alec, blinking her beautiful doe eyes.

Myra stopped gesturing to the other crew and looked at Alexa in disbelief when she heard her mention returning everything. Alec looked at Nadia, and her expression reminded him of his own mother's whenever she was upset with him. He turned back at Alexa and flashed a tight smile. "Keep it. Keep it all."

Behl clapped a hand to his forehead, making a strange little strangled sound, and Wolf gazed upon him as if Alec had saved him... which in fact he had. Myra grinned frightfully and engulfed both Alec and Alexa in a giant hug, lifting both of them off the floor.

"Put us *down*, Myra." Alec scowled. "And make sure we can still load up all the important stuff, or you'll lose some of your shi..."

Alexa looked at Alec. "Important?"

Alec realized he had lost yet another battle, and decided to regroup very far away, leaving over a hundred women cheering and talking loudly about all their loot. Alexa was still holding onto his arm, and tried handing one of his debit cards back to him.

"Keep it, love."

Her sloe eyes brightened; she wrapped her arms around his neck and kissed his face all over.

"Relax!" he laughed. "It's just a debit card."

"No, not that, silly. You called me your love."

"No I didn't," Alec defended himself. "I just, I meant..." Alexa looked confused, so he kissed her. "Yes. Yes, I did say that."

"Thank you, love...I'll respond to that when we're all alone with one of my little rituals." Alexa gave him a mischievous smile. She felt his member stiffen and turned around, letting her firm buttocks graze his masculine pride. Then she put the debit card into his chest pocket and tapped on it.

Alec swallowed hard and stuttered, "I said you could keep it. Use it for emergencies."

"Why? Stupid thing won't work anymore. Tota told me to have you refill it, or for me to sign a credit, and I know what a credit is... well, what it means. Back to the old slave block. I don't really understand the little guy, but I couldn't carry more stuff anyway. Besides, I want to get something ready for the dinner ball tonight."

Alec slid a new debit card into her breast pocket, grinning. She gave him a pat on his cheek and strutted back to claim her share of the loot.

Nikko Behl's voice rose behind him. "Tota said *what*? Wait until I get my hands on that sniveling little pants pisser!"

"Not piss, sweat," mumbled Alec to himself, leaving a Behl with a questioning expression.

"You're learning, young master."

Alec turned to face Nadia.

"Thank you for allowing them to go shopping, sir. This gives them a rather different outlook on life to counterbalance the theft and pillaging they've been used to. They needed this, and besides, you can afford it."

He snorted. "Nadia, never tell me what I can and cannot afford. Do I make myself clear?"

"Crystal." She bowed her head. "My apologies if I have offended you."

"Nadia, your intentions today were noble, but letting them spread money around like there's no tomorrow won't do them any good on the day they have to fend for themselves."

Nadia nodded her head, understanding. "You're wise, sir. I am honored to learn from you, and I hope that I can still be part of your crew and that my actions today may be forgiven."

"Your actions don't need my forgiveness, dammit, and yes, you're part of this crew. And yes, *you* will be the one explaining to our younger crew members the concept of spending limits." Alec smiled as he gave Nadia a quick hug, demonstrating to the onlookers that there were no hard feelings between them, and Nadia accepted it.

She met his embrace, whispering, "You are a good person, and in time I hope you can trust me and all Grisamm with your soul."

Alec looked Nadia in her eyes and nodded.

ADMIRAL Cook spent two days recovering from flash burns and decompression injuries in the infirmary on board *Crusher 5*. Since the *Unity 1* was now just so much space debris, he designated the *Crusher* his new command post and temporary flagship, much to Captain Copola's great dismay; the captain figured he'd see much less action as a result.

By the time Cook bulled his way out of sickbay (against medical advice, of course), both Alec and Admiral Busch had visited and debriefed him on everything. He'd hardly listened to a word at the beginning, but expressed his relief over finally having found his nephew. All of them agreed to keep Alec's newfound career a secret, and to definitely not tell his father—at least, not yet. Any information about Alexa must be kept away from his parents as well; Cook had insisted, not wanting to remind Alec about the bride-to-be his parents had arranged for him. He didn't care to spoil the young man's first true love, knowing it could never last due the political realities of the situation. Of course, Alec could always keep the girl on the side as a concubine, assuming his wife agreed; otherwise, she would certainly end up dead.

Cook concealed his emotions and let the young man in front of him continue with his incredible story. When Alec told Cook about his mad idea of going to his friends' rescue, it was to Cook's great relief when he subsequently announced that he would no longer continue in that direction, but wanted to return home as soon as possible. There was a brief argument when Alec refused to join Cook on the *Crusher*, but Cook was too tired to argue. He reluctantly allowed Alec to continue his command aboard his own ship.

Captain Copola joined them then, charging into the room, embracing Alec in a huge bear hug. Alec's former teacher was twice his weight and a head taller, and Alec felt his feet leaving the ground and his ribs cracking from the strain. Captain Copola would have ended up putting Alec into the bed next to Cook's, if he hadn't dropped his beloved hat, which he grabbed at before it could hit the ground. In so doing he dropped Alec, who hit the deck on his ass.

After he'd calmed down, Cook ordered Copola to help Alec upgrade and refit his weapons and supplies on the *Predator*, and to supply him with 100 elite troops.

"Finally," Copola muttered as he brushed off his hat with his forearm. "Your father, uncle and I have looked forward to seeing you in action for a long time, kid." Then he turned abruptly and left to fulfill his admiral's orders.

Cook had difficulty fathoming the enormous size of the treasure Alec had captured; but Alec had expected this reaction, especially after Busch's initial response when he had heard about the treasure. When he fished up a tritonium silver bar from his pocket, he felt a rush of contentment at the shock on Admiral Cook's face. Both Cook and Busch looked at it suspiciously, and neither seemed especially enthusiastic to touch it. After a while, though, they took turns holding it and staring at it in disbelief. Meanwhile, Alec regaled them with tales of all the other loot he'd taken back from the pirates.

FOUR

INSIDE one of the grand mess halls on the Star Dice were three large circular tables, each located atop a podium. The lowest table held the highest-ranking officers and Tota's VIP guests, while the other two levels bore lower-ranking officers and less important guests. A band was playing from a balcony, and several singers replaced each other in turn after performing a few songs each. The walls were masked with vast red draperies, and the lighting changed colors, depending of the type of music. Most of the guests mingled on the dance floor, telling battle stories for the most part. The general ambience was stiff, given the presence of soldiers and officers from both Federations, not to mention a dozen Predator captains.

Servants and androids moved with quiet grace among the guests, serving drinks and snacks. The discussions among the various groups were wide-ranging, covering everything from the latest scandals to religion and sports. The one subject every single military guest avoided was politics. The one thing they all looked forward to, on the other hand, was some real food, instead of the ship rations they'd been forced to endure during the long days of fighting. Even the everyday chow aboard ship, they all agreed, was little more than pig-slop.

The majority of the military guests were clad in their dress uniforms or battle fatigues, though some of the higher-ranking officers were dressed in their parade uniforms, making the room even more colorful. Tota wanted to avoid any tension, so he had his own staff intermingle with everyone on all levels. Many of the young men and women working the crowd worked for old lady Pulp.

Alec was dressed in his dark blue uniform with the odd boots, which drew attention from many eyes as he wandered across the great room, exchanging pleasantries with civilians and military alike. The belt, with its strip of unusual hair, also drew some attention. When he passed near Myra—who was dressed in what appeared to be acres of overstressed pink taffeta—she raised her large nose in the air and sniffed with an expression that conveyed fright, dangerous anger, or possibly both. After a moment her glare landed on his belt and boots, in turn; and then she grinned and suddenly hugged him, whispering into his ear, "We'll make a pirate of you yet, you cold-blooded little Oman."

She planted a wet kiss on his cheek, then returned to her friends and started to whisper to them. Thereafter, a dozen of the female crew came up one by one and thanked him, though they never made clear exactly what they were thanking him for. He guessed it had something to do with their shopping spree earlier in the day. *We'll make them all work it off, though*, he thought to himself. But when some of the women came up to him—staring at him from top to the bottom—and started to touch his belt, he looked at Alexa nervously, hoping it wouldn't upset her.

Alexa was dressed in standard shipsuit, and was more or less ignoring him. At the moment she was engaged in an intent conversation with Admirals Cook, Nass and Busch, several of the Predator captains, and various friends and associates of Tota, who were all laughing as she told them some kind of wild story. Her hair was put up and looked more messy than organized, and a smudge on her cheek suggested that she'd just returned from working in the docking bay.

He had to admit to himself that he was a little disappointed that Alexa hadn't taken the time to freshen up and change into something nicer, perhaps even sexier; after all, she *had* been shopping. But he realized after observing her from a distance that even dressed the way she was, her charm radiated through the entire room. He felt a sick jolt inside, and was suddenly tremendously jealous.

The diminutive Tota, who seemed to be talking to everyone at the same time, stopped right in front of him all of a sudden. "Alec Horn, my favorite Oman," he shouted, jumping up and down like a demented toad. Tota's distraction made Alec forget about his uncomfortable feelings towards anyone looking at Alexa, and he smiled as he kneeled to bring his face level with the little fellow's. Tota leapt into the air and landed in Alec's arms.

He whispered, "Told you I'd find you some pirates, yeah?" and then continued, "So why act as if you're no longer joined with her, my friend? Be grateful for what you have. Thoughts like the ones you're having now will pass, just like the storm outside. If they don't, then you might feel the next storm *inside*...and that is never a good thing. But should she choose not to continue without you, then treasure your memory of her and move forward. Always move forward and never look back, except to enjoy the best of your memories." Tota ended his soliloquy with shouts of joy, calling out to everyone to see the mystery prince, who had crushed the pirates just for his mystery princess!

He jumped down on the floor, demanding everyone's attention; and when he didn't get it, the little man demanded that Nikko Behl, who stood near Alec, pick him up. Alec shook his head in disbelief; the little elephantoid had earned Alec's respect more than once, but if he didn't know better, he'd think he was just some silly little man. He reflected that he'd never seen a better actor, as he smiled towards Alexa, who now was in the center of many hungry gazes—male as well as female, from every Oman and omanoid species present.

Myra and a number of the women from the *Predator* crew were looking at him similarly, eyeing his belt and boots with satisfied admiration. When they noticed Alec's jealousy towards Alexa, though, they looked at each other and nodded, intermingling with the other guests and taking up station near the ones obviously hungering for a taste of the dark-haired, gold-skinned beauty.

As he lifted Mr. Tota, Behl growled, "If you piss on me, you little shit, I'll keelhaul you from here to bloody New Frontier 16, you hear me?"

"Indeed I do, my funny friend." Tota clambered onto Behl's shoulders and patted him on the head before standing up and shouting, "Attention everyone! Welcome, all my beloved friends! Have a seat, and let us all forget the evil outside and instead focus on a wonderful dinner! Enjoy!" Tota launched himself in the air and made an agile landing on the deck, hurrying away to assist his servants with the seating.

In the background came the sound of laser and particle beam lances pounding away at the larger meteor fragments (and other debris) whenever they came too close; but it had become so constant that it was nothing more than background noise by then, ignored by all. Once everyone was seated, Tota jumped onto a table and held a short welcome speech, in which he thanked everyone for fighting off the scum of the universe who had tried to destroy them. In thanks, he gave all the soldiers a 1,000-credit bonus, to be used in his casino only. His next words were drowned in applause, so he stood there, beaming, until the clapping died down, then tried again: "Now, before we start, Rear Admiral Jonas Nass of the great Florencian Federation would like to say a few words." Tota gesturing for Admiral Nass to join him on the table.

Busch glanced at Admiral Cook, who looked back at him, both cursing themselves for not thinking about speeches of their own.

Nass clambered up onto the table. He was dressed in a white parade uniform covered with medals and insignia; his black knee-high boots shone like obsidian mirrors. His personality and charisma reflected the authority his rank held, and the room fell silent almost immediately. He held a confident pose while looking over the room and moving in a small circle, making sure he had everyone's attention.

"A unique historical event has occurred here at the Battle of New Frontier," he proclaimed, and by saying that, he made history himself by giving the battle its official name. "Military forces from the Florencian Federation and the Nastasturus Federation have fought as one, under a single command, against a monstrous fleet of pirate ships. Even though the battle is not entirely over, I feel confident that we will prevail when we are reinforced by several fleets from both of our federations, and also from the famous Predators." The crowd ended his sentence with wild applause, and Admiral Nass took the opportunity to pause. When the storm of clapping had passed, he turned to look at Alec. "One man, a civilian, was able to regroup and save both our fleets in the midst of chaos, and perhaps avert a disaster. His name is Alec Horn."

Thank Gull he doesn't know Alec's real name and his family background, Admiral Cook thought, tugging at his collar.

"Mr. Horn almost singlehandedly combined our forces and configured a battle strategy that completely overwhelmed our enemies, scattering them, while simultaneously decreasing their numbers enough for them to think twice before they attack again. It is my honor and duty to present Mr. Horn with the honorable rank and commission of a commander in the Florencian military, as well as the Grand Order of Florencia."

Admiral Nass smiled broadly at Alec, who, after a brief hesitation, climbed onto the table with the Admiral. Nass handed him a small box containing several computer cards and a medal, while saluting Alec, who as an ostensible civilian only nodded his head and shook the Admiral's hand. When Admiral Nass placed the silk band holding the medal around Alec's neck, he whispered, "Keep my command card for the CBR unit, son. It might protect you should you ever travel in our space...and thank you for saving my life, not once but twice." They looked at each other, and Alec took a step back.

Well, Admiral Cook couldn't be outdone by a Fish Fucker, no matter how honorable. He reached over and snapped a medal off Captain Copola's broad chest (he had plenty of them anyway), and hurried to the central table, climbing up as Nass climbed down. Drawing himself up, he announced grandly, "I, Admiral Hadrian

Cook af Hornet of the Grand Federation of Nastasturus, would like to take the opportunity to thank everyone for their assistance in the ongoing fight. May we all one day fight no more, and enjoy the rewards and prosperity that come with everlasting peace."

Admiral Cook's little political speech was met with less enthusiasm that Nass's, but he ignored the crowd's reaction (or lack of it) and continued. "It is my duty and honor to present to this young man, who has performed a duty above and beyond any civilian's call, this Medal of..." Admiral Cook looked down, and noticed that the medal he'd taken from Copola's chest was actually a campaign medal, older than Alec was; hoping no one would notice his mistake, he continued smoothly, "...Bravery, and the commission of Captain in the Nastasturan Space Navy, should he choose to accept a *real* military commission."

Admiral Cook smiled at Admiral Nass, and Alec had difficulty containing his amusement as his uncle placed the old campaign medal in his hand and whispered, "Put the damned thing in your pocket, and we'll have a talk or two later."

Alec took a step back, and nodded his head to both of the Admirals. Someone in the background shouted, "Speech, give us a speech!" Behl looked at Captain Zlo in horror; Zlo looked back, equally frightened. Both remembered the first speech they'd heard Alec give, the one that had cost them millions of credits back in the slave market.

Alec glanced at them and smiled. "Why, thank you. I don't know what to say; I'm not much of a speaker. I feel that all of us did well under the circumstances we've endured and are still facing, and I hope that all of us will soon see an end to this conflict...but right now I'm hungry." Alec's last words were meet by cheers and more applause than either of the Admirals', and he climbed down from the table to get to his meal.

As seemed the local custom, the dinner was accompanied by several different shows—magic, aerobics, and even a popular comedian, who cracked everyone up with his spot-on impersonations of the leaders of both the Federations. After the first course was served, along with wine and strong liquor, some of the tension and stiffness began to abate. By the time the second course was served (accompanied by a rather erotic dance from two dozen Marengan ladies), people were cheering and laughing. The wilder the dancers performed, the wilder the guests became, slamming their fists in unison on the table, breaking glasses and clanging cutlery.

When the music reached its peak it stopped, and so did the dancers. The room darkened, and the dancers lined up in a circle, moving their bodies like snakes. The formation opened up and a podium rose out of the floor, revealing the famous celebrity duet of Panristo and Passena, who began singing a famous Oman opera so old that no one knew where it had originated. The crowd fell silent, and many teared up as the singers belted out their parts with brio, weaving a tale of the end of war, and the beginning of a much-deserved peace. Panristo represented the dark shadow of hate with his basso profundo voice, while Passena, representing the light of love, soared above his grim pronouncements in a trilling mezzo-soprano. As they continued, they moved toward one another, and their voices fell more into unison, both in tone and theme; and as peace prevailed over war, they sang as one, arm in arm.

Not everyone was impressed. Next to Myra sat a somewhat drunk Florencian officer who could have cared less about the music, and shouted something about capitalistic propaganda. Myra slapped him hard in response and left him with his ears ringing; tears trickled down her face.

Alec himself sat next to an empty chair. Alexa had excused herself over an hour ago, after the first course, and as the meal went on, he had nearly forgotten about her absence. As the third course was removed and the dessert was placed in front of him, he looked around for her. He gestured, and Bax leaned forward. "Where's Alexa?"

Bax tapped a button on the torc around his neck and spoke briefly in hushed tones. Then he leaned forward and murmured, "Everything is fine, sir. No worries."

Alec twisted around to look into the huge man's eyes, but Bax merely stared forward, motioning toward the floor in front of them. Alec looked puzzled, then turned around, shaking his head. *I can't believe I've become so possessive about her*, he thought.

Panristo and Passena had just finished their last aria, and were being inundated with applause and shouts of "Bravo!" as they were lowered back into the floor on their dais. Immediately thereafter, another platform rose into view with seven svelte young women kneeling on it. Mist flowed across the floor like waves in an ocean, lit dimly from below. The band began playing a soft, calming song, as searchlights stabbed up from below the mist, their flashing beams resembling lightning within clouds.

The seven stood; all were beautiful women, dressed in outfits that left very little to the viewer's imagination. They looked like goddesses standing atop the clouds, their faces painted in silver, black, and white, highlighted with strange jungle patterns similar to camouflage. They began moving agilely and seductively with the rhythm of the music, twisting and turning in slow motion in ways that most certainly weren't suited for minors. As soft and delicate as it was, their dance seemed to radiate orgasmic joy.

Everyone stared in silent disbelief.

The dancers moved to the center of their dais and begin to dance while touching each other erotically. One of them stood spread-eagled, while the other women gyrated around her arms and legs. Two of them knelt as the others wove their bodies around the women in the center.

The moved in a circle, allowing everyone to see all the details. The dancers traded places occasionally with the one at the center, kissing and touching each other's breasts while moving with the increasing beat of the music, breathing louder and louder. There were many encouraging shouts from the crowd, though the shouters were quickly shut down by their neighbors, who had learned from Myra's reaction.

Alec grinned. *Alexa should be here to see this. Maybe she could learn a thing or two.* Alec had been thinking about what Nadia had lectured him about, regarding Alexa's innocence and lack of social knowledge, given the harsh upbringing she had endured.

All seven dancers had well-shaped bodies, and they knew how to use them. The music began to beat faster, and the dancers began moving faster as well. They turned on each other, tearing apart each other's garments in a false-fighting scenario, leaving only a few shreds to save them from full nudity. As it turned out, their fantastical facial art continued down across their bodies.

The dancers split up and moved seductively toward the front table, crawling and sliding on all fours. When the music changed rhythm, they stopped, kneeling in front of the guests at the table, moving even more seductively.

The sound of dropping jaws and popping eyeballs was practically audible, and Alec looked on with vague envy as one of the vixens began to dance in front of Captain Copola. To the amazement of everyone who knew him, she was soon wearing his battered hat as she seduced the captain, who smiled at her like there was no tomorrow...until he realized the current location of said hat. His expression changed from satisfaction to horror, and he lunged after her in a futile attempt to snap back his most precious possession. She slid gracefully away, shaking her head and grinning; then she spun away down the circular table, as Copola leapt to his feet and got himself ready for some serious rescue action. Laughing lightly, the dancer tossed his hat with a surgical precision in his direction, and it landed backward on his head, eliciting laughter from the crowd.

Holy Gull, that's Tara, Alec thought; she was easier to identify than the others, since she wore less makeup...and well, less of everything.

"Don't forget to pick up your eyeballs on the way out, son," Admiral Busch whispered to Alec, who turned towards him with a confused expression. He noticed Nadia, who stood next to Bax, looking upon the display like a proud mother. When Alec turned around, he found that the dancers had moved in unison to new locations around the table—and in front of him was his own personal vixen.

Alexa gifted Alec with her shyest, most innocent and yet most seductive smile as she eased down onto her stomach, knees bent and crossed behind her, feet curled. She blew him a kiss and lunged up onto all fours while moving back and forth, faster and faster with the rhythm of the music, arching her back, curving her spine almost unnaturally. She flexed her athletic, well-defined body, revealing the most perfect set of buttocks in creation. For an instant the music stopped and the students looked to Nadia; and the dancers, who in addition to Alexa and Tara clearly included their cohorts Nina, Kirra, Muhama, Miska and Zicci, emitted soft cries of ecstasy.

Alec leaned over Lady Pulp's shoulder and muttered to Busch, "Remind me to have a little chat with their teacher about their physical training classes." Busch shook his head and gestured towards the show.

Each dancer vaulted onto the table and grabbed a large clay bottle full of wine, clearly placed there for the purpose. While a stunned audience watched, they poured the wine over their heads and bodies, each standing on one leg while extending the other forward, offering to anyone the wine that spilled off their delicate toes. Several guests held their silver cups out for refills; others tried to grab a girl's ankle and drink directly from the source, but when that happened, the young lady gave them soft kicks on the forehead while sliding away. To intensify the moment, the girls smashed the soft clay bottles over their heads, and wine mixed with bits of clay—which turned out to be a kind of candy—splattered everywhere. Loud shouts of encouragement erupted from the audience, most of whom were standing and applauding.

The girls jumped backed to the floor, gesturing at the seated people to join them on the floor. Alexa waved her hands to Tota, who tossed his silver cup into the air. A servant snapped it out of the air with an experienced hand. Tota hurled himself over the table, and to everyone's amazement, danced like a professional with the beautiful girl, who was easily two heads taller. A few of the more venturesome guests joined them on the dance floor, and soon it was packed.

With quiet precision, the entire room altered its shape, and soon transformed into a nightclub. Walls opened up, revealing extensive bars with waiting bartenders, as well as quiet, comfortable lounges.

Alec lost Alexa in the crush of the crowd and pressed through the other guests, looking desperately for her. He was contemplating asking the Grisamm guards for their help, but changed his mind as he noticed Nina and Kirra dancing with a group of Nastasturan and Florencian officers. Zicci was nearby, gyrating to the beat with a female Predator captain; Tara was in the middle of a circle of giggling, jewelry-bedecked civilian women. He saw a long tail snap suddenly, and realized that Miska had slapped someone who had tried to grope her buttocks. Her sister Muhama patted the chastised fellow on the shoulder.

Obviously, Alexa had to be around her somewhere. As Alec pushed his way out of the melee on the dance floor, he noticed some cages being lowered down from the ceiling, filled with more dancers.

Shrugged, he made his way over to a bar and ordered a drink. Just as he was about to take a sip, his glass was yanked out of his hands. "Thanks, I could sure use that."

A second later, Alexa slammed the empty glass on the bar and bellowed for more, as she let out a discreet little burp and dried her mouth on her forearm. Alec was overwhelmed by her surprise attack, and could do nothing but stare. She focused her own attention on the bartender, waiting impatiently for him to refill the glass, and emptied it just as fast when it was placed before her. With a sour expression, she demanded some water from the busy bartender, and turned to her waiting knight. "Did you like our dance?" she asked, grinning.

"I think you gave some of the old ladies of both genders heart attacks." He grabbed her and kissed her hard, lifting her off the ground. Her legs were kicking in protest until she clamped her arms around his neck and returned the kiss.

He set her down gently. "Come on."

"But my drink!"

"I'll give you plenty to drink."

Alec pulled her aside in a firm grip, and slammed her up against the wall in a dark corner a few paces away from the crowd hanging onto the bar. Before she had time to react, he kissed her neck fervently, making her body scream for more. He whispered in her ear how beautiful and adorable she was, then looked around, making sure no one was looking, while Alexa went for another sip from her glass.

When she looked up, her knight was gone...or so she thought, until she felt an insistent nudge between her legs. As she felt his tongue jab at the pearl of her clitoris, she reared up and slammed her head in the wall, emitting a low cry of pain and pleasure intermixed.

A few people nearby turned around, and Alexa smiled at them while rolling her eyes. She hurriedly adjusted a bar chair in front of her, concealing Alec, who was apparently working on an advanced degree in, ahem, cave research. He lashed out with his tongue, while making short circles with his finger over her belly button; and when he noticed she was near an explosion, he stopped.

Alexa, by then, was doing everything she could not to scream out in ecstasy; so she was rather puzzled and certainly disappointed as she looked at her knight. He took his glass from her and emptied it in one gulp, then handed it back and leaned close. "There you are, my little pirate," he whispered into her ear. "I hope that will teach you a thing or two about tantalizing someone. Oh, and now you have something to look forward to."

Alexa wrapped her arms around his neck and kissed him. "Sure, I'll think about it as I dance with all the dozens of horny toads out there," she motioned her head towards the dance floor, and noticed her knight's desperate expression. She grabbed his crotch and massaged it.

A moment later, Alexa noticed Captain Copola standing impatiently behind Alec. "Someone wants to see you," she murmured. "See you back at my suite."

"You mean *my* suite," Alec insisted.

Alexa frowned. Then she let out a quick laugh, and hurried back to the dance floor.

Captain Copola gestured to Alec to join him, so he followed the Captain to a small group of several waiting people. "Time for a little chat," Hadrian Cook said, as he gestured for Alec and Busch to follow. Admiral Nass and several officers also caught up with them, including some of the Predator captains. They walked into a private lounge, and the doors behind them clicked shut.

Two exhausting hours later, after a grilling that left virtually no minute of his life for the past two months untouched, Alec hurried back to his suite. The wild event was still in full swing, and he noticed that some of Alexa's partners in crime were making out with the same people they had danced with earlier. When he flagged down Nadia to ask her about it, all she had to say was, "Wish we had some younger men, too. They make excellent spies." Being too exhausted to consider the implications, Alec had left it at that.

When he finally closed the hatch to his suite aboard the *Predator*, he was grateful that Lady Fuzza had rebuilt her quarters—now Alec's—to a friendlier (and larger) design than military ships usually enjoyed. He stepped into the small pantry area and took a bottle of water from the fridge. When he entered his sleeping quarters, he looked down at the beautiful woman taking up the entire bed, hogging all the sheets, with amused eyes. She was still wearing that strange paint all over her body. He slipped out of his clothes, and pulled a thin black rope from his wardrobe. He tied one end around his ankle, and the other around hers.

"What are you up too?" she mumbled. "It's not fair taking advantage of a lady when she's at a disadvantage...especially since the bed is moving something awful." She lifted her hands to her aching head.

"Just one of my new rituals, love, now that we're one. But if you don't want to..." he trailed off, disappointed, realizing that she'd passed out. Then he smiled gently, rearranged her on the bed a bit, and lay down next to her. A moment later she opened her eyes and slid atop of him seductively. "About time you came back," she whispered, resting her head on his chest and apparently going right back to sleep. Her curls tickled his nose, but he didn't care; he didn't want to wake her up. Soon he joined her in deep sleep; and for the first time in months, his dreams were pleasant.

Alec slept very heavily, and it took him a while to realize that he wasn't dreaming anymore when a wonderful sensation shot like electricity up and down his spine, tingles progressing throughout his entire body. He opened his eyes, very confused, then sat up, looking around.

"Don't move," hissed someone underneath the sheets.

He sensed the warm sensation of a mouth and teasing tongue slithering around his erection; he calmed down and slid back down on his pillow, lifting up the sheet to see a pair of eyes glittering in the darkness as she attended to him. "Sorry if I woke you," she murmured. "I couldn't resist, and besides, I needed some breakfast."

He grinned, dropped the sheet, and let her do her thing. She paused occasionally, asking him what he liked and if she was doing it wrong, playing with him while driving him absolutely crazy.

"So, did you like our little dance, my dear, and did it turn you on?"

"I loved it, and are you kidding me? I had no idea it was you girls at first, but when I did, I..."

Breakfast forgotten, Alexa tossed the sheet aside and sat up, looking at him suspiciously. "You didn't know it was me on the floor? You didn't recognize me right away?"

"Well, um, no."

"Oh, is that right? So some other slut could have been turning you on?"

"Well, no, but...wait, where are you going?"

Alexa untied the strap around her ankle and tossed it on the bed. "Sorry, I have a dental appointment with Doc today."

Alexa stormed into the bathroom, slamming the door hard, leaving Alec to wonder what the hell he'd done or said—just like most men did most of their lives.

"**FASTER!** Faster, you no-good harpies from hell!" Nikko Behl shouted. In the forward fighter bay, fifteen women ran like mad and dove into their fighters. Other crew members elsewhere manned the cannons and missile turrets on the two gun decks. Myra's voice sounded like rumbling thunder when she bellowed to her mid-ship gun crew to move faster, faster, *faster*! Myra had proven to be one of the better non-commissioned officers, especially after Alec had paid for her new cloned legs, much to the crew's relief. They were sick of listening to her prosthetics making all types of noise, followed by Myra's curses whenever they broke down.

The entire crew repeated their drills relentlessly, despite the complaints. After the hard exercise, the entire crew had to do physical training, weapon drills and, finally, ship maintenance. The Grisamm monks were exceptional military experts, and eagerly passed on their knowledge to the entire crew. Whenever someone lacked the enthusiasm to continue, the Grisamm monks had several eventful surprises for them, from scrubbing toilets to cleaning and repairing the hull of the *Predator* from the outside, something most crewbies absolutely hated. This did, however, allow them to hone their skills at fighting in pressure suits, using jet packs and various weapons and tools adapted for the vacuum. Alec had overheard some of the veterans from the original crew confide to Lady Fuzza and Captain Zlo that they had learned more in the past month about space warfare than they had in their entire careers previously.

Alec and all the officers, except those on duty, participated in all the drills in order to maintain morale and sharpen their own skills. He noticed that he was never placed in a group with Alexa, and he never asked the Grisamm monks why.

After two days of intense drilling with very little rest, they received a warning from the command bridge that the convoy would be passing out of the annoying meteor swarm the next day; and they all knew that the battle would surely be rejoined as a result. All exercises ceased, and the crew was ordered to rest as much as possible and to get themselves properly nourished. Any shore leave to the casinos was canceled.

That afternoon, Alec ambled toward his quarters, thinking about Alexa. He wondered if she still might be upset with him, and what it was that had made her so upset in the first place. He wanted to freshen up and change before attending a final staff meeting several hours hence. The meeting was to be held aboard the *Predator,* so that any tension between Admirals Cook and Nass might be avoided. Both couldn't attend in person; they would be present as holograms transmitted from their respective flagships.

After he finished a quick shower, he wrapped a towel around his waist and headed for his bedroom—where he found Alexa sitting on the bed with her head in her hands, tears pouring down her cheeks. In alarm, he thought, *I hope the instructors aren't too harsh on her because of me.* He approached her with care. "What's wrong?"

He sat down next to her at the end of the bed, but she pushed him away. He grabbed hold of her shoulders and turned her toward him, looked at her with a serious expression...and she started pounding her fists into his chest while crying. "Don't you ever do that to me again, you big brute!" she cried. "Don't you dare think of another woman ever again!"

"But, but I..."

"And don't you ever let me leave the room upset like you did the other morning!"

Alec looked even more confused than before, at a loss for words, so he did the only natural thing that came to his mind: he kissed her, thinking, *Maybe I should have spanked her instead?* He could taste her salty tears when their lips met. She grabbed him hard and pulled him tight to her body. "I promise, I promise," said Alec between kisses, not really knowing what he was promising.

After they'd made up and snuggled for a while, he asked, "So how was your dental appointment?"

Alexa looked a bit confused, then shot him a mischievous smile. She leaned forward in front of him, running her nails over his muscular chest. "The good doctor prescribed a lifetime of very intense oral workouts, as often as possible, while working my neck muscles. He tells me that should help me take everything down to the bottom without choking, and that I must swallow all the medicine, never spilling a single drop."

She moved down on the floor, running her fingers up his thighs under the towel. "And in the event I might spill some of my medicine," she continued, "then I should be punished. Oh, yes, then I must be punished very hard; she insisted. She really did."

She gave him a questioning look, running her tongue along her upper lip in a seductive way. She giggled when she noticed the tent that suddenly appeared in the towel in front of her. "I'm going to promote the Doc to General, as soon as I can," Alec whispered, as Alexa knelt before him.

A few moments later, she looked up smiling, swallowing hard. She pretended to spill some of his juices...but the fantasy became reality as a few drops splattered on the deck. She looked down on the small spots, then looked up at him in horror. "That doesn't count. Hey, did you hear me? It doesn't count."

Alec was all over her before she could fend him off. She curled up into a small ball on the floor, but she was no match for Alec's strength; he lifted her up and placed her over his lap, while Alexa protested louder and louder over his rough treatment on her fragile body. "This is *not* what the doctor meant! Now, listen to me and be reasonable! Owww, wait, that hurt..."

Alec had never dreamed of laying his hands on a woman this way, but he didn't count this as abuse; and neither did she, apparently, as she promised to get back at him as he spanked her bare rear. Finally he stopped. Apparently his cure didn't have the same effect on her as his mother's had once had on him. He tossed her on the bed and smiled at her. "I have to run, staff meeting, but we'll continue your treatment as soon as I return, you bad little girl."

Alexa stood up, massaging her tender buttocks while looking over her shoulder into a large mirror on the wall. No bruises. She muttered, "Better than being tickled," and covered her mouth with her hands as she saw Alec's evil grin reflecting in the mirror. She looked at him, eyes pleading. He threw her a kiss and turned to leave.

"I didn't mean that, do you hear me, darling...?"

Alec ignored his vixen's explanation.

"Shit!", followed by the sound of someone kicking something, was the last thing he heard before the hatch to his suite hissed shut.

Alec was in a great mood. *Finally! I've won my first battle against the little beast,* he thought, hurrying away to the staff meeting, followed by his Grisamm shadows.

―――――o〇o―――――

THE very last thing that went through Key Administrator Zala's mind was the large profit she had earned, and then everything went black. Well...in truth the last thing that went through her mind was a collapsteel blade wielded by an overzealous pirate, but by then she was too far gone to notice.

Zuzack glared in disappointed disgust at the bloody dead thing tied to the desk—her own, as it happened—and then turned his irritated gaze on the two pirates next to her, both of whom were blaming the other for going too far and killing her. He couldn't care less; his main concern was contacting his brother Horsa. He turned around suddenly and swept his sabre out of its scabbard, cutting down both the idiots in a trice, and thrust the sword back into the scabbard without bothering to clean it. Horsa's words echoed in his mind: "Remember, no witnesses, and the fewer partners we have, the more spoil we get." Zuzack looked around in the office and smiled, then headed back to his ship, which was docked to the main security complex.

Hughes and Grotech waited. "We're checking out," Zuzack bellowed, laughing grimly.

An hour later the *Bitch* was approaching Horsa's flagship, which headed a group of about 500 ships in two large convoys. Almost a thousand more pirate ships were still attached to the New Frontier 16 like great metallic leeches on a giant, and the pirates were still looting. He looked into his holotank past the station, toward the hundreds of ships keeping station a thousand kilometers away. "Ogstafa, you old cow, why don't you take the bait?" he grumbled.

He shrugged, and ordered, "Zozo, maximum power to all our deflector shields and engines. Get us the hell away from here." He turned off his communicator before his strange engineer had time to respond, and turned to Hughes. "Inform my brother that I have finished my task and gotten the information we need. Tell him to order the rest of the clan to get as far away from New Frontier 16 as possible, and that we will meet up with him later."

The rat-man gave his captain a poor excuse for a salute, and headed back to his seat on the command bridge as large metallic plates began to iris shut over the forward ports. Zuzack glanced at the image in the holotank, which displayed the New Frontier 16 on the far left; there was a red line arcing across space near the middle of the image, and a small white dot that represented *the Bitch*. When the white dot passed the red line, Zuzack pressed a button on the panel before him and cried merrily, "Hold on, everyone, here we go!"

The New Frontier 16, with its millions of inhabitants and hundreds of thousands of visitors, transformed into a brilliant white supernova as shaped magnetic fields released quantities of antimatter measured in the kilograms. Residents, diplomats, gamblers, traders, tourists, maintenance workers, soldiers, security personnel, whores, and slaves of all classes and species, belonging to dozens of polities, were vaporized in an instant—as were fully half the pirates who had been in on the initial attack. The shock waves from the explosion spread through local space at half the speed of light, immolating hundreds of smaller ships and stations, and crippling hundreds more to a distance of tens of thousands of kilometers. The violent destruction of so many ships just added to the shockwaves spreading through local space, ultimately overtaking even small conveys of ships and independent stations that were still running away from the battle, and adding to the casualties.

Nearly half the combined Nastasturan/Florencian fleet, and nearly all the Predators, were stationed within twenty thousand kilometers of the New Frontier 16. As soon as the first flash of brilliant light flooded their sensors, the fleets scattered. There was no time to worry about formations or containment; all they could do was get safely away without colliding with anyone else, and then attempt to regain control of their ships. Despite their immediate action, some were destroyed immediately; fortunately, most had military-grade shields in place, so they were instead hurled helter-skelter into space, intact but completely out of control. The Star Dice convoy and the remaining ships of the Federation fleets were located nearly one hundred thousand kilometers from the blast, but were still within a dangerous range.

When New Frontier 16 exploded, things were business as usual on the command bridge of the *Predator*. Alec was sitting in his command chair, enwrapped in a green-tinted holographic image that allowed him to conduct a private conversation with Admiral

Cook. It wasn't going particularly well. At the moment Cook was saying sternly, "I'm well aware of your right to go after the pirates that took you and friends. Revenge is right and proper, and if I know your father, he will give you permission to do so in the future."

"I don't think my friends will have that much time," Alec argued.

"The three of you who made it out should be grateful, son. As for the rest, we'll just have to see if we can locate them and buy them back."

Alec's eyes widened. "What do you mean, 'the three of us?'"

Admiral Cook looked puzzled at first, and then realized that Alec didn't know. "You don't know about Lieutenant Bow and Major Nesbit?"

"Say what?"

Cook took a sip from a cup. Then he took another deep gulp and refilled the cup.

"Major Nesbit and Lieutenant Bow returned a week before the 11th received our marching orders. Didn't Admiral Busch tell you that?" Cook didn't wait for Alec to respond; instead he continued, "They said they managed to escape during the chaos when the pirates were engaging two of our frigates, which ambushed them."

Alec stared at his uncle's image in disbelief.

"We lost one of the frigates in that fight, and the other picked up Nesbit and Andrew as the pirate ship...the *Bitch*, that's the name, right?"

"It is, but..."

Admiral Cook continued, "Before the *Bitch* turned to flee."

There was an eerie silence; Alec could hear his pulse pounding in his ears. His eyes narrowed and he hissed, "Arrest them. Arrest them now."

Cook looked shocked—but not, perhaps, as shocked as he might have. "Come again?"

"Admiral, I don't know about Nesbit, but it would have been impossible for Andrew Bow to have 'escaped in the confusion.' He would have had to been removed. Almost the entire time I was a prisoner, he was sitting next to me. They only reason *I* escaped was because I was released by Alexa in the first place. And I remember the attack you're talking about, though we never knew who attacked us. During the attack, and for a long time after, we remained together in a so-called VIP block. It's impossible to escape from one of those, because they include measures that effectively disable the prisoners. We were all on the same damned slave block, Admiral. Have you ever been in one? You're crunched down with your feet and hands in front of you, locked into a bloody stock. You can't move. After a while you can't feel anything but pain, the blood pools in your ass and feet, and you shit yourself...

Alec stopped talking and squeezed his eyes shut, trying to erase the horrible memories.

Over the next hour, Alec repeated his entire story, and Admiral Cook observed the young man with calm, cool eyes. When he was done, Cook said, "That puts things into a much different light, doesn't it? Apparently, you escaped—much to their surprise. Nesbit and Bow were released. It also explains how the pirates got our shield codes; someone aboard our fleet clearly gave them to them. I knew that, and now I know who it was."

"Dangerous accusation. Nesbit is powerful," Alec pointed out.

Cook glared and spit out his next words: "I'm going to kill that traitor."

"You and me both."

"We have to be careful, son. If Nesbit and Bow find out you're alive, they're likely to try to kill you, or worse. We have to come up with a plan before we contact your father."

Alec nodded thoughtfully, then took a deep breath and told his uncle about the map and the treasure, letting it all out. He no longer cared; although he was doing his best to hide it, he was blinded by hate and wanted nothing but revenge. When he had finished, his uncle observed him in quiet amazement.

"About that map. How did you find it?"

"It was inside the cockpit of the escape shuttle in a small wooden case. The thing works something like the computer programs for our emergency probes. You program the computer with the coordinates and your ship takes you there. I haven't figured it all out yet, but I believe that once you go to one of the map's five hundred points, you receive the coordinates to another point. That way you have to travel all over the place, for a long time, to collect all the treasure. Some of the points and coordinates are missing; I think the pirates have already recovered that part of the treasure."

Admiral Cook nodded and said, "We can go over the map and its function later. Is it in a safe place?"

"Yes, very safe."

"Good. Keep it to yourself, Alec…wait, it isn't on your ship, is it?"

Alec snorted. "No, I launched it in a probe to specific coordinates before Captain Behl and I arrived at New Frontier 16. The only place the coordinates are recorded is here." Alec pointed at his temple.

"Don't tell your father about the map, Alec, do you understand? His loyalty to the Federation supersedes his loyalties to his family. You know this, right?"

"What else is new?"

"Good. Let's keep it between us for now, along with the enormous treasure you have in that shuttle. No one's going to question that, unless you start talking about finding fifty or so tritonium bars. Just tell the authorities you found five or ten. The ones you've deposited with the Merchants and Traders no one will know anything about, unless you die and someone inherits them. They're probably your best retirement fund right now. The Federation will tax over half of the treasure you account for anyway, so be careful you don't hand them a fortune."

"And just where is your loyalty, uncle?" Alec asked coolly.

Just as coolly, he replied, "My loyalty lies with myself."

"Now you sound like Frances."

"That's because we belong to the same Order, and we share similar beliefs about freedom and independence, something most Nastasturans have more or less forgotten about. Oh, they claim our people have it, but the Grisamm don't accept that. We can discuss that later. You might want to leave some of the treasure from the shuttle in one of Tota's banks on his station, incidentally, and let me hide some of it for you."

Alec nodded, knowing he could trust his uncle.

"Now, about your Alexa and the other crew members with questionable backgrounds. I'm sure you realize your secret is safe with me. Since she and her closest friends were forced into piracy at a young age, they've known no other life and can't be held responsible for everything that's happened here. If we can tame them, we can always adopt them into our or some of our friends families' houses. But you need to get rid of the older and more infamous pirates, like Myra. Just drop them off with Tota or something; for Gull's sake, don't bring them back to Nastasturus, whatever you do."

"Aye aye, sir."

Cook rolled his eyes and modified his tone somewhat. "Now, park your ship in Captain Copola's dry dock, and say your goodbyes to whomever. We have a long journey back, and our relief columns will be here in a few hours. Expect our departure within a day. I can't stress this enough: make sure you let most of your crew go before we leave, or we'll have to drop them on one of the next spaceports we run into. You decide what you want to do about that. And about Alexa..."

"There's no negotiation on that subject, sir."

His uncle looked at him with a jaundiced eye. "Well, I guess that can wait for now—"

The holoimage vanished as the *Predator*'s sensors reacted to the sudden bloom of radiation from the gaseous remains of New Frontier 16. The electromagnetic shields hardened, and metallic covers fell over any open viewports. It took precious seconds for anyone to realize what had happened, whereupon Alec snapped, "Any crew members outside?"

"Nossir, everyone's inside," Captain Zlo said calmly.

"We're scanning, trying to see what's going on," Behl said, even as the forward viewer flickered to life. It hadn't failed, as it turned out; it had just gone black to save the vision of the bridge crew from the intense flash of New Frontier 16's death. Now, they could see the bright, burgeoning death-blossom of the massive station, and officers cried out and began praying all over the bridge. Behl snarled, "Bastards!"

Seconds later the shockwave hit, and a cosmic giant picked up the *Predator* and smashed it into the *Crusher 5*. Fortunately, the shields on the two ships clashed, and they bounced apart. There was some damage to ships and crew, but no one was killed on either vessel. Zlo and Behl soon had the *Predator* back under their control, and they watched, helplessly, as several ships crashed into the Star Dice deflector grid, causing tremendous damage, and others in their convoy twisted uncontrolled through space, tumbling in all three dimensions. The *Predator* was doing fine until a cargo vessel slammed into her amidships, whereupon chaos took hold and all communications were lost. Zlo and Behl worked frantically to gain control—again—and as the lights failed, Alec heard Behl bellow, "Zlo, we need more power to the engines!"

Then something else hit the *Predator*, and the frigate was tossed like a rag into the Big Dark.

FIVE

HIS Imperial Majesty Salla XII, absolute ruler of Marengo and the Greater Sun Empire, gazed at the shiny silver object in his hand. A small wooden box lay open by his feet.

The throne and the staircase leading up to it were made of pure gold imbedded with platinum plates. Yellow, red-white, and black gold sheathed the walls and surrounding pillars. The entire grand hall in which the great throne was ensconced was itself a masterpiece, constructed almost entirely of precious metals and gems. In those few places where more yielding material was required, purple koa wood—the most expensive wood in the galaxies, fabled to originate on the forgotten homeworld of all the Oman races—was used. Even the floor was covered with baroque tiles cunningly carved from giant bioengineered white and black pearls, and the décor in general was evidence of extreme luxury and power.

Despite the cost of the throne room, which would have bankrupted whole nations, none of those things was as valuable as the small thing that the Emperor held in his hands.

Twenty steps down from his throne knelt his beloved subject the Lady Fuzza, her grizzled head bowed. She had heard rumors about the enormous golden palace, but she had never imagined what the reality was like. The truth was that ostentation on this scale, while impressive, somewhat sickened her. She realized that it had originated during the height of Marengan power, more than five hundred years ago, when the Sun Emperor controlled hundreds of worlds. But she found it somewhat hard to take nonetheless, as an example of reckless overindulgence—she, who was accustomed to wealth, especially now that she had hitched her star to Alec von Hornet's.

The enormous palace was not actually made of gold—gold was far too heavy and soft to use as a construction material on that scale—but it was certainly *covered* with it, nearly every centimeter. She and most people in the universe knew the magnificent building very well, as it had been featured in innumerable films, tri-dee sequences, magazines, and books. But to actually be inside the semi-mythical place was something Lady Fuzza had never imagined, and to her surprise, while impressive, it was less than enjoyable.

Hundreds of young slaves, mostly Oman or Oman-derived, hung around looking pretty. Actually, the term "slave" was a misnomer, a relic of the Imperial past. Each was actually a free person employed for a year at a time, and each earned more in that year than most people would in a lifetime. The Emperor and Empress loved their presence, and their joint appetite for sexual games and orgies was notorious. Given that and the pay, the palace drew comely young people from all over civilized space. Lady Fuzza even recognized several celebrities, from as many different worlds.

At the moment, in fact, Lady Fuzza could hear the sound of lovemaking emanating from some corner of the giant room. The civilian staff and politicians paid no heed; nor did the hundreds of advisors and officers on the Emperor's staff. All were all focused on the emperor and his wife, Empress MoSalla.

Without saying a word, the Emperor stood and gestured to his wife; she joined him as they retired to a room behind their throne. Purple curtains heavily embroidered with gold slid aside unbidden as they approached the chamber, sliding shut behind them. An advisor gestured for Lady Fuzza to remain; and two so-called slaves of Lady Fuzza's own species, one male and one female, approached, whisked her to her feet graciously, and escorted her to another chamber hidden beyond a stand of large pillars. She dared not protest, and her trembling made the two slaves giggle as they exchanged looks. Lady Fuzza was all too familiar with the rumors of people who had vanished inside these golden walls, never to be seen or heard from again.

"**ZANCHES.** Bring my son Zanches," the Emperor ordered.

His wife whispered something to him, and the staff of thirty in the antechamber, arrayed in seats around a large triangular table, waited with great anticipation. After a brief silence, the center of the floor opened, and a young man in his early thirties rose up on a small dais. He wore a forest-green military parade uniform encrusted with gold braid and medals. He saluted the couple before him, ignoring the Emperor's council, and stood there with grace, a confident expression on his handsome face. He smiled to his mother, the Empress, who returned a more serious expression.

Emperor Salla handed the silvery object to a waiting servant, who nested it on a red silk pillow with gold plumes and took it reverently to Zanches. He received it quietly, and looked it over with amazement for a long moment before handing it back to the servant. From there, the servant carried it around the room for each of the councilors to peruse. Some picked it up, gasping when they observed the engraved sigils of Marengo and the ancient Sun Empire, as well as the date imprinted on the silvery bar. None of them gave away any of their inner thoughts, however, as they examined that previous metal. Tritonium silver: not only the rarest of rare metals, but also one of the most useful. Strong, light, and conductive on several quantum levels, it could be used for everything from subspace electronics to constructing indestructible spacecraft and impenetrable fortresses. It was as close to the mythical adamantium as science had ever been able to come, and just as precious.

"This is the property of Marengo," Emperor Salla intoned, "the stolen treasure of our golden age, when the Sun Empire was at its peak. It is quite literally worth more than worlds. Its loss led to our downfall." He looked around at his councilors. "We must take action to reacquire this Imperial treasure *immediately*, before those two beasts—or anyone else, for that matter—discover that the Black Moon convoy has been found. More than Marengan pride is at stake here, people. Should this hoard fall in the wrong hands, then the universe will be faced with an unheard-of catastrophe, financially and socially. We might even descend into another universal-scale war. I don't have to remind you that we're still rediscovering worlds trying to crawl back up from the last one, and that was thousands of years ago.

"Needless to say, we *must* prevent this from happening—and we must do so without drawing any attention to our actions. Councilors, you will give my wife and me your input and opinion about this highly delicate matter. In the meantime, we shall send our youngest son to find the young man who has returned our property to us."

The Emperor turned to his son and said formally, "Count Zanches of the house of Salla, you are hereby commanded to take your flagship and one fleet group and locate Master Alec von Hornet. Request the presence of this young man, and invite him under escort to us. Never forget that he is the scion of an Elite House and the son of the prime military commander of the Nastasturus Federation, and treat him always with the respect he deserves. However, use any means at your disposal to persuade him to join us here. *Any* means. Am I clear?"

Zanches extended his right hand into the air and saluted his parents, as his heels met and a metallic click echoed in the room. He remained saluting, at attention, as the platform was lowered. He never said a word.

THE surviving ships of the Florencian 9th Galactic Fleet cruised slowly through the massive debris field, all that remained of the hopes and dreams of millions of sentient beings. The enormous station known as New Frontier 16 had been thoroughly destroyed in a few horrible moments two weeks before, and though it seemed hopeless and everyone involved was exhausted, the 9th was doing its best to continue a standard search-and-rescue mission.

Four massive chunks of the space station remained somewhat intact in the middle of the debris field, spinning and tumbling in their own new erratic orbits, but it seemed unlikely that anyone could have survived the horrendous shocks that had ripped them asunder. Even if they had, the radiation released by the matter/antimatter explosions and several breached fusactors would have killed them in seconds. The surviving portions of the station were still glowing, and some appeared to be melting and sparkling as trapped volatiles cooked off. Countless millions of debris fragments, many organic, were accreting around the remaining large fragments, attracted by their considerable gravity; if given time, they might coalesce into grisly new planetoids that would continue on through space, to reach their intended destination in a few tens of thousands of years; if, in fact, the brown dwarf in the far distance didn't add them to its own family of asteroids and minor planets.

Heartsick, hoping for miracles, Admiral Jonas Nass himself oversaw the SAR mission, remaining ensconced on the bridge of his temporary flagship for most of each ship day. The only time he left was for his infrequent rests. During the last two weeks, fewer than five hundred people had been found alive, all from outlying stations and escaping ships that had been brushed by the explosion as they accelerated away from New Frontier. Star Dice Station, itself badly damaged but gamely limping along, was being used as a temporary hospital and R&R area for the SAR group while their ships underwent maintenance and repair.

In the weeks since the catastrophic destruction of the New Frontier 16, ships had arrived from all over civilized space to assist the Florencian 9th and the Nastasturan 11th in the rescue operation—or to salvage the wreckage, which was the legal and acceptable term for what, to Nass's mind, amounted to looting. Hell, what was left of the station was still warm, for Gull's sake! Then there were the ghouls: the curious who arrived in everything from tiny ships to large cruise liners to revel in others' misfortune. Reporters and news organization ships were clogging local space without any consideration of the rescue efforts. In their quest for ratings, all they did was make things harder for the volunteers. Military ships from both federations and several other polities had been forced many times to fire warning shots across the bows of the ships causing problems. Fortunately, they had all taken the hint and backed off—so far.

The infamous Brakks, the ultimate leaders of both the Federated Merchants and the Commercial Traders, had sent ambassadorial parties from each organization to investigate and determine who was to blame for interrupting trade. Each ambassadorial staff resided onboard an Ambassador-class heavy cruiser, escorted by a fleet of military ships. Neither had made any contact with either of the federation fleets…or, for that matter, with anyone in the vicinity of what was left of New Frontier 16.

Insurance adjustors, on the other hand, made their presence known to everyone as soon as they arrived in their small, fast ships. With Tota's permission, they set up a large office on Star Dice, and were sending out small shuttles with experts to investigate and gather as much information as possible before they started making settlements.

Tota's station was among the first in line for said settlements. One of the larger Florencian cruisers remained embedded in the lower hemisphere of the Star Dice, twisted unnaturally into the superstructure and piercing the station's shell in a number of locations. Tota's engineers and architects had talked to Admiral Nass at length, and after a long, testy discussion, Tota had purchased the cruiser at cost. There was no other choice: it was so tightly interpenetrated with the station that it would mean the end of Star Dice if Florencia tried to remove it. Once the classified material had been removed, it would become another part of the station—an odd and ugly excrescence, but better that than no station at all. Tota had succeeded in talking Admiral Nass into leaving all the weapons platforms in place; since none of the weapons were classified, Nass had consented. He made sure that the fleet removed the various missiles, rockets, and ammunition, however.

Tota assured him that the weapon systems would be removed from the ship and strategically placed around the station for future defense needs, making Tota's Star Dice one of the more powerful civilian space stations in known space. The cruiser itself would be rebuilt from the inside, adding three thousand new rooms and suites, while a small portion of the ship would be turned into a museum commemorating the Battle of New Frontier. Tota's business sense was incredible, and he wasted no time profiting from the disaster. Nass found that a bit distasteful, but he couldn't help but like the weird little man.

And the fact was, Tota had done everything he could for the few survivors they had found so far. Most had lost everything; he provided anything from money to jobs to sympathy to medical help, though he could not give them back what they really needed: their loved ones. Word of his generosity grew, and it wasn't long before the obligatory vultures appeared and claimed they had been on the New Frontier 16. Within days the number rose to over ten thousand, all of whom vociferously clamored for their fair share. After Tota kicked several of the worse out of airlocks without suits—with the full support of his friends in the federation fleets, of course—the others quietly dispersed, escorted out of the system by Tota's friends the Predators.

Not all of the vultures were from out-system. Even as the curious arrived in droves to see the "battlefield," several surviving stations that had escaped unscathed scuttled back toward the debris field, their owners more interested in making money than helping out with the long, exhaustive rescue effort. To the disgust of the SAR personnel and Tota, guided tours had begun literally days after the blast—and somehow, the tour guides knew more details about the battle than anyone who had actually taken part in it. That most of those details were fictional didn't faze them at all. As the second week waned, the tour shuttle traffic was the biggest problem for those trying to get things done in the region.

BARELY noticed, a mid-sized civilian cruiser, bearing the markings of Florencia in addition to the military ensign indicating its status as the flagship of the entire 9th Galactic Fleet, docked with Star Dice. When he got word of its arrival, Admiral Nass was in the process of inspecting the remnants of the cruiser intertwined with the southern hemisphere of the Star Dice, ensuring that all classified material had indeed been removed from the former Florencian vessel. He and Tota were deep in a discussion about how much longer they should conduct the SAR work when the Admiral's aide scurried into the room and whispered something urgently to Nass, who suddenly looked like he had swallowed Captain Copola's hat. "Where is he now?" the Admiral growled.

"He's about to dock, sir, and demands that you report to him at once."

Nass nodded sharply and said to his companion, "Tota, I must leave for now to greet my...commanding officer."

Tota looked at him speculatively, no doubt having noticed that Nass never concealed what he actually thought of his commanding officer, who had managed to avoid the entire conflict two weeks before. The little man asked curiously, "Admiral Nass, may I join you? I would certainly like to think High Admiral Rimez for his efforts on our behalf."

Nass cast Tota a frustrated glance, but when he saw the fat little fellow grin invitingly, he gestured his consent.

"**DID** I win, did I win?" a querulous voice demanded. "Where is my claim of status for my victory, and where are all the spoils and prisoners? Where? Answer me, you idiot. Vera! Vera, make him answer or else!"

Admiral Nass stood at attention as the High Admiral Rimez hovered around, drowning him in questions and not bothering to wait for answers. So it went. The young moron was squeezing his hands greedily, all but drooling; and it wouldn't have been all that unusual if he had. Due to centuries of inbreeding among the ruling families, Rimez wasn't the sharpest arrow in the quiver, and with his vapid expression, he looked even stupider than he was. Luckily, he had Vera. The older woman stood in the background, looking friendly and sympathetic. Nass looked at her pleadingly, but before he and a chance to answer his commanding officer, he was barraged with more questions and demands.

"This station I will take into my possession as my part of my victory," Rimez said, gesturing grandly, "and everyone inside shall be sold as slaves for compensation of our losses and expenses and..."

Rimez stopped, blinking in surprise as he became aware of the sound of people arming their weapons all around him.

Feeling a grim sense of satisfaction, Nass said quietly, "My lord, we are in neutral territory, and in any case this is an independent space station owned by this gentleman here." He gestured at Tota, who looked at the young Admiral like an excited little puppy and waved cheerfully. He seemed unaware that his security offers were fingering their weapons, not looking nearly as happy as their employer.

Tota's grin widened, and he jumped up and landed in the very surprised Admiral Rimez's arms, in his excitement pissing all over himself and somehow making sure the liquid stained the young snob's perfectly pressed uniform, which was covered with baubles of all kinds that the idiot probably thought were medals.

"Welcome, welcome to the Star Dice Hotel and Casino, young Admiral Rimez! Forgive my exuberance, please, I am just so happy to see you!" He wiggled in the surprised young man's arms. "My new friend, we open up our arms to such an honorable person as yourself! Now, do you like boys or girls, or both? Oh, I shall enjoy introducing you to Lady Pulp, and introducing you to the pleasures of our gaming rooms! May you spend many credits in our casinos while you're still alive!"

The little fellow's last words finally penetrated the fluff. Perhaps it had something do to with the fact that, despite Tota's clownish attitude, the eyes that stared into his reminded the young Admiral of his father's. "Admiral Nass, explain," Rimez said slowly, his deeply buried common sense finally asserting itself.

"Mr. Tota here is a hero of the Federation. Without his help, our entire fleet would have met its demise during the recent battle—"

Alas, common sense's victory over the young Admiral was all too brief. Interrupting sharply, Rimez rolled his eyes and snapped, "Spare me, Nass. Just hand over the claim of status for my victory." Tota jumped down, still grinning broadly, as Rimez extended his hand towards Admiral Nass.

"There is no claim of status, Sir. It went to a civilian."

"Nonsense," Rimez snorted. "It's mine and mine alone, as you well know. The presence of Nastasturus and other combatants will be denied by our people, and you are responsible for our economic losses. The victory is mine alone and that is final. You will gather up enough credentials and signatures to transfer the claim of status to me, and collect whatever funds are necessary from these civilians to pay for us rescuing them. In the event they can't pay, then you will send them to our labor camps so they can start working off their debt. I have already had two hundred of them arrested aboard your flagship for owing us rescue fees, incidentally. By the way, why are you giving them free medical assistance? None of them are citizens to Florencia. And you should have come and picked me up rather than making me come here. I'm beginning to think you wanted credit for this simple victory all for yourself. Now, we are moving the fleet soon, and..."

Nass listened to his Admiral prattle on with weary eyes, displaying no emotion.

Poor man must be used to the idiot, Tota thought, tapping a command into his wrist computer, ordering his staff to stand to. Several Predator captains withdrew unobtrusively, hurrying back to their waiting ships. They needed to be ready in case the inbred young admiral decided to give some stupid order for his people to board the station.

Rimez turned his ire on the owner of Star Dice. "And *you*, Master Tota," he sniffed. "I shall report your hostile attitude to our Federation, and make sure we collect a proper rescue fee."

Tota's grin broadened. "If you try that, my little man, I will have to kill you. With my bare hands."

There was an uncomfortable silence.

Tota seemed to swell as he advanced on the young Admiral, still grinning. "You really *are* as stupid as you look, Quillion Rimez. I, however, am not. I happen to have contacts in the highest levels of your government, including your father by the way, and I shall inform your government of the truth, backed up with unassailable documentation. Powerful family or not, I doubt you will last very long after that, you jelly-spined coward. I will also make sure that every news reporter from here to Florencia, including your own propaganda spewers, finds out the truth, you sniveling little shit—that the claim of status for this victory falls to a Nastasturan civilian named Alec Horn, *and not you*."

Cheerfully, Tota waited for Rimez respond. The young admiral had turned pale—quite a feat, considering his mahogany skin—and he started to tremble as sweat poured down his face. Rimez got his confidence back a moment later, as glanced out a large viewport across the room and noted the Florencian fleet massed outside. "Whatever," he said shakily. "We will leave. But know this, Master Tota: neutral space or not, we will meet again. And I shall issue an arrest warrant against this Horn for stealing my claim of status. After I capture him, I shall send his skin to you as a reminder that you will be next." Rimez spin on his heel and walked away, gesturing for his staff to follow.

When he was gone, Nass bend and said urgently to the little man, "Get your station away from here. I'll do what I can, but his father is the real leader of Handover, and he has great influence with the government."

Tota glanced at him, his smile gone. "I know who his father is," he said flatly. "I wasn't bluffing when I said he was one of my contacts in the Florencian government."

Nass looked started, and his amazement grew when Tota offered, "Stay here with us, Nass. Defect. You're too decent to be a part of the current Florencian regime."

"I can't, Tota." Nass sighed heavily. "I have family back home, and they would suffer. Don't worry about me...I have a good record and history behind me. Besides, his father and I are friends."

Tota harrumphed. "*That's* why he has you as the idiot's babysitter?" Tota gestured after Rimez. "Ties of blood are more important than ties of friendship. Someday the elder Rimez will betray you if the son pushes him hard enough."

"He's just a lot of talk," Nass said uncomfortably. "Soon he'll miss his social functions and his strange friends, and then he'll leave me alone. His father knows everything about him."

"And yet he lets him get away with this kind of stupidity. Why?"

"No idea."

Total harrumphed again. "Perhaps he *wants* him to die. You realize that young Admiral Rimez would be dead right now if I wanted him to be—and that there would be no serious repercussions as a result?" He glanced up at Nass, who nodded unhappily. "In any case, my Florencian friend, I'm about to leave this region of space permanently. There is much...business to be done elsewhere."

Nass found his feet, realizing that the business Tota was touting wasn't just of the mercantile kind. "Very good, Tota. I'll make sure my fleet group won't bother you, despite the High Admiral's threats. Please, just get away from here, in case the young fool does manage to convince someone with real power that we should start taking prisoners and loot to compensate for our losses. You're better off in Nastasturus space anyhow."

Tota looked up at him, surprised. "With *their* taxes? Hell no, I'll be in a different part of neutral space or in some Merchants or Traders sector. I have plenty of powerful and influential friends there, too." He stuck out his hand. "Until next time, Admiral."

As Tota shook the Admiral's hand, he said darkly, "You know, if I were you I'd kill the little bastard, or maybe just lose him in space."

"Perhaps I will someday," Nass replied. "Will you warn Alec that he might get a warrant, in the event I can't talk some senses into our leaders?"

"Consider it already done...assuming he can ever be found."

Nass headed down the boarding tube to his shuttle, and Tota watched quietly as the shuttle undocked and headed back to the Florencian flagship. He glared as the coward Rimez's pinnace entered a docking bay on the same ship, then glanced at a Predator who worked at a terminal a short distance away. "Captain, can you send a ship or shuttle to warn Admiral Cook about the impending threat from Florencia? I doubt Rimez will do anything while they're still around, but I'd hate to overestimate his intelligence. Cook should probably know about the pending warrant on Alec too, so he can warn him when he's found."

The woman nodded her head and proclaimed, "I will personally make sure they find out, sir, and I will also warn all our brothers and sisters about Rimez."

Tota nodded and smiled. That was taken care of, at least.

ONE entire InterGalactic Fleet, the Nastasturan 64th, secured the outside perimeter of the New Frontier debris field against any new looters and scavengers. Admiral Busch had ordered the more damaged ships from the 11th to the nearest military dock in Nastasturan space for maintenance and repair. What remained of Admiral Cook's fleet was spread out through local space, aiding the Florencians in finding survivors. Meanwhile, the Nastasturan 31st Galactic was pursuing one of the two pirate convoys heading away from New Frontier—the one probing deep into Nastasturus space. Unfortunately, they hadn't yet been able to close with the raiders.

Meanwhile, over a hundred Predator vessels followed the second column deeper into neutral space, waiting with great anticipation and patience for the column to scatter, whereupon the Predators would start picking them off one by one. The intent was to do so as gently as possible, so that any prisoners might be recovered; but that was considered less important than destroying the pirates.

Hundreds of bounty hunters trailed both the 31st and the Predators, hoping to profit once the pirates were scattered or stomped by their pursuers, whatever the case might be.

The 31st was crippled by the fact that the pirate column was larger than the military fleet, and composed mostly of larger ships. As long as the column remained together, the 31st could do little more than follow, wait for reinforcement, and make occasional probing attacks on individual ships. The idea was to find a way to put the ships out of commission rather than simply destroy them, given the hundreds of thousands of captives and all the loot the pirate ships were laden with. But as with the Predators, they would destroy any pirates they were forced to without compunction.

Meanwhile, the premier Nastasturan Omega-class cruiser, the inimitable *Crusher 5*, was carrying out its own unique SAR mission: it was looking for a small Marengan frigate called *Predator*, after the commissioned pirate hunters who had come to New Frontier's aid during the recent battle. If not the *Predator* itself, they were hoping to find its lifepods and, in particular, one young man who called himself Alec Horn. But it had been nearly two weeks, and there was little hope left. On the command bridge, a dead silence reigned, punctuated by the quiet sounds of the bridge crew carrying out their duties. No longer was Captain Copola invigorated by the thought of war; he sat in his command chair at the forward viewscreen, where the ship's sensors displayed various perceptions of space in every direction. From time to time he glanced at his commanding officer, who paced dourly back and forth in front of the viewscreen.

Captain Copola suspected that the conversation between Admiral Cook and his older brother had been less than pleasant, given that Cook had finally found the Marshal's son and then promptly lost him again. To top it off, intelligence had reported that the highest bounties in history had been placed on an Oman fitting Alec's description. Not one bounty but two, originating from separate sources, both untraceable. Naturally, this drew in ships from all over the inhabited universe; there were already thousands clogging the region, and more were arriving constantly. In response, Cook had broadcast a warning on all communications channels, hoping Alec would somehow hear it, warning him to take evasive action and return home as soon as possible. The message had of course been encrypted with most recent family codes—although eventually, even the most advanced encrypted code could be broken. Admiral Cook no longer cared. He just wanted his nephew found and returned home safely.

A dozen Predators followed the *Crusher 5*, all reliable personal friends of Tota. That didn't necessarily mean much, given the threads of betrayal running through this entire affair, but at least they were helping. Each had volunteered for the search, expressing great respect for the young man who had fought the pirates to a standstill before that final, crippling blow had trumped everything. Each of the Predator ships maintained constant contact, primed to come to the *Crusher*'s aid in the event of a fight.

So far, however, there hadn't been the slightest trace of the *Predator*. They'd never had a great deal of hope to begin with, but as the search entered its third week, their expectations went downhill rapidly. It was clear that Admiral Cook was prepared to end the search for the *Predator*. Copola himself had all but given up, though he still prayed that Alec and his crew would eventually show up. He just hoped that somehow, they were hiding in a forgotten corner of a nearby system, licking their wounds and gathering their strength.

MEANWHILE, the entire Federation waited with eager anticipation for their heroes to return and celebrate their victory. Admiral Cook and the 11th fleet had crushed the pirate threat in one of the greatest space battles in modern history, and surely deserved and expected to be feted in style! Both Copola and Cook were sickened when they read or watched the news reports regarding the "victory," especially when the mighty Nastasturan propaganda machine was at its best. There was no end to the reporters' lies: by now, the pirate fleet had grown to more than 20,000 against 11th Fleet's two hundred. Little mention was made of the Florencian presence, the Predators' assistance, or Alec's contributions.

Naturally, both federations took the opportunity to point to the destruction of New Frontier 16 station as a typical example of the other's failures. One especially dangerous rumor floating around in Nastasturus was that all the activities at New Frontier 16 had been a front for a major invasion from Florencia that had backfired, thanks to Admiral Cook and the 11th Fleet. Representatives from Florencia, of course, denied any such allegations, asserting that NF16's destruction was the result of the catastrophic failure of a scandalous group of running-dog non-believers who satisfied their greed by stealing from the hardworking common people. This was their punishment; after all, there could be no pirate activities among any true believers.

Nastasturus quickly responded that over half of best known pirate clans were either from or supported by Florencia. Florencia's response to that allegation was, "Prove it!"

And so the recriminations and lies washed back and forth. It was obvious that, eventually, the truth behind the pirate attack would be buried, never made clear to the people who needed to understand what had, in fact, happened, so that they could learn from it.

Several witnesses claimed that a civilian had organized the two Federation Fleets, strategically attacking the pirates and destroying them. Those poor deluded individuals were met with laughter and derision; no reporter of any influence followed up the story, hence it brought no ratings. However, when an obese but charming little elephantoid stepped forward and claimed in an interview that the shitstorm had been triggered by a secret prince rescuing his beloved princess, the idea took off like a rocket. No one could resist the thread of romance that twined through a story of such magnificent violence.

It was said that the prince, variously from Marengo or some other neutral world, had searched the universe for his princess, who had been kidnapped by an evil pirate. The pirate had taken her to the slave auction on the New Frontier 16, at the Commercial Traders market, and the Prince had followed and broken her free; and that was how the entire incident had started. Rumor had it that the Prince was enormous wealthy, though no one knew where his wealth had come from. Perhaps, it was whispered, he too was a pirate, or even one of the old dark warlords returning from the dead as they were wont to do...

What happened to the Prince and his Princess no one knew, but some speculated that they had died in each other's arms when New Frontier was obliterated, blown to atoms like so many others. Some preferred to believe that they had left the system, and perhaps even the galaxy, to settle on a quiet world and live happily ever after.

In any case, very little was known about either of them. There was a bad photo of a young man in some type of blue uniform, standing beside a beautiful young woman sheathed in pearls, an exquisite tattoo inked onto one side of her head. In the background were two officers: one from Nastasturus, the other Florencian. The reporter who released it claimed that the picture had been taken at a major art function moments before the battle began.

It was a simple matter to enhance the photo, and within a few days after the battle there was a pixel-perfect image of Nina and Alec floating around the ether. Soon, a similar story emerged—but this time, it involved two non-Omans of different species. It didn't take long before reporters from different news organization slandered their competitors, accusing them of racism and sensationalism, and before long the image of Nina and Alec was forgotten by most...though not by the few who knew the truth.

One news organization claimed that an exotic who had been working for the pirates organized everything, and this was one reason that their number one hero, Admiral Hadrian Cook af Hornet, hadn't yet returned to bask in his well-deserved fame and status; he was, instead, hunting the perfidious pirate. Several different images of individuals from different non-Omanoid species were shown, but none of them looked anything like Alec. "My brother's work," Cook mused, as he studied yet another crazed report from a reporter who claimed to have a "reliable source" who had survived the massacre.

The media touched very little on the contributions of the Predators, and said nothing at all about Mr. Tota's assistance. Anyone with any sense, though, knew that if it hadn't been for Tota and his space station, both the Nastasturan and Florencian fleets might have been lost. But not even Marshal van Hornet wanted to provide too many outsiders with too much accurate information.

As soon as their insurance adjustors had arrived in the system, the various Brakks from the Federate Merchants and the Commercial Traders opened negotiations to restart local Galactic trade;

Intergalactic trade was business as usual, of course. After making sure that all was as it should be, they blanketed the ether with their own news bulletins, in which they proffered two main witnesses as to what had occurred: the Federated Merchants' Key Administrator Tobbis and NF16's former head of security, a Marengan woman named Cabelle. Once their statements had become public, and the recorded evidence had been uploaded into the public infosphere, all former reports as to how NF16 had met its fate were thrown out the window. Their detailed descriptions of what had actually happened on the station were straightforward and believable.

Of course, accurate as they were, their stories formed only one part of the big picture. Given their desperate situation at the time, they knew nothing about any major assistance from either Federation. Once they had managed to escape, they detected no signs of the presence of either fleet. Key Administrator Tobbis made it clear that he was convinced that both of the Federations were in cahoots with the pirates in yet another attempt to control the trade in neutral space. The loss of his wife and daughters was a tragedy, and he offered a huge bounty to anyone who could provide him with information on their whereabouts—assuming they had survived.

One of the Brakks from the Commercial Traders came forth with his suspicions that a wealthy Oman might be the brains behind everything, but there was no evidence to support the claim. When asked if the Oman had any funds invested with either the Merchants or the Traders, the Brakk saw an excellent opportunity to advertise, and responded that if the person in question *did* have accounts with either the Traders or the Merchants, then they were nonetheless protected no matter what. She also assured her viewers that access to all accounts of those who had lived on or visited New Frontier 16 would be reopened as soon as possible in banking facilities around the universe, and that the trade would return to its normal levels within days.

She added that in the event anyone might have evidence or information about any of the pirates' involvement, then they would be handsomely awarded, should they step forth to assist in the hunt for the villains. She also offered privateer commissions for anyone with suitable spacecraft to hunt them down.

To assure the public that everything was in fact copacetic between the two powerful organizations, several Brakks lined up for pictures, shaking hands while smiling for the cameras. The Brakks avoided apologizing for the trade probe that had been launched, stopping all trade, by the former Key Administrator Zala, who unfortunately must have died in the explosion of the New Frontier 16. It appeared that she had gone mad, they insisted, and they promised to look over the trade probe safety features, in order to avoid the possibility of a similar event occurring in the future. The cautious suggestion that they might just order the warning probes to be altered or simply removed was met by applause. Representatives from both Nastasturus and Florencia were also present at the meeting, and took the opportunity to eagerly inform their citizens that all trade was secured and insured.

———————○○○———————

THE purple Unsanti slammed its thick erection into Andrew's rectum, causing him to jerk involuntarily. Nesbit slapped the young man and shouted angrily, "Don't bite, Gulldammit!" Nesbit squeezed Andrews's nose, cutting off his oxygen, and shoved his erect penis back into the boy's mouth. Andrew took it from both of them with a ravenous appetite, kneeling on a large thick pillow, his hands and head secured in a waist-high pillory.

The torture club took up an entire basement of a vast building that lay beneath Nesbit's staid and rather ugly old palace. It had several rooms and levels, all decorated like dank pre-Space dungeons. It was heaven for anyone with a sadistic or masochistic bent.

Currently, there were some two hundred guests enjoying themselves with all types of erotic games, along with a few others who were simply practicing their art of torturing their victims for real, often followed by applause from the onlookers. The poor servants—or, in most cases, kidnap victims from other worlds—weren't shy about screaming out their pain and horror; but to no avail, because whoever screamed loudest was rewarded only with more applause from the crowd.

A dozen people had gathered around their host, Colonel Nesbit, cheerfully watching as he and the Unsanti ravished young Andrew. A number of them became so aroused by the tableau that they moved away to different parts of the basement to join in the fun.

There were beds and comforters placed strategically on small platforms alongside the walls, and scattered in islands around the rooms. Some rooms had only a large mattress on the floor, for those who preferred to be more intimate, away from all eavesdropping. Servants dressed in slave attire threaded their way among the guests, serving up refreshments—and occasionally becoming the refreshments. For those who preferred to fetch their own drinks, there were several bars with android bartenders. A few levels up, the establishment was more reminiscent of a nightclub.

Some guests were dressed up in old-fashion dom costumes, heavy on the leather, with others pretending to be slaves—though of course, when "tortured," they were dealt much less painful punishment than the real slaves, and never faced any danger. This could not be said for most of those undergoing torture, however, for they were either kidnapped enemies or nobodies picked up off the street. Their screams quite ruined the music for most of the patrons, but what could you do? Those in charge were in charge, and besides, it wasn't as if they cared what happened to the poor wretches. Take, for example, the woman strung up in her wrists in the farthest room, someone's ex-wife apparently. Guest took turns whipping her naked body, cutting deep lashes into her bare skin. Bets were being made on how many strokes she could take before she died.

Then there was the young man, barely out of his teens, who was attached to a rack further along; several women and their daughters were working the wheel, stretching him out to the limit. They cheered the victim on whenever he screamed, making funny faces and mimicking the sounds of his tearing joints. After he passed out, one woman handed her teenage daughter a dull knife and instructed her on how to castrate the shackled victim, cautioning her to wait until the medical android had woken the victim up. The mother slapped her daughter when she cut off the man's penis by mistake, and threatened to put her on the rack next. But the young girl didn't hear her; she was trembling with pleasure as she sawed off the scrotum, blood squirting all over her face. The women clapped happily, their cheers drowning the shrieks of the victim, who was now very much awake. The daughter looked at her mother proudly, waiting for her approval as she handed the older woman the bloody pouch.

In another room was a floor that seemed to be paved with heads; they were living, those of guests buried to their chins in a dark gel while other guests glided around naked on the oily surface, playing with them. In the dining area lay several beautiful young people covered with food as the guests helped themselves.

But those things were tame. Less so were the several triangular table devices with pyramid tops. Each bore a woman sitting on the peak, hands tied behind her back, legs spread out on each side with weights attached to the ankles and a noose around her neck. It was clear that they were each in horrific pain, but were forced to remain immobile lest they die. Some of them were gagged, while others weren't. All that the women had in common was the horror and utter agony of their expressions.

Most horrendous of all were the young children who ran around playing and chasing each other, thinking it was all a game. There weren't many, but they were there, and even some of the guests found that repugnant. Those guests were well aware of the fate that would eventually face most of these children: many of the young people being raped, tortured, and gruesomely murdered in the back rooms were the offspring of other guests, in some cases the siblings of the playing children. Fortunately, as the time grew late and their parents become more violent and sexually aggressive, the children were escorted away by their respective nannies or servants.

Some guests preferred a subtler version of torture, of course, tying each other up or linking themselves together with strange devices while petting, teasing, tickling and caressing, holding off their orgasms as long as they could endure. It didn't matter. There were more brutal activities occurring elsewhere. What many of Nesbit's guests didn't realize was that after this night, many would never see their homes again. They would serve as the victims during the next function.

A popular event at functions like these, generally as the evening's finale, was always the main execution. Tonight a young vixen would stand, hands bound, on an ice block in her bare feet, a noose around her neck. Either she would eventually slip on the ice and hang herself, or she would suffocate slowly as the ice melted. That was a particularly inventive death, though on a few rare occasion a few victims had even been tickled to death, mingling pain with pleasure. This was extremely popular among Nesbit guests, and was why he seldom let the guests witness the treat, making them crave more. Besides, it was very difficult to find a beautiful person who wouldn't start crying just because they were about to die.

Nesbit's masterpiece finale would be to have someone on their back with their neck on a guillotine's chopping block, with the rope to the blade clamped in the victim's mouth as they were tickled. Eventually the victim would let go of the rope and watch the blade slide down before separating head from body. This was Nesbit's favorite way to murder; he had practiced it alone with servants and kidnap victims, and whenever the victim had been ticklish, it had worked very well. But only if the victim was very ticklish.

Once he had even had sex with his secret lover on the guillotine. He had mounted her from behind as she crouched on hands and knees, her hands tied behind her back, her head secured in the stock device, both of them aroused to the point of near-insanity by the threat of danger. But unfortunately, when she had orgasmed, both he and she had forgotten about the rope in her mouth...and she never knew what happened. Too bad it had been the President's wife! She did have a smile on her face, though, as she had looked up at him from the basket.

The thought made him orgasm powerfully now into Andrew's mouth. He pushed the idiot away roughly, then took a cloak from a servant and tossed it over his shoulders. He walked away and intermingled with his guests, leaving the leashed Andrew to be buggered to a fare-thee-well by the Unsanti. After enjoying a drink at a nearby bar, he noticed that they were finished for the moment, and returned

HUNTED | 171

to lead Andrew along on the leash, while the Unsanti followed like the good servant he was.

He smiled as he thought about the dead Jasmin Petrius, whom he had been obliged to incinerate after their little accident. The President still had no idea what had happened to his wayward wife. But she paled to insignificance, of course, beside Andrew Bow, the love of his life. He loved Andrew, and he loved especially being in control of him. That hadn't been possible with Jasmin. But Andrew...oh my, yes. Nesbit's secret functions were becoming notorious, and not especially secret among the extremely wealthy of Nastasturus. These days, people were lining up to be part of his secret club.

Nesbit picked a young woman out of the crowd, pushed her over a table, and began fucking her from behind. He gestured to the Unsanti, who forced Andrew to watch. Oh, how it turned him on to watch as Andrew fought the exotic angrily with teary eyes, demanding to participate. Nesbit only laughed, inviting several other young women and men nearby to take part, including one of the sons of the woman he was plugging. This turned Andrew mad with jealousy, and he redoubled his efforts to escape the Unsanti.

The woman Nesbit was pleasuring happened to be one of the local Senators, but no matter; he had numerous senators, congressbeings, and even a few Governors among his guests. Many of his guests—indeed, most of the ones who would return home safely this night—were very influential in the political arena. The knowledge that he was in control of all these power-hungry flunkies made him orgasm and scream out in ecstasy as he showered the five open mouths by his knees with his thin semen.

Well, there was more where that came from. He removed a tiny canister from an inner pocket of his cloak and inhaled more of the highly illegal love gas within. It was a drug he had been introduced to by his colleague Zuzack, one he would sell to all his drug lord contacts, earning him a quick and massive profit. Within five years, if all went well, he would have enough to purchase his own fleet and buy an admiralty.

As he stood there swaying from the powerful hit, he caught a glimpse from the corner of his eye of someone newly arrived, who stood looking flabbergasted at the entrance, flanked next to two guards. Shit. His arrival would probably spoil the rest of his night.

Nesbit looked at the head sticking up from the center of a nearby round table; it was that of the Chief of the Federal Police, Lady Cleta Miseba. Her joyous expression was no doubt due to the fact that she was being pleasured from underneath by someone or something...even she didn't know what, and that made it exciting for her. She would have been horrified, in fact, to discover what it actually was. Several guests sat around the table enjoying the show, sexually pleasing themselves with robotic toys.

As long as she stays there, I have nothing to worry about, Nesbit thought. He strode up to the waiting messenger, and motioned for him to follow to an adjacent room through a secret passage.

Nesbit tossed his cloak on a sofa and put on a robe. He peered at the monitors arrayed along his desk, displaying every part of his club under the basement of his palace. Said palace was built on top of a high mountain, of course, so that he could look down on people. His main estate was located on the opposite side of Tallas.

As he poured himself a drink, he said drily, "It must be urgent for Zuzack to send you here...not to mention dangerous, should some of my guests learn of your profession." He gestured towards Lady Miseba, who was featured on one of the monitors. "If that were to happen, I doubt if even I could save you. Pirates aren't very popular right now."

"It is an emergency," Grotech answered stiffly.

"Isn't it always? Next time, use the standard procedure for contacting me, no matter what the emergency is. By the way, what the hell were you idiots thinking when you attacked New Frontier?"

Grotech shook his shoulders and ignored the question. "Your price got away." He shrugged, then took a sudden breath as he noticed that the trophy heads on the walls were those of Omans and other sentients—females on one side, males facing them.

Nesbit dropped the drink on his priceless carpet. "He did *what*?"

"That cadet you wanted us to take care of managed to escape. He's the reason we attacked the space station."

Nesbit was all but speechless for a long moment. When he found his voice, he growled, "A simple cadet caused millions of pirates to attack New Frontier?" Ignoring the dropped drink, he set up another, then looked sidelong at Grotech and said icily, "I am unimpressed by your Clan's utter incompetence." He slapped the marble bar and shouted, "*We had an agreement!* Alec von Hornet was supposed to be sold to Zoris af Sun! By rights, he should be one of her art pieces by now!"

Nesbit stopped himself before he went too far. "You blithering idiots, how in the *hell* could anyone get away from you?"

Grotech stared at him. "How he got away isn't important. How we find him is."

Nesbit sat down in an overstuffed chair, looking suspicious. "You mean to tell me you attacked and destroyed an entire New Frontier space station because he escaped from your clutches?" Nesbit raised his eyebrows and waited patiently for an answer.

Looking a bit uneasy, Grotech seemed to fumble for his words. "There is a bit more to it than that," he finally admitted. "However, Horsa will pay you two hundred million in addition to the original bounty of a billion if you can help us find him."

Nesbit eyebrows moved even higher up his forehead. "Two hundred?"

Grotech nodded. "And a million canisters of the drug, easily worth five times that on the street."

"What do you need from me?" Nesbit said solicitously.

"Anything you can give us that helps us locate him. We understand that all Elite citizens have transmitters implanted in their bodies, and we need his frequency."

"Impossible," sniffed Nesbit. "I don't have it. What you're talking about are nanobodies in the bloodstream, and they're nearly impossible to find without official equipment that I have no access to. In any case, the individual codes work only when the person is being actively scanned, and for that to take place you still have to find him. No, forget about that. I will figure something out—but in the meantime, you need to leave. Tell Zuzack I'll do my best for you to find

Alec, and remember, don't come here ever again. In future we will meet as we always have, is that clear?"

Grotech muttered agreement, then left through another secret passage, escorted by two waiting androids.

Nesbit looked over the monitors, bored. Unless he had some beautiful celebrity he could tease and torture, it wasn't any fun or interesting any more. His secret functions had begun to bore him. It was a problem many of the Elite citizens in the Nastasturus Federation, with their enormous wealth, were faced with: sheer boredom, the sort of ennui that rarely affected ordinary productive people who had to stay busy just to get by. Many turned to strange sex games, or exploited themes much more violent, similar to those from the pre-Space era, when gladiators fought each other or large animals in life-and-death contests in large arenas. Several secret societies did just this with prisoners, often abducted from worlds that either didn't have space travel, or had lost all knowledge of it. This had been interesting for a while, but like most youths, Nesbit was at the peak of his career and wanted something new, something exciting.

The military academy had been acceptable, and Nesbit had been one of the better students in his class; but there had been no major conflicts in or near Nastasturan space at the time, so when he returned home, it didn't take long before he sank back into boredom. He soon got tired of his parents nagging at him to build up his own fortune, since his oldest brother and sister would get to split their entire inheritance. The way things were set up, he and the other siblings would only receive about four estates each and a few hundred servants for life, plus a minor trust paying for everything for five generations. Nothing significant.

He had taken care of all that long since, of course. But even so, Nesbit had never cared much for the properties. He was a realist; he believed that what happened now was all that truly mattered. He was convinced that religion was the root of all the evil in the universe, and that totalitarian beliefs were wrong; though why, he didn't really know or care about. He wanted a career in politics, so that he had the opportunity to make history. This was one of his main ambitions in life—at least, until he got bored with it.

Nesbit never thought of himself as a sociopath; he thought of himself, rather, as a very misunderstood person. Really, he was no different from most of his colleagues and relatives, and in fact he was very attentive to his one and only true love, Andrew, and his more intimate friends. He didn't care one whit for anyone else, and why should he? Other people were just things, really. When thought of how he'd eliminated his parents and arranged to sell his two brothers and three sisters into slavery, he felt quite a bit of satisfaction and gratification.

He'd gone to visit his enslaved siblings from time to time. He didn't want them dead; then he would be all by himself, and Nesbit hated being alone, unless he was studying or doing research. (His biggest weakness, he admitted to himself, was his passion for science, especially biology and human physiology; he especially enjoyed researching how much pain and suffering various species could endure before they simply died.) He had become great friends with all his siblings' owners. The long, hard space journeys he had to endure every few years was evidence that he still loved them, wasn't it? He felt he had done them all a favor, really. Now they would never have to be concerned about the future or the everyday problems of Elite life ever again.

Nesbit missed taking care of his family. He especially missed his youngest sister; she was quite attractive, and he had contemplated having intercourse with her more than once. As kids they had played often with a slave block toy their father had purchased for them, but when he had cut off his favorite sister's right foot, his parents had punished him hard, sending him away three years to a hospital for very wealthy and very sick children. He never forgave them for that treachery. Well, he had done for them, hadn't he? And there was one bright spot: that was where he had met little Andrew—eight years younger than himself, but the perfect lover.

Nesbit looked up at the jar with his sister's foot inside. He had cut it off, again, before he sold her. The new owner had stimmed it back, to his dismay, but what could he do? Life wasn't fair at all.

Nesbit had never cried from pain or sadness, not even whenever he got seriously hurt; nor had he ever shed a single tear from happiness. Instead of crying, he adopted a strange expression, and eventually he started to laugh. It was something that his family, friends, and doctors had never understood: he adored the sound of laughter, and never understood why people cried. It was the only thing that still amazed him, the way people wailed and moisture poured from their eyes, and it was one of the reasons he continued his research. Why would they cry out in pain when they could laugh? Didn't pain make them feel good? He just couldn't comprehend it, and had promised himself to find the secret behind this biological phenomenon. Tickling itself was a torture, this he knew for a fact; but somehow it didn't affect most people the same way as applying intense heat or cold, or removing body parts, or simply playing with the exposed nerve of a broken tooth. Tickling was perceived as more innocent somehow, a kind of welcomed agony.

It simply didn't make any sense.

Observing his research objects screaming and crying from pain had actually become a bit dull for Nesbit. He liked to think himself as a more delicate and cultivated sort of scientist, with more class and sophisticated skills—not just a simple brute, like most of his guests.

Nesbit's general belief in life was simple; one plus one equals two, and that's it. Tears belonged to pain, not laughter. Next time he met his friend Zoris af Sun, he and she would engage in a serious discussion about the subject, and perhaps she could shed some light on this most bothersome question. Nesbit didn't know if he was ticklish, but he was very tempted to find out. However, his pride, and his refusal to allow anyone to have that sort of control over him, had kept him from doing so.

His mind turned back to his cousin, Alec. Nesbit's hatred for Alec derived from nothing more than the fact that it gave him something to do and feel. Something wasn't right with his cousin, but he could never put his finger on it. No doubt it was due, somehow, to the inbreeding that was startling to riddle the Elite culture of Nastasturus with the depraved, the mindless, the psychotic, and the sociopathic. He had the intelligence and perspicacity to understand that he was numbered among the latter. It did not bother him; nor did it bother him to arrange for and put into motion the ruin of one of the most powerful families in the Nastasturus Federation.

It wasn't so much a conspiracy to get his hands on the inheritance, and the status that came with it, as it was a chance to destroy that overbearing old fool, Marshal Guss von Hornet. He didn't dislike Alec personally; in fact, he was rather attracted to him. But Alec made an excellent pawn in Nesbit's game of life—or should he say, a better research subject? Nesbit rubbed his chin. Well, to be honest, he hated Alec just a *little*. But he would never murder his cousin; it would spoil the fun and take away the challenge…plus, after all, one did love one's family, as long as they didn't betray one. As the elder Nesbits had tought their son.

Selling Alec to Lady Zoris, knowing he would always be alive, if somewhat immobile…well, that really did turn Nesbit on. He could come and visit Alec whenever he wanted, just the way he did all his brothers and sisters. This thought alone convinced Nesbit that he was at least as loving and caring as the average sociopath. It saddened him that Alec knew nothing about his secret club; since they were children, he had wanted to have his way with his fresh young cousin.

He thought back to the day when Marshal Guss and Lady Beala had learned that Alec was missing, taken by the pirates, that day when he and Andrew had been presented to the Marshal as survivors of the raid. Frankly, hearing Alec's mother cry had aroused him much more than he had expected; and when he and Andrew had left the Marshal's presence, he had forced Andrew to perform orally on him right there in the Marshal's backyard, behind a screen of trees, a scant few meters from that room full of babbling people. It had been terribly exciting, standing under the window and listening to all of them.

At least he had forgotten about having to marry that cow Michelle Oranii, which was something he had to do, because his father's old nemesis was her father. That she was promised to Alec upset Nesbit, but it didn't make him *jealous*. He wanted her as his toy, and was going to do his guillotine finale on her eventually. But he wouldn't be screwing her; no, he would be tickling her. He knew that she was extremely ticklish on the soles of her feet. Now, the idea of watching the blade come down on her—*that* aroused him tremendously, and he couldn't wait for it to become reality.

At the moment, she was inside his dungeon, on the sacrificial ritual table (which he normally used for staged sacrifices on kidnap victims or incompetent servants) where anyone who wanted could have his or her way with her. Like so many Elites, she was wired to enjoy playing the submissive. Nesbit found it very strange that so many of his powerful friends liked to be victims; again, there had to be some misfire in the genome, due to overzealous inbreeding, that resulted in this particular flavor of depravity. He himself could never allow that; the thought of someone dominating him was sickening. Andrew liked it, because he himself had trained his true love from the beginning, when he was just a little boy at the hospital. Andrew accepted it as fact, and part of his and Nesbit's life together.

Contacting the pirates was the ultimate thing Nesbit had ever done, and he had had more sex that month than he could remember, just out of excitement, and it had been the best he had ever had. For almost eight years he had planned this; he had planned everything down to the last jot and tittle, and not once had he been truly bored. But he was getting bored now, as the endgame played out; and of course, he was more than a little frustrated that much of his hard work and carefully planning had been spoiled by his own cousin. Something had to happen, or he might just get upset.

A thought struck him, as he picked up a riding crop and turned it over in his hands. *I shall help the pirates with my cousin...but I'd better relocate for a while.* Slapping himself on the thigh with the crop, he muttered, "Especially after Lady Miseba's warning that I'm being investigated by Guss and the Federal Military Police." Perhaps he should seek a commission to one of the rebel worlds. "Not a bad idea," he said calmly; and slapped himself harder, this eliciting a breathless laugh. "I shall contact my favorite Aunt Lucy and see if she can get me a staff position in an InterGalactic Fleet." He looked over his monitors with dead eyes, that strange expression on his face, and hit himself again.

SIX

THE *Predator* tumbled uncontrolled through space, spinning in all three dimensions, like the wreck it very nearly was. On the command bridge, a lone figure desperately fought the controls. Almost everything electronic was dead, so Captain Zlo was forced to use manual controls when he could and jury-rig what he couldn't. He had no one to turn to for help; everyone on the command bridge was unconscious or dead. He had no idea how long time they had been drifting—it seemed like hours—and from time to time he shouted desperately for someone, anyone, to wake up. His head was pounding, and his anterior crest was pasted to the side of his head by dried blood. It had been that way when he had awoken, an eternity ago now, evidence that he had been out for hours—possibly as long as a day.

He'd just managed to tweak the main port thruster into action, taming the ship's erratic roll, when a large hand grabbed his shoulder. He looked back into the eyes of Frances, one of his employer's Grisamm guards. "Are you all right?" the big man asked.

Zlo sighed with relief. "For now. But I need you to take Behl's place and help me get control of the ship." Frances just nodded and started unbuckling the straps holding the unconscious Captain Behl in his seat.

The old man stiffened and his eyes flew open. "Get your hands away from me!" he hollered, "I ain't dead! Now what's happening? What happened?"

"I think New Frontier 16 blew up," Captain Zlo answered dully. "Frances, see if you can get the sensors back online. Better yet, see if you can wake up some of these others."

Frances nodded acquiescence, then clambered over to a bulkhead and removed a first aid kit from a small compartment. While Frances passed among the crew, providing succor and waking those who were wakeable one by one, Behl worked to bring the electronics back online while Zlo wrestled with the manual controls. Behl cursed up a storm as usual, elucidating a long list of details on a recipe of what he would do to the bastard or bastards who had caused this disaster.

"Hiding his fear," Captain Zlo muttered, only realizing that Behl had heard him when he stopped cursing and shot Zlo an irritated glance.

Frances paused to close a dead crewman's eyes and looked up into Alexa's. The young woman lay propped against the her paramour's command chair, battered but alive, holding Alec's head in her lap as she stoked his hair and spoke softly to him. Trying to hide his irritation, Francis said softly, "How long have you been conscious?" He didn't wait for an answer. "Alexa, I need your help. We need to get everyone up and back to work so we can get the ship back under control."

Her eyes bored into his and she said, in a tone that brooked no disagreement, "Bring that medkit over here now. He's in bad shape."

Frances didn't argue, hurrying to her side. He winced when he realized that either Alec hadn't strapped himself in properly, or one of the straps had broken at some point. Then he realized that wasn't the case at all. As Alexa pawed through the medkit and began treating Alec's skull with a bone-knitter, Francis snapped up the broken strap and examined it closely. *Someone cut this,* he mused, *enough for it to fail during that rough patch.* He decided to keep that thought to himself and went to help Alexa with Alec, who was indeed badly injured.

By then there was some movement on the command bridge, as the conscious began to help those Frances had not yet gotten to. Shortly thereafter the lights flashed, there was a deep thrum that was felt throughout the ship, and both Captains cheered. The *Predator* was back under control, the electronics were up, and life support was fully online. Voices babbled from hidden speakers and loose earbugs all over the bridge as damage reports came in. When everything was sorted out, it became clear that nearly two days had passed since the blast wave from the NF16 had struck them like a sledgehammer; only the emergency life support system, which had flashed-cocooned them within an impenetrable nano-wall and injected a cloud of medical nanos into the atmosphere to stabilize all those not killed outright, had saved them all from certain death. That it had taken so long for any of them to come out of their stupor was an indicator of how bad it had been; the radiation alone should have cooked them.

In those two days, the *Predator* had drifted very far from its course, and it was a miracle that none of the pirates had boarded them. In the far distance they could detect the blazing yellow pyre where New Frontier 16 had been, shrunken by distance to little more than a pinprick. Meanwhile, sensors detected thousands of ships and larger pieces of debris all around them.

"Probably what saved us from being boarded," Alec mumbled much later, as Captain Zlo recited a rather depressing damage report.

"Indeed," the crested Marengan noted drily. "Now, to summarize, Master Horn, we'll need to dock and refit most of the ship. There's not a system aboard that hasn't been severely damaged, and some are pounded to junk, frankly. The problem is, there's no decent spacedock anywhere nearby, now that NF16's gone. That's a serious problem, given the state of our engines. We might be able to go as high as half speed, but not for very long. That's going to be a problem if we need to outrun anyone. Plus, the deflector shields are down to a minimum, and we..."

Alec listened distantly as he watched a pair of ships gliding by in his one intact holodisplay. They were news media, according to the transponder codes, and they ignored the crippled *Predator* as they hurried towards the former battleground. He scowled as he noted their bristling communications arrays, and that sparked an idea. He tapped on his chair arm, a signal to Zlo that he wanted to interrupt, and said excitedly, "Captain Zlo, I know how we can get away from here undetected, and join up with the others without drawing any undue attention—in case the pirates are still out there looking for us."

Captain Zlo lifted elegant eyebrows. "Sir?"

"We need to rejoin the others as soon as possible...but from what you've have told me, it'll take almost half a day to return to the Star Dice, and we can't afford to run into any trouble. Right?"

Zlo nodded.

"So I was wondering, we can disguise the ship as a news ship?"

Just then Frances joined them, interrupting Zlo's inevitable question. "Forget about returning, Master Alec. There is something I want you to see." He gestured for them to follow him into the conference room just off the bridge; it was filled with rubble from the command bridge, but it had already been determined that the room's features had more or less survived intact, including the lock and the privacy field Frances snapped on as soon as Alec and the Captain were inside. He brought up monitors on one of the bulkheads, displaying several Galactic news channels, all of which were reporting on the battle and the subsequent destruction of the New Frontier 16.

"Look here." Frances tapped a few buttons on a computer console, and a coded text appeared superimposed over one of the broadcasts. "That station is secretly receiving and retransmitting special news bulletins, most of them illegally. They're probably an independent organization, and this is a side business. It took me some time to hack in, but I finally did it."

Alec glanced anxiously at the monk. "And what does the message say?"

"There are numerous messages, actually—mostly inside information about secret trades and rates of various types. It's not always clear what's being traded, though trading of some kind is always involved. But these two messages are different." He tapped a specific feed on the screen. "They're from two different sources, but they involve us. Well, you and Alexa mostly."

Frances hit a key, and the messages were immediately decoded and translated, highlighted on the screen in large sigils. What Alec read gave him chills. "There are bounties on us? But why, and from whom?"

"I think Alexa's bounty is from the woman who bought her—legally, according to the Commercial Traders," Francis responded gravely. "The bounty on you seems to be from one of the pirates. I'm not sure, but I *will* investigate, and I'll see what we can come up with. And let's keep this quiet. As you can see, your bounty is high enough to tempt even the most steadfast allies."

Alec nodded, his mouth dry. "And Alexa? You're sure this one is for her?"

"Yes, I've found similar official messages from several traders who are offering awards for her return to her rightful owner. That would be Zoris af Sun, the bitch we liberated her from. The one who wanted to use her in what she calls 'an art function.'" Frances scowled. "The Traders have already confirmed the transaction, making Alexa officially stolen property."

Alec looked at Zlo, who told him forcefully, "I think we should go through with your plan, Alec. We need to alter the *Predator*'s appearance."

"I agree," Frances said stolidly.

Nodding thoughtfully, Alec took a deep breath. "Very well. Frances, inform the crew that no outside communications are allowed for the duration, and immediately shut down our receivers, except for those on the bridge and whatever we need for navigation. Disable our transponder; better yet, alter it if you can. Except here on the bridge."

"Good idea," Zlo said. "No need for anyone to catch one of these broadcasts and get any ideas."

"Yes. And as soon as we can, we're going to get to a safe harbor and split the crew up. As much as I'd like to chase down the pirates who captured my friends, I need to go home."

A day later, Behl located a suitable asteroid in the brown dwarf's poor excuse for a planetary system, and as easily as if he were handling a personal hovercar, brought the *Predator* down into a wide gash on the surface, stashing the ship beneath a rocky shelf on the rill's floor. It was the closest they were going to get to a spacedock. Behl never cursed once during the operation, which suggested to those who knew him that he it was a much trickier maneuver than it looked. Once the ship was in place, the crew swarmed out of the ship in pressure suits, along with dozens of repair andies, and proceeded to make over the *Predator*—converting it from a sleek (if battered) vessel of war to a clunky news ship. As a precaution, Behl himself led a flight of all the remaining fighters out of the frigate and over the surface of the asteroid, where they set down on the surface surrounding the crater the *Predator* was ensconced within. They would be the first warning system in the event some ship ventured too close. Fortunately, the fighters were equipped with chameleon paint, which soon took on the color and craggy texture of the asteroid itself.

Not every crewmember was outside; some, including Alexa and her posse, were sitting inside Cargo Bay Five, cursing Alec Horn roundly as they altered the outfits they'd just purchased with his money. The bastard had insisted that they sacrifice their new clothing for the cause, adding them to the decoy that they were constructing. That every extra stitch of clothing, blankets, sackcloth, and any other fabric anyone could find on the ship was also being used didn't enter into the equation.

Nadia assisted the girls in their sewing, making sure the job got done. She made no attempts to warn them about their language, even when Alexa accused Alec of being a chauvinist pig because he'd forced *them* to do the sewing. Nadia knew they were just blowing off steam, and she did giggle a bit at Alexa's antics, because they brought a little comfort to everyone in the bay.

Nina cried out as she stitched one of her favorite outfits to a ratty old blanket, and Tara joined her. "This is the worse torture any dude can perform on a lady," Zicci muttered, receiving supportive comments from everyone. Her skin shifted from blue to red as her anger swelled.

"I know how we can get back at him, though," Kirra purred mischievously.

"Tell us!" demanded Alexa. She tried to slide a skirt under her jacket, but stopped when her eyes meet Nadia's.

"We get one of his debit cards and go shopping."

Cheers and laughter greeted the proposal.

"I see that all of you have gotten over the initial shock, and that's good," Alec said quietly, as he stepped into the cargo bay. He was dressed in a pressure suit sans helmet, which he carried under one arm.

"Pig!" Nina shouted.

"Tyrant!" Zicci added.

"Inconsiderate dickhead!" Tara let out.

"May you lose your balls next time you zip your pants, you bastard," Kirra commented calmly.

Muhama and her sister Miska icily ignored Alec.

"Asshole!" Alexa screamed at top of her lungs, and the rest of the girl's cheered her on—except, of course, the twins.

Alec's eyebrows rose as he looked at Nadia. "And here I thought you were educating these young ladies in proper manners. You're lucky this is a *civilian* ship."

"Some things take longer to teach than others, sir."

"I'll bet."

Alec walked away from the little group of mutineers, wondering why he felt like he'd just lost yet another battle.

"You ain't gettin' any tonight, prick," Alexa said loudly as he left.

Alec stopped and turned around slowly. His eyes bright, he said quietly, "There's always the block, darling."

Alexa stopped sewing and glared at him. "Bastard! Nadia said that when a person makes threats to a free being, then it only demonstrates that individual's poor character. Most likely he or she suffers from rape-syndrome, and is a totalitarian thinker."

"Sure it does, but you're not free. You're my little mutineer, aren't you." Alec shook his head as he turned away and put on his helmet, ignoring Alexa's cheeky comments. He turned around at the entrance and threw her a kiss with his gloved hand. Alexa stood with her legs wide apart, her fists clenched and at her sides. Her mouth was moving, but he couldn't hear a world. Ah, bliss.

He strode away down the corridor, cheerful. The only reason he had put the younger crewmembers on the sewing detail was that, frankly, they didn't have enough experience spacewalking in a dangerous environment like the asteroid. All of the girls had proven to be excellent pilots, but they displayed dismaying gaps in their spacer knowledge. On most practice spacewalks thus far, they'd managed to get themselves and others into trouble. The more experienced crewmembers had been relieved when Alec ordered them to remain inside the ship and sew the decoy. So had Alec.

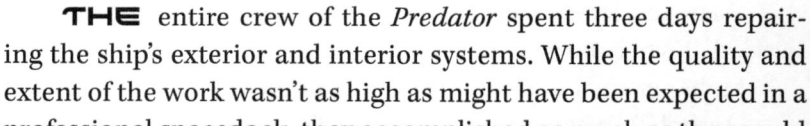

THE entire crew of the *Predator* spent three days repairing the ship's exterior and interior systems. While the quality and extent of the work wasn't as high as might have been expected in a professional spacedock, they accomplished as much as they could with what they had. Alec and his staff were more than pleased with their efforts.

He was especially pleased when the engineering officer informed him that most of the engines were restored to normal power. "However," Chief warned, shaking a finger at him, "Don't push this ship and its engines too far. Save all the capacity you can, in case we get in a scrape with someone. Your pirate friends, for example."

It took nearly the entire crew two more days to build and attach the large metallic framework that served as the basis of their disguise, and then Behl was forced to move the *Predator* into open space so that fifty crewmembers could attach the huge circular decoy radars, assisted by dozens of repair andies. The crew also made several other changes and alterations on the ship's hull, most of them with no specific function; the main purpose was to make the ship appear different from its original configuration to any scanners or probes with a hostile intent.

Meanwhile, seven young crewmembers held a sad ceremony for themselves, but for anyone to see, as with teary eyes they made their last farewells to something in space. Each made a solemn vow, each swearing some sort of blood-oath against a cruel monster.

Once the *Predator* had been reconfigured, the crew was informed that their main mission was now to find some safe harbor where they could disembark. All would have their contracts paid out in full, complete with a bonus. They could go wherever they wanted to after that. Alec did point out that if anyone wanted to continue on with him to Tallas, they would receive a large bonus and be invited to stay as a guest at his home...assuming they made it back safely, of course.

Most of the crew were exhilarated at this news, but Alec failed to see the concerned expressions on Myra and some of the older former pirates. Frances and Bax did not fail to notice their concern, however, and took careful note of it.

The *Predator* left the New Frontier region behind soon after, making its cautious way to a nearby jumpgate and diving through in the typical brilliant white flash. Despite their disguise, Alec's first action was to send out an advance probe to collect data on the new region before advancing to the next jumpgate system. This time, they launched a false probe with the *Predator*'s original electronic configuration and transponder codes, and sent it on its way through a series of jumpgates on a course that would last weeks.

As for the Predator *itself*, for the next week it followed a convoluted path toward Tallas, jumping through half a dozen gates. It launched over twenty false probes, some through other gates and some into interstellar space. From time to time, they took refuge on an isolated space-rock, or hid behind an asteroid or in the radiation shadow of a gas giant. Eventually, they located a small moon with a cavern of the proper size, where they parked and spent another week while they finished up most of the repairs.

The only damage that remained was to the decoy they had built onto the ship at their previous dock; it was ruined on the cave ceiling at the entrance, for the ship's internal warning systems never warned them that it was in trouble. After all, the change hadn't been programmed into the *Predator*'s mainframe, and it had been a miracle, according to Lieutenant Brown, that the "umbrella-device," as he called it, had made it this far. Everyone else just pretended it had never happened.

When not busy repairing the battle damage, the younger crewmembers were trained in spacewalking by Nadia and Wolf. All seven had decided to mourn their ruined clothes, and so they created yet another pointless ceremony that, if nothing else, took their minds off the boredom of their training: they collected the remains of their ruined garments from the decoy radar and buried them in a shallow grave on the moon's surface. Each gave a short speech, while cursing the monster who had forced them into such straits. Several of the men from the crew elected to sympathize with the young vixens—anything to get into their pants, especially as news of their famous dance on the Star Dice spread. Nadia kept a watchful eye on her students, while keeping another on their fan club.

Their mood changed somewhat when Wolf set up a large, clumsy-looking machine he had built himself, then handed them a plasma rifle each and instructed them on target practice in vacuum. A small target was launched from the contraption into space, and the girls had to hit it as it whizzed away. Sometimes more than one target was launched, usually in different directions, making it all the more difficult. Soon this became a very popular sport among the entire crew. It didn't take long before Pier and Wolf had organized a competition.

Alec and his staff welcomed the respite. They all needed a break from all the work and the relentless drilling the Grisamm monks were putting them through.

The overall attitude among the crew was positive, though Alec's was not. He missed Alexa, who had moved to her friends' quarters without saying a word. One day when he'd returned to their quarters, he had noticed that all her belongings were gone. Alec suspected that this was another one of her little games, or perhaps some female hormonal thing that he didn't understand. At first, he was simply sad and somewhat jealous; but as time went by he became more aggravated and hostile. He kept it all inside, though, letting it grow and feed on itself; combined with the fierce headaches he kept having, this worsened the situation.

Phalaxor scanned him several times and put him into a healer twice, and finally came to the conclusion that it must be psychological. He had offered Alec counseling, but Alec turned him down flat. Whenever he confronted a crewmember or any of the officers, he put on the perfect mask, concealing his aching head and his worries about the woman he loved. Something that Alec had learned at the academy was to never show any emotions to crew or fellow officers. He was forced to put his personal thoughts aside; the ship and the entire crew needed him, and he felt like the weight of the world was on his shoulders.

Worse, he began to feel all alone, in a way he never had before.

Although the entire crew had their meals in the ship's galley, he usually ate his alone in his ready room, or wherever he was at the time. He was always doing something. He and Alexa had hardly talked to each other in weeks, and they hadn't made love since before the destruction of the New Frontier 16. Anytime he tried to meet her alone she was either doing her chores, or attending classes held by Nadia or, sometimes, Frances or Captains Zlo or Behl, or doing her homework, or she was asleep. Once he had made arrangements for a private dinner in his quarters, but she never showed up and she never said anything about it. When he had confronted her about it, she had only snapped at him, saying she sure as hell wasn't *his* bloody property.

Alec had been left standing there confused, not understanding where she'd gotten such a crazy idea. When he made a third attempt to communicate with her later that evening, reminding her that he had promised not to allow her to leave him angry again, she let him know that he could just find another sex toy and had slammed a door in his face.

That night, when he finally was alone, Alec wept—the first time he had genuinely done so in years. He couldn't sleep, food tasted like ashes in his mouth, and his emotions didn't improve. He kept himself busy studying star and jumpgate charts—and in the morning, as he haggardly prepared himself for a new day, he made a pact to himself to move on. He thought he had finally met the love of his life, but evidently he had been wrong...something that, frankly, seem to occur all too often lately. He wasn't going to get back at Alexa, but neither was he going to let her get the better of him. He was going to move forward, focusing only on returning home to his family. Soon all this would just be a bad memory, the only good coming from it a lesson in life. And all that money, of course, but he'd already been wealthy.

Thereafter, Alec kept busy with his work and staff meetings, driving his officers on like mad, making sure everything was double-checked and checked again. For the most part he forgot about his situation with Alexa, but whenever he took more than a brief pause from work an unpleasant sensation invaded his mind, and his chest tightened like someone was squeezing his heart. But thanks to his impartial mask, no one knew about his personal demons; and as far as he could help it, no one *would* know. He would face those demons alone.

In one of his more introspective moments, Alec told himself that it was like the first time he'd burnt himself on a hot plate. It hurt like hell then, and as much the second time; but the pain didn't last as long the second time, and the experience taught him not to touch a hot plate again.

He welcomed the idea of the shooting competition when it came up, as he too needed a break. He had no plans to participate, of course; he just saw the competition as an excellent opportunity for some of the crew to leave the ship. The walls of the *Predator* seemed to be closing in. He wasn't sure that he agreed with how the winners of the competition would be awarded, though. Frances had come up with the idea that the losing team would act as servants for the winning team during a victory dinner later that night. Alec had a bad feeling about that. "Explain," he told the Grisamm.

"The crew has requested a little party later on, and..."

"The entire crew should get drunk? No way."

"Not the entire crew, sir. We would divide them into three groups, and..." Frances noticed that Alec was leaning against the wall, holding his head. "Are you well, sir?"

Alec straightened abruptly. "Yes, Frances, I'm fine. Now, listen up—do whatever you and the other officers think is appropriate. Just leave enough people on stand-by duty in case something comes up."

"Yes sir, of course, I'll see to it. But truly, are you..."

Alec made an impatient gesture and hurried away. Frances watched as he left, puzzled.

The pounding headache was increasing as Alec hurried to his ready room. After easing himself into his chair, he gulped down some medication in pill form, hoping it would help. As he awaited its effects, he considered the shooting competition. The rules were simple: each team had to hit as many moving targets as possible using as few shoots as possible along a course of ten contraptions that Wolf and Pier had build the night before. Each team would be divided into smaller groups of ten, and the one-third of the crew remaining on the *Predator* would get their turns as soon as the first team finished. The winner would decide the destiny of the losing teams; either they would be on stand-by half the night, or they would be serving the winners. After dinner, they would have a party, and the two losing teams would take turns standing by.

Several crew members had already helped the ship's cook, a Cupan named Latoff, with the decor in the galley. The bulkhead separating the officers from the crew had been removed and, to the crew's joy, the officers' bar made available to everyone. The entire area looked more like a nightclub than part of a battleship. The music had fallen to Myra, who had volunteered as the "disc jockey"—given that her sheer size would likely cause damage to the other crew if she decided to dance. In any case, the position assured that win or lose, she wouldn't be a servant. Another reason that had made Myra volunteer was her passion for music—any music. She felt it was a gift from Gull, and her knowledge of the music from many different worlds was impressive.

During the subsequent staff meeting with his officers, Alec spent most of the time listening to their reports, quietly pleased with everyone's performance. A low electronic buzz from the door interrupted a report from Nadia, who looked at Alec questioningly. He nodded his head to Bax, who stood by the entrance. He opened the hatch—and in walked Alexa.

Alec's heart jumped, and he sat up. He had more or less forgotten about her over the past few days, considering he hadn't seen her at all; but now that he had, his soul felt injured. Alexa walked over to Nadia and handed her a clipcomp. The two whispered, Alexa pointing at the comp from time to time, for several moments before Nadia thanked Alexa and motioned for her to leave. Alexa gave everyone a brief smile—except for Alec—and walked out.

Alec managed to maintain his mask, and motioned for Nadia to continue. She intoned, "And in conclusion, overall the crew are doing very well, and the five patients remaining in the autodocs should, according to Dr. Phalaxor, be back on their feet within days—and I would like to add that the doctor apologizes for not attending this meeting."

"As usual," snorted Captain Zlo, and those around him laughed.

"Has Phalaxor *ever* attended a staff meeting?" Brown asked.

"Who cares?" Behl commented. "He's devoted to his job, and he has a lot on his plate lately."

"We all have a lot on our plates lately, yet here we are," Brown pointed out.

Behl nodded, then glanced at Alec. "And what team will you join for the tournament, General?" He had to repeat his question when Alec didn't respond; he had turned his seat to pretend to look out a viewport as he rubbed his aching head. When the question finally penetrated, he swung around, smiled, and said, "No team, Captain. I'll be watching the ship, making sure we don't have any...rodents."

There was a brief pause as the people in the room digested the odd comment, followed by a few half-hearted laughs. "If you don't compete you don't get to party," Nadia commented drily, focusing on her computer pad.

Alec leaned forward suddenly, his face grim. "Don't you ever tell me what I can or can't do on my own bloody ship! Is that clear, Sergeant?"

The silence this time was one of thunderstuck surprise. Everyone remained silent, focusing on Alec and Nadia. "Yessir, it's crystal clear," Nadia said blandly. "I would..."

"You're all dismissed," Alec said abruptly. Relaxing into his chair, or at least trying to, he stated, "I wish all of you well in the competition, and may the best team deserve whatever it gets."

Alec failed to notice the surprised expressions worn by his fellow officers as he turned his chair fully toward the viewport. They cleared the room slowly, but within a minute they were gone—except for Frances, who cleared his throat quietly.

"What?" Alec asked, with his back turned.

"What is wrong, sir?"

"Nothing, Frances. Return to your duty."

After a brief pause, Frances nodded and left the room. He was very concerned at Alec's sudden, strange moodiness. When he stepped out of the conference room, he found everyone who had just left standing in the corridor, each with a questioning expression.

"I have no idea what just happened," he said, looking around at his fellow officers. "Do any of you?"

"I know he has some kind of constant headache Doc can't cure," Behl muttered.

"Anything else?" demanded Zlo.

No one replied.

"Well, it's probably just the headache, then," Behl reassured them all.

Everyone walked away muttering, except for Frances, who walked up to Nadia and asked, "Is there something I should know?"

"Not that I can think of."

"And how are things between him and Alexa?"

"Good, I suppose."

"Are they?"

"Yes. What's your point with all this?"

Frances lifted a shaggy eyebrow. "Well, Nadia, you *are* her first instructor and teacher, and something of a confidante. Perhaps you have some information you haven't passed on?"

Nadia was quiet for a moment before she said, "The only thing I can think of is that she moved out of his quarters."

"She did *what*?" Frances rasped, more loudly than he'd intended. He lowered his voice and grabbed her shoulder. "You didn't think that was something major? I told you to keep me updated on *anything* that might affect Lord Hornet, or have consequences in his life. We both know what we're really doing here—or should I have to remind you, *instructor*?"

"Sir, it never occurred to me that..." Nadia trailed off, then started from the beginning. "I wanted to get closer to her, to get her to start to trust me so that we might continue studying Lord Hornet, and I told her that it would be better for the crew if she didn't share the same quarters with the ship's commander. I'm..."

"An idiot." He thrust her away. "This is the last time, Nadia, that you will ever mix personal matters with your professional duties. You have parted them, and Gull only knows what that will lead to. You are a disappointment to the cloth, monk."

"But my intentions were only..."

"Your intentions are no longer of any concern here, Sergeant. The only thing that concerns *me* is that he recovers fully without any major incidents. And you will put your hatred for the male gender aside whenever you represent the Grisamm. I realize that you have had some unfortunate experiences in the past, but so have we all. You will not allow that to affect your work."

"What about her?"

"She is *not* why we are here, as well you know. Besides, from what I recall now when I think back, she is the one who has been evasive towards *him*."

"Well, yes, he had said something about her being his property."

"Are you referring to the incident at the docking bay, when you and the young women were sewing?"

"Yes, how did you know that?"

He rolled his eyes. "Surveillance cameras, Nadia. And for your information, he was clearly joking."

"But..."

"Nadia, return to your post and forget about this entire incident—and hope that I do as well. I will wait and see if there is anything we can or should do. Sometimes the Holy Mother and Father Universe sorts these things out." Frances walked away from Nadia, disappointed, mostly at himself for failing to notice that Alec had needed someone to talk to about the situation with Alexa.

———————oOo———————

IT was unusually quiet on the command bridge during the ship's night cycle; only a skeleton crew was present. Alec stood in the CBR wearing the cybersuit, hovering in cyberspace, practicing battle scenarios. A electric buzz echoed inside his helmet, making him lose concentration. "What?" he snapped.

"May I talk to you?" Alexa's voice was neutral.

After a pregnant pause, Alec replied, "I'm busy. Is it urgent?"

"Why aren't you going to compete?"

"I said I'm busy."

"I need to talk to you. Right now," she said, sounding agitated.

"If there's something personal you want to discuss, make an appointment with Bax."

"It's an emergency! You once told the entire crew that anyone could come and see you if they had a personal emergency!"

It took a few minutes before the pressure door to the CBR opened. Alec stood with his helmet under his arm. Alexa noted his pale, thin face and weary look, his eyes underscored by dark shadows, and was taken aback. But she decided to ignore his unhealthy appearance, unwilling to fall into what she considered a trap. "What's going on between us?" she asked coldly, locking his gaze with hers.

He sighed. "Nothing anymore, and that's thanks to you and you alone."

"Now, wait just a minute here," Alexa protested, waggling an index finger at him. "I moved out because I know what our relationship can do to the crew, and…"

"Get to the point."

Alexa, surprised by the harsh interruption, hesitated for a second before she continued. "It takes two to tango, pal. It's not fair for you lay all the blame on me."

"Wrong, Alexa. I've never 'tangoed' with you. You meant more to me than just a dance. If anyone was dancing, it was you. I tried to communicate to you on several occasions after you left, and every time, you ignored me or treated me like dirt."

She tapped her foot on the floor, her expression oddly vulnerable. "Please, try to understand that I'm not used to all this."

"What?"

"Freedom!" she blurted. "I want to try everything Nadia's taught me for a while! I want to live without having to follow anyone's orders!"

Alec gave her a puzzled look. "Whatever you want, just do it. I'm really not up for this discussion at the moment."

"So is it acceptable to you, then?"

"Is what acceptable?"

"Me trying to find myself. I need some time, I think. Nadia told us that for a person to find herself, she has to grow with the environment and develop her own personality and become an independent, free-thinking individual. I want to do this for me so that I can be a better person, using my intellect instead of my muscles. You have to understand."

Alec looked irritated at first, especially after hearing Nadia's name; but then he relaxed a bit. "You don't need my permission to make a personal decision."

"Alec! What I meant was, will you wait for me?"

There was a moment of silence as the two looked at each other. When he had first heard her voice through his helmet, moments before, his heart had vaulted in his chest; but then pride had taken over, souring that good, clean emotion.

Looking worried, Alexa continued, "Um, Nadia asked me what I expected from our relationship, and I said..."

Alec interrupted her, and this time he had difficulty hiding his irritation: "I never expect anything from anyone. That way I'm never disappointed." Alec thought about his father's use of those words, not realizing how powerful they were when impacting on a third target. "Look, we should be in a safe port soon. At that point you're free of any obligations you signed up for when you boarded this ship. What happens after that with you and the rest of the crew is none of my concern. Just do whatever you have to do. But if you expect me to be your punching bag whenever you want to vent some frustration or anger, or want to accuse me of using you as a sex object in front of the entire crew..." His disgust at the thought was clear in his expression, and Alexa tried to take the opportunity to interrupt; but he motioned for her silence and continued, "...well, then you're wrong to think I'll wait for you 'find yourself.'"

He squared his shoulders, then said, "If that's the deal, then good luck with your search, Alexa. I hope you find whatever it is you're looking for—and if you get lost, you can always ask Nadia or one of your other buddies for directions."

Alexa gave him a wondering, confused expression; and after a long moment, she leaned forward to kiss him. Soon she was nibbling his ear, whispering, "I have a surprise for you tonight."

Alec never moved or responded; his pride—twice hurt by the young women before him—didn't allow him to do anything. Alexa stopped and leaned back, looking disappointed. He stood there stiffly, like a statue, something very cold in his deep blue eyes, staring straight back at hers. Chills went down Alexa's spine—not the type associated with love, but the type associated with horror. She was hesitant and fumbled clumsily when she backed away from him, avoiding his eyes. When she reached the hatch to the bridge, she turned her back towards him and, with a trembling voice, said quietly, "If you change your mind about tonight..."

But by then, Alec had already turned around and put on his helmet. He never saw Alexa's tears.

Alexa stomped out of the bridge, cursing herself for all the mean and stupid things she had done out of anger—or love, as Nadia had called it when she had confided in her about her problem with Alec. It had started as a joke, but had turned into something very ugly. Alexa had wanted to stop and embrace Alec when he had confronted her with those sad, dark blue eyes, but something inside her kept pushing him away, and she couldn't understand why. She supposed just wanted to be by herself for a while before she jumped into her final relationship.

All the stories she and her friends had heard from Nadia and the other instructors had made her and her friends eager to try a new life. They all wanted to travel to exotic places and get educations, so they might learn as much as possible. There were so many more things to life than gadding about space killing people.

But she wanted Alec too...and she didn't know if she could handle a real relationship right now. Nadia and her friends had insisted that she take more time, rather than rush into something she might not be able to handle in the future. Instead, she should learn more about life in general, they said; if Alec loved her unconditionally, then he would wait for her and stand by her side when the time was right. Everything Alexa would learn could only help their in the relationship in the future; or at least, that was the impression she had gotten. The idea had made sense to her, and she still believed in it. Alexa felt she was doing something not only for herself but also for Alec...but she just couldn't express herself properly. Whenever she'd tried, he had harshly interrupted her, and she had lost track of her long, overdue, prepared speech.

Alexa's personal background included very little regarding family, friends and values, the trust between parent and child, or the concept of parental experience passed on to a child. Her life had been one long struggle of survival and scoring plunder. All she knew was this: if it hurts, don't do it; if it feels good, do it. Whenever the pain inside becomes too much, use drugs to make the pain go away. Wake up and move on with your life, and whatever you do, always make sure to be alive at the end of the day.

When she'd started telling Alec off, it had been a new experience for her. She loved his reaction whenever he was craving her. It made her feel wanted by someone she loved, and the feeling was wonderful. No one had ever made her feel like that before and been sincere. Oh, the pirates on the *Bitch* had had their way with her and her friends many times, especially in the beginning, when she was considered little more than fresh meat. But after a while, they turned their attention to new victims. To Alexa, sex was a physical act that sometimes made her feel good; she loved the sensation of having or giving an orgasm. She hadn't experienced that many herself, at least not with men; most of those experience were rapes enacted purely for someone physically stronger to relieve himself or herself, using her as a tool so that they could demonstrate their own selfish power over someone weaker. She was used to it and it didn't bother her so much anymore...or so she had thought.

In the last few years, she and her friends had been left alone by most of the pirates, with a few exceptions, and whenever she had pleasured herself with one or all of her closest friends, it was mostly whenever someone needed to be cheered up. It wasn't until she had met Alec that she had realized there was more to the love act than just the physical interaction and the sensation that might follow. Especially after the first time he had kissed her for real.

"Just here," Alexa thought, when she noticed the railing where Alec and she had made love. When he had nibbled on her neck, whispered into her ear how beautiful she was, and then finally kissed her, he'd given her her first mental orgasm ever. Never had she had an orgasm from just a kiss; and when she had told her friends about her new experience, they'd all laughed at her and called her a liar.

Alexa held on to the railing and trembled. She couldn't control the tears pouring down, and she used all her strength to hold back her sobs. Soon, her entire body was shaking, and she felt dizzy and sick. She knelt down on the hard metallic deck, still holding on to the railing with one hand, and covered her face, muffling any sound with the other. She cried quietly, thinking over and over, *I lost him!*

The competition was a success, enthusiastically participated in by the entire crew...except, of course, for one man. The third team, led by Frances, won; Alexa was a member of that team. There had been some minor delay whenever the teams had replaced each other on the *Predator*, but ultimately everything worked out quite well.

The second team received the great honor of acting as servants while the first team had to return to their duties. The teams later took turns attending the party at the mess hall and the galley. The crew praised their officers, while several crewmembers gave spontaneous speeches. The chef, Latoff, had prepared a true gourmet dinner with four courses. The losing crew members had to eat standing by the buffet, after they had acted as servants.

The party afterward started wild and got wilder. Myra was the perfect musical host, and she altered the music constantly, depending on the crowd's mood. As the hour grew later, the music became soft and calm, and several couple matched up for slow dancing. Then, just as things were getting a little too slow, Myra altered the musical beat to something more challenging.

Someone who had seen Alexa and her friends dancing at the Star Dice shouted encouragement for a similar performance. At first, the girls were hesitant. None of them were wearing the proper outfits; but when the crew members who had missed the show began clamoring for them to dance, they gave in. This time the music was different, but their dance was as erotic as ever, with the exception that girls danced solo. The crew went nuts, and after a short while most of them were involved, dancing as dirtily and provocatively as they could.

Alec watched the festivities from a monitor in his quarters, stone-faced, thinking of something that Carter Copola had told him before they had parted after the Battle of New Frontier: *"A ship's captain who envies something or someone is a bad captain; but a ship's captain who is jealous of a crew member...that would be as disastrous as me trying to run the* Crusher *without my hat. You think about that, Alec. It might be my last lesson to you, son. Be warned by it, and learn from it, or be destroyed by not acting—because that can happen, too. Never ever become involved with any officer or a crewmember in your chain of command. Hurry back home to marry her and get back into the saddle, if you must, but whatever you do, leave the little beauty back home."*

Alec didn't really know or understand what he was feeling about Alexa anymore. Perhaps his initial attraction had been a simple infatuation based on her exceptional beauty, and the way she spoke; or perhaps it was all that and the great sex combined? Whatever it was, he felt better after the confrontation with Alexa, but something was still missing. He felt empty.

He missed her and everything about her, but his injured pride couldn't go unheeded. He had cried himself to sleep for a week, waking up feeling like a weak-minded, scared fool; but for the last two nights he had slept without crying, possibly because of lack of nutrition and rest. He had started feeling alone, no longer a part of the ship's team. He avoided everyone, except when he had to do his duty, though he always smiled and put on the perfect act. He had cursed himself several times for allowing himself to get too personal with the crew, and had repeatedly sworn to himself never to make the same mistake again.

Alexa's treatment of him was unfair, and that was that. *One day I will write the thickest book about the female species in the entire universe,* he vowed to himself, *containing everything there is to know about them. The book will be over a thousand pages from cover to cover, and not a damned word will be written inside.* He smiled at his own joke, and then began to meditate.

An odd part of him, deep within, didn't care about Alexa or anyone; that part of him seemed dead. He hated the feeling, but he couldn't help himself. His headaches had started to come and go as they pleased, and even when they were pounding his skull, he didn't care about the pain. Something else was growing inside of him, he thought; he was afraid of it, because he didn't understand what it was. Was he going insane?

And yet, somehow, he welcomed it. The sensation helped him put aside his feelings towards Alexa. The love he felt for her, and the pain that seemed to come with it, kept fading away whenever he allowed this newly discovered dead zone to take over.

Something out there in the deep, dark universe was calling for him; whatever it was, he must find it.

Alec came out of his meditative trance and stood smoothly from where he'd been sitting on the deck. He moved to his rack and lay down, thinking about what Alexa had said. Images of them making love cluttered his vision. He rolled his eyes, as he knew that his pride was about to take a turn for the worse and allow his second head take command over his actions—as happens with most young men at such times.

Expressionless, he got up and walked over to one of his closets. He looked at the contents and closed his eyes, almost changing his mind about going downstairs to the party. Just as his newly found pride and strength—or was it weakness?—was about to take control again, he noticed the thin black cord lying on the bottom of the closet. He picked it up and touched it to his cheeks; he could smell her on it. The prideful feeling vanished as quickly as it had come. Alec put the cord in his pocket and pulled on a jacket, then left his quarters and strode confidently to a lift and went down a few levels. He crossed the corridor to call a second elevator...but when the doors opened, he was presented with the sight of a couple making out. Flustered, they stopped abruptly and stood at attention, while Alec motioned his hands for them to continue. He waited for another elevator.

He found that his reserve of patience was running low as he made his way toward the galley. He met several couples or groups heading towards their rooms or otherwise away, but most of them were too caught up in each other to notice him. That, or they simply ignored him. The thumping music got louder and louder as he approached the galley. As he entered, he nodded to several people who greeted him; they seemed happy to see him.

Alec stood at the entrance, looking for his true love, his heart racing; but that feeling lasted only for a moment. His heart made a somersault and his breath whooshed out of him when he saw Alexa's arms wrapped around the neck of one of the young lieutenants—one of Zlo's original officers, only three years older than Alec, a fellow named Beck. Their gazes were interlocked. After a moment

Alexa gave Beck a gentle push and turned her back towards him, to begin dancing with Nina.

Someone—who it was, Alec never saw—pushed Beck against Alexa's back. Alexa kissed Nina first, and their tongues met, teasing the young lieutenant; and then Alexa gave Beck a small peck on the cheek. She tossed back her head and laughed, while dancing very lewdly the two of them.

Everything seemed to move in slow motion for Alec, and he felt faint. Images flashed before his eyes—of the time Alexa, Nina and their former captain had rutted like dogs in front of him; they clogged not only his vision, but his thinking as well.

Myra noticed Alec standing next to the podium by the main entrance, and quickly changed the music to a softer tune. Nina turned and danced with Wolf, while Beck grabbed Alexa hard around her waist and forced her closer to him. Alexa, taken off-guard, laughed and turned her back towards him, moving her body rhythmically with the music like a snake, rubbing her body up against his. She reached out behind her and grabbed his neck, while Beck begun caressing her own graceful curved neck. Alexa moved her body more seductively and challengingly—and wasn't expecting it when Lieutenant Beck kissed her.

At first she was overwhelmed and upset; she moved her head back, turning to Beck with a surprised expression. Beck kissed her again. This time, they kissed for a while, and then Alexa turned around and forced him back, emitting a short giggle—and that's when she looked straight into pair of dark blue eyes. She thought she could read love in them, so she smiled back; but then she realized what she had just done. Her heart nearly stopped and her face turned pale as she saw the staggering pain in the two most beautiful eyes in the universe.

———o○o———

ALEC couldn't remember how or when he returned to his suite. He thought of nothing, and he moved like a programmed andy. He'd locked down not just his own hatch, but also the only entrance to the passageway leading to his quarter. He left his clothes in a mess on the floor and took a long shower. When he finished cleaning up, he put on his new battle suit, a customized gift from Cook and Copola. The suit could be worn inside a ship or outside in space; it served as body armor, and came with its own electromagnetic shield.

Dimly, through his stunned grief, he realized that something was happening; a tiny red button on his wristcomp kept flashing, and eventually the comp started vibrating against his skin. Alec pressed the red button, but the light wouldn't go off.

In his bedroom was a secret compartment that Copola's crew had installed under his bed—along with various other surprises throughout the *Predator*. Scowling, Alec tapped a panel on the wall and the bed slid aside. He jumped down into the cramp area beneath and begun working the computer there, peering closely to read the tri-dee monitor. What he saw sent chills down his spine. *How can that be?*

The warning read: *"Communication Alert. Foreign Transmission Detected."*

Alec removed a memory drive from the computer, scrambled out of the secret compartment, and hastily shut it behind him. He hurried next door to the office built adjacent to his private quarters, slid the stick into a computer slot and, while it downloaded the information, armed himself. When the computer *dinged*, he carefully read the warning information. Apparently, someone had been covertly transmitting and receiving messages repeatedly during the past two weeks. The antiviral programs installed by his Nastasturan experts had been extremely effective; still, Alec cursed that it taken weeks before the system had teased the errant, intermittent signal out of the *Predator*'s datastream and brought it to his attention.

"That can't be right," he breathed, as he noted the distance the incoming transmission was estimated to have traveled before being received, based on its power and attenuation configuration. Once received, it tended to vanish too quickly for anyone else to pick up or hack into. "Must be extremely advanced."

Tapping insistently at the keys of his computer, he linked into the ship's sensors and scanned the space around them in every direction, in every portion of the radiation spectrum the ship could detect. He found nothing...but he expected that there was something out there to be found. The warning system they had launched prior to landing should have given them well over twelve light hours' warning if a ship was approaching at full in-system speed... but the signals that had been received originated no more than six light hours away. Maybe they were hiding behind the asteroid; but of course the detection system should still have picked them up... "Wouldn't want to be out of line-of-sight anyway," Alec muttered. "Wouldn't want to lose their prey."

He glanced at the helmet to his pressure suit, which stared at him from a shelf across the room. *What do I trust?* Who *can I trust?* He stood up with sudden resolve, crossed the room, and put on the helmet. After he'd dogged it down, he checked his weapons and then his pulse, and smiled dangerously when he noted the slow, steady beat.

He hurried back into his private quarters and removed what looked like a first aid kit from the concealed area under his bed. Inside were three hypospray tubes, each marked with a colored stripe: white for sleep, red for paralysis, and black for death. He removed the white tube and inserted it in a small opening on the bulkhead above his bed. The thing inside his head was back; it wasn't talking now, but he knew it was guiding his actions. Wondering if he was going mad, he programmed his wristcomp for three hours and pushed a release button on the tube.

He mused on the words of one of his favorite instructors back at the military academy. He hadn't really agreed with the man's statement then, but it rang true now. *When all else fails, fall back on the Captain's Privilege. When you have no more strategic choices, never forget: as a ship's captain, it is your responsibility to yourself and our Federation to survive—even if it means sacrificing your entire crew's survival. When there is no more trust between you and the crew, then like any field commander, you are alone. No matter what, you must take the proper actions. Put the crew out of commission, whether through sleep, paralysis, or death; the choice is always yours, and a military tribunal can never hold the decision against you. Your training and preparation forbids us, your instructors, from signing off on your diploma in the event you are not mentally fit for command. When in grave personal danger at the hands of your own crew, you must protect yourself, return to the nearest Nastasturan port, and report your situation. This protects you against any form of mutiny or from the need to scuttle your own ship. If you are a captain on a civilian ship, of course, the laws are different...*

Alec watched on the holomonitor as the gas spread through the ship, the green dots representing life signs turning white one by one. When they were all white, he marked a spot on an emergency map of the moon's surface with a code, then removed from his computer a memory stick containing a copy of the ship's log. *Enough of this running shit. Time to fight. No more Mister Nice Guy.* He keyed overriding commands into the computer, sending out orders to the mainframe and all the backups.

For a moment he stopped long enough to think of Alexa, then shook his head in a desperate attempt of clear his mind of her. "I hope that someday, you really will find your knight in shining armor," he whispered.

He stood and turned his mind back to the matter at hand. As it turned out, his father was right about the Grisamm: they interfered too much in the lives of others, ruining things for everyone with their talk of freedom and self-determination. "This will be the last time I ever work with them," he growled. "And incidentally, where the fuck is Bax when I need him?"

He tapped hit a few buttons, and a reference image of Bax show up on the screen. The image roved around a blueprint of the ship before stopping at a white blinking light outside his suite entrance. *How did he get there? I locked the outer hatch. Bet you're in on it too, aren't you? Ha! That's what I get for trusting Tota and my uncle.*

ALEC hadn't been at his quarters, on the command bridge, or any of the other hundred places she'd tried. As Alexa hurried down the corridor, she dialed his communication code, *1, on her wristcomp; but there was no answer. Where could he be? The ship wasn't *that* big. As she turned down the corridor leading toward the docking bays, she wondered if he might have gone outside. That didn't seem likely, but it was possible; yet there was one place she hadn't checked: Cargo Bay Five. Maybe...

Alexa ran like mad through the ship, hopped on the first lift she came down, and went down to the cargo level. There was nothing in Cargo Bay Five except several man-high crates and, of course, the damned slave blocks. She cursed. "Where can he be?"

Alexa had only one thing on her mind, and that was to throw herself into her knight's arms and beg his forgiveness; and if she had to, to become his personal slave for life. She begun to sob, and didn't give a shit who saw the tears pouring down her cheeks. She became desperate and headed back to her quarters, in case anyone there might have seen Alec.

She encountered a number of the crew still partying as she passed through; most were paired up as couples, heading for more intimate places. As she pushed through the crowd in the narrow corridor outside her quarters, she cursed herself for not having told Alec that she loved him, for not taking the time to do whatever it took to make him realize that. She hit the keypad to her place, hoping as the hatch slid back that her roomies hadn't returned yet...but that hope was smashed by what she saw. "Typical," she snarled.

Kirra was busily giving head to a female exotic, straddling one man's erection while another penetrated her from behind, her eye glazed with excitement. Tara, meanwhile, rode a muscular stallion while jerking two guys off, even as a fourth shot his love juice all over her face. Zicci, who had always liked to be the one who dominated, had a woman on her knees with a sex toy attached to her private parts and a wide metallic bandana strapped around her head, sending electrical impulses into her body and brain. The woman screamed with pleasure as her body trembled in convulsions.

Zicci, Miska and Muhama wore similar sensory bandanas on their heads, allowing them to sense what the "victim" sensed. Meanwhile, several crew and a few officers cheered the participants on, eagerly awaiting for their own turns.

It seemed to Alexa that the entire room was filled with naked bodies and torn clothes, with broken bottles and smashed cans adding to the décor. The android usually programmed for maintenance had been reprogrammed, and was now simultaneous satisfying a man and a woman with its robotic hands in one corner of the room.

Alexa turned around to leave, aggravated, but was pushed back inside by Nina, who surprised her from behind from the hallway. "Get in and find some love birds!" Nina ordered, shoving her playfully. Alexa fell on her ass in the middle of the love nest—and when she tried to get back up on her feet, several helping hands pulled her back down. Nina had Lieutenant Beck's penis in her hand, in a hold Alexa had taught her, and pushed him inside while tearing off his trousers and attacking his rod with a hungry mouth. He let out a moan of pleasure.

From hidden speakers in the walls came loud music with a fast, syncopated beat, intensifying the mood in the cramped room. Cursing, Alexa got back up on all fours—but now several helpful hands tore at her clothes. Nina helped them eagerly, leaving Beck behind. Someone jammed a finger into Lieutenants Beck's anus; he jumped up and lost his footing, falling forward. He immediately saw an opportunity and took it. He grabbed onto Alexa's head in a firm grip, and forced his erection deep into her throat.

Alexa was taken by surprise, and tried to get away—but again, several sets of hands held her tight as they removed her clothing. Meanwhile, Lieutenant Beck looked down into the beautiful vixen's eyes, happy he finally had her. Beck had tired of their young commander getting all the best of everything...but not anymore. Now he had the little cock-teaser right where she belonged. Beck nodded to one of his sergeants, and smiled when he saw Alexa's surprised look of pain as she got her anus filled up. It didn't take long before Beck exploded, shooting deep down her throat. The sergeant worked Alexa hard from behind. Another soldier wanted to get in on the action, and started scuffling with a third.

Alexa bit Beck hard, making strange gurgling sounds. He pulled out his injured erection, swearing as he shot the last of his juices on her face. He slapped her several times, and was encouraged by several onlookers.

"Here, have some more!" Beck shouted. He was blinded by a sudden rage, and by the excitement of being in control over the so much talked-about little tease. He'd loved every moment doing her in the mouth. He knew she didn't want him, and that feeling aroused him even more.

"Hold her tight!" he bellowed to his friends, who all wanted to give the commander's whore a night to remember. Beck aimed a clenched fist at her, and was just about to teach her a lesson in manners when everything went black.

THERE was a strange and eerie stillness throughout the ship; the only thing that could be heard was the music beating from the speakers in the background. Alec hurried down a long corridor; he had to jump over several bodies, but he paid them no attention. He took a shortcut on his way to Cargo Bay Five, and passed the crew quarters where Alexa had moved. He looked with disgust over the naked bodies in the corridor. When he reached Alexa's and her friends' quarters, he hesitated. *Shall I see if she's there*?

After hesitating for a split second, he decided to continue with his primary mission of protecting the ship, so he never looked inside the quarters. The hatch was half shut and he ignored the people lying by the entrance...but from the corner of his eye he thought he could see her. He shook off the thought and forgot about what he might or might not have seen, and hurried towards his destination.

When he reached Cargo Bay Five, he was short of breath. He looked at the timer on his wristcomp: less than three hours. He had to hurry. He tapped a few buttons and intoned, "Guards, guards. Activate."

There was silence in the cargo bay for a long moment, and Alec could only hear his own heavy breathing inside his space helmet. Then there came a rustling from two of the larger crates, and seconds later they burst into showers of splinters and packing foam. Ten large battle androids emerged and lined up in front of him. They were two heads taller and five times heavier than himself, armed with a variety of vicious weapon systems. Their black metallic bodies, with their red, staring oculars, combined with the electronic whine of their movements to create a truly frightening impression to anyone who encountered them—an impression that they could back up very easily with the least of their weapons.

Alec ordered one andy to secure the bridge, and another his personal quarters. He sent two to the docking bays, and two more to patrol the ship. Two were stationed outside in space in guard positions. One android was ordered to activate secondary defenses, while the last battle android was ordered to follow him. The androids moved very quickly to their respective locations.

The andy ordered to activate the secondary defenses began his task by opening several crates stored behind the two slave blocks, revealing two dozen smaller hovering guards and battle droids shaped like large flying disks. Once they were activated, they relocated to strategic positions throughout the ship.

Alec and the last battle andy hurried to the smaller of the two docking bays, where they boarded a speeder and exited the *Predator*. His face grim, Alec directed the speeder towards a small mountain outside the cave, where both he and the andy disembarked in silence. After ordering it to remain on guard at the base of the mountain, he climbed the several hundred meters to the top.

It was a simple matter in the microgravity; within minutes he was at the peak, staring down at the battle android next to the speeder. He turned in a slow circle, scanning the moon's pitted surface, to make sure they were alone; he saw nothing, and neither did the sensors imbedded in his suit. Satisfied, he turned to the small radar probe he and Captain Zlo had planted there just after their arrival. Everything seemed copasetic. Moving quickly, always aware of time ticking away, he jacked in a clipcomp and started scanning the space surrounding the moon in both normal and subspace bands. He found nothing except the expected space debris, none of which was of any consequence. Nodding to himself, he set the scanner to scan automatically, and decided to use an old-fashioned approach to confirm its findings: his eyes. Tabbing a button with his chin, he dialed up the magnification on the helmet's faceplace and peered into the Big Dark itself. He changed the settings several times, zooming in on different regions in different ranges of the spectrum; nothing. He changed his position repeatedly, just in case the minute parallax shift might make something jump out at him; again, nothing.

Alec hesitated for a moment, then hammered a piton into the surface of the mountain peak and jetted upward on a long, thin line about half a kilometer. He peered over the curve of the moon with his enhanced vision, clicked over into infrared—and that's when he saw them: three ships, one cruiser and two destroyer class attendants, which would have remained out of sight if he hadn't left the surface. They were very far away, on the backside of the small asteroid that served as this moon's moon, and soon orbited out of sight; but he caught enough of a glimpse to be sure. His heart started pounding fast, and he felt a strange nervousness; but the voice returned just then, and all thoughts of stress vanished.

"There's some type of decoy in front of the cruiser," he muttered as he winched himself back down to the cliff. He grabbed the radar probe and dashed down the slope, making about three giant leaps before he hit the ground next to the waiting andy and the speeder. He checked a timer on the helmet readout that estimated the speed and distance of the approaching danger, and estimated they had less than two hours before they were within striking distance—unless they increased their speed. In that case, they could arrive much sooner.

Thirty more precious minutes passed as Alec and two of his battle androids made preparations for their arrival. They managed to move into place at the lip of the cave one of the large and extremely lethal Florencian T-Star mines, with its eight stubby ZZ-2 missiles. A computer interface with false ship configurations was emplaced next to the mine, and a dozen of the smaller battle andies now hovered alongside the *Predator*.

In lieu of the unconscious crew, Alec set dozens of his androids to the task of preparing the ship for takeoff, then made his way back toward the command bridge, followed by his attending battle andy. Without knowing quite why, he took the longer way back to the command bridge, passing the corridor next to Alexa's quarters. When he did, he stopped and looked at the people crowding the floor, then made his way to the quarters Alexa shared with her friends. He had to push aside a couple of bodies to get the jammed door opened—and when he did, he wished he never had. He found her intertwined with several other people, half-naked, with Lieutenant Beck's soft erection in her mouth. From the looks of things, another man had been taking her from behind when they all collapsed. Her face was stained with their semen, and it looked as if she were smiling, taunting him.

Alec felt a sharp sting inside him, and thought, *I should be used to this by now.* He remembered the thin black cord he had tied to his and her ankles just before everything fell apart between them; it was still in his coat pocket from earlier. He pulled it out and tied it hard around her left wrist, muttering, "I see you finally found your knight...or knights. I hope you enjoy your new freedom." He stopped himself from kissing her stained forehead and stepped back.

He waited for the voice inside his head, but there was nothing. Alec was surprised by his calm reaction; he no longer felt any jealousy or enmity towards Alexa; rather, he felt disgust and pity, nothing more, and promised himself that he would give her no more thought, at least on a personal level. *Should we survive this, then two or perhaps three more weeks, tops, and I can leave all this behind,* he vowed to himself.

After leaving Alexa's quarters, he verbally programmed the battle android to patrol all the living quarters on this deck, and told it and all the other battle androids to stun any reviving crewmember who showed signs of mutinying. The remaining androids were ordered to remain on station inside the cave after the *Predator* had left, hopefully giving the impression, through means both physical and electronic, that the ship was still inside the dark cavern.

Five minutes later Alec was in the CBR, strapping himself into a sturdy command chair. Computer keyboards folded out from each armrest, both parts of the cyber-suite that included the gloves attached to his spacesuit. A few taps of the keys and the *Predator* lifted out of concealment and left the cave slowly, its camouflage cloaking device dialed to mimic the moon's surface.

A holomonitor flickered to life before Alec, showing him the two large battle androids still inside the cave. Both they and their lesser companions were busily setting traps; and as he watched, one of the big androids hurried away towards a more secure location. Alec mused over his plan and hopped for the best. It was difficult for him to control the entire ship alone, so he had to focus on that rather than worry; that was good. He worked the controls before him with a speed that others would have found uncanny, fighting to keep to *Predator* as close to the moon's surface as he dared. The AI could have done a better job, but he didn't trust it at the moment; it might have been compromised. He kept the ship high enough for it not to leave any traces in the regolith from the engine turbulence, but not high enough, he hoped, for anyone to detect it immediately.

The countdown was at minus three minutes. "Any time now," he breathed. "They've got to be somewhere near." He was breathing hard inside the helmet; the salt irritated his eyes a bit, turning them red and moist. He didn't have time to worry about it, though; it took all his concentration to fly the ship. It would be almost an hour yet before his crew woke up, and at least several precious minutes after that before they could be battle ready—probably longer. In the meantime, he was just going to have to do what he'd planned to do with the help of the androids alone. Of course, if you wanted something done right, you had to do it yourself...

He set the *Predator* down two kilometers away, between two small hills, facing the cave entrance.

He and his android helpers were able to set the weapon batteries on automatic, but not as quickly or effectively as when the crew had worked them, and he was limited to the missiles and mines— and not even all of those. The fore missiles and torpedoes, normally under the pilot's and copilot's control, were very effective weapons; but he couldn't effectively control them from his position in the CBR. Oh, he could lock them on a target and launch them; but any enemy with an up-to-date computer could scramble their electronics, intercept them, or simply avoid them. At the moment, they were point-blank weapons only.

The longer Alec waited, the calmer he became. The voice was back, and soon his crew would awaken.

A quarter-hour later, he saw blurry movement at the cave entrance, and dialed up the magnification on the holodisplay. He was able to make out two camo-cloaked troop shuttles as they settled down on the surface. At least two hundred armored figures, with as many heavy battle androids, poured out of two shuttles. A third came into view above the cavern, and hundreds more pirates—he assumed they were pirates—disembarked from two large bays in the sides, descending with jetpacks. Another hundred or so appeared over the top lip of the cave and rappelled down on ropes.

The ships shuttles had come from hove into view; one of the destroyers took up a supporting position a few kilometers from the cave entrance, while the second hovered a dozen kilometers above. Meanwhile, the pirates advanced along a disordered line with care. One of the leaders gestured with his or her arm, and fifty pirates and as many andies charged into the cave. A dozen small, heavily armed speeders took up a defensive perimeter around the cave.

Alec glanced at a timer: thirty minutes left before the crew would wake. He fired several monitors into the air above the original; taken together, they provided a panoramic 360-degree view of the landscape outside. The way the *Predator* squatted between the two rounded hills, it created the illusion of one large hill; or that was the intention, anyway, and with the camo-cloak on, it seemed to be working fine.

Two Triple-X missiles were already locked onto the larger battle cruiser, which was still hiding behind the moon's moon in the same location as before. "Coward," he muttered. Didn't matter; despite the loss of a line-of-site connection, Alec had no doubt the missiles would find their target when the time came. He tapped the air beside one monitor and looked into Alexa's quarters through a cloaked surveillance camera; everyone and everything inside the room floated in zero-gee. Alec had dialed the artificial gravity control down in an effort to protect the defenseless crew; they would be safer in zero-gee, he reasoned, if the ship took enemy fire. He had sealed all the doors to the various areas and compartments, preventing the crew from moving around the ship. He hoped that all of them would wake up almost at about same time, so that he could order them to hang on to something until he turned the gravity back on. He realized that a few of them might be injured when he did that, but it was a risk he was willing to take.

He shut off the monitor and closed his eyes. He was still thinking about her. "No I'm not," he assured himself, then pressed a button on his armrest.

Several pirates ran out of the cave waving their hands in an effort to warn their fellow pirates to take cover. But it was too late: the dozen flying battle androids that he'd left behind erupted out of the cave and begun picking off the pirates and their battle androids one by one with laser lances and magma blasts, seasoned with the occasional anti-personnel torpedo. The pirates who had waited outside as a reserve force responded immediately, charging the cave despite the rain of fire and explosions. If nothing else, they were brave.

Meanwhile, the support destroyer moved closer, its captain sure of a quick and easy victory.

The first large explosion lit up the world with white light as a cloud of regolith and rock erupted out of the cavern, sending tremblors through the moon's surface and ringing it like a bell. The entire cave collapsed as a fireball bloomed above it. Several ZZ-missiles, just bright streaks due to their speed, emerged from the morass, sprinting in various directions; two struck the destroyer near the cave, and it vanished in a coruscating fireball so bright that the holoimage blanked. When the screen winked back on, he saw the remains of the destroyer down on the surface. The illicit ZZs had easily penetrated the shields, and the ship was completely gone except for a few scraps of metal. Some of the debris from the explosions was pattering down now, but he imagined the blast had helped most of it achieve escape velocity.

He tapped some keys and reoriented the viewer; it was clear that the ship in the space above the cave had been incapacitated by at least one missile, though it hadn't been destroyed. Grinning, he turned the view back to the destroyed cavern and tapped in a new command; two more missiles exited the debris and set a course for the hidden cruiser. Another command sent a final missile straight up into the incapacitated destroyer; it twisted apart into two unequal halves, spewing flame and atmosphere.

By now the battle cruiser had wised up, and had somehow identified the nearby "hill" as the source of its troubles. A hail of large caliber magma bursts fell on the location, eroding the *Predator*'s protective cliffs, followed by several missiles that completely altered the hill's shape, turning the center dead black. The *Predator* had lost its camo-cloaking. Wasting no time, Alec launched the *Predator* into space in a whirl of dust, leaving just in time to avoid being pulverized by another flight of missiles. The cruiser accelerated into attack speed, and took up pursuit—and never knew what hit it, twice, as the Triple-X missiles turned the ship into glowing dust.

Alec looked confident and pleased as he steered the *Predator* into deep space, leaving the devastated moon behind. Preliminary reports indicated minimal damage to his ship, and he directed the repair androids to swarm by the dozens over the several breaches and ablations in the ship's hull. Fortunately, nothing had penetrated through to the interior of the ship; but the exterior damage weakened the hull sufficiently that it needed to be seen to before they made any attempts to pass through a jumpgate.

He was just about to relax and remove his helmet when several warning indicators began flashing, and an annoying piping alarm warned of incoming traffic. Snarling, he reached into a holodisplay and yanked forward, magnifying sharply; at the very edge of detection range, he saw a swarm of ships—surely numbering in the hundreds—boosting for the *Predator*'s current location. More annoying piping, and hundreds more ships appeared from all directions, flanking the *Predator* in all three dimensions. "I must say, Tota did a hell of job when he spread that rumor about our intended mission," Alec muttered. He was damned close to being hoisted on his own petard.

It took another two hours before the crew of the *Predator* began waking up, and Alec promised himself that he would inform his Uncle Hadrian about the delayed effects of the sleep gas. It just might end up killing them all. By then, several of the pursuing ships had closed in, and Alec knew that it would be only minutes before some of them would engage. He was fairly close to a jumpgate, and thought he might be able to make it to the event horizon safely; but there was no way that he could negotiate the gravitational shear zone in a ship this size without the help of a trained crew.

His people awoke more or less all at once. When Alec heard the commotion over the com freqs, he triggered off a klaxon that alerted the crew that he would soon be re-engaging the artificial gravity. Most were able to brace themselves on the deck before it came back on, but there were the inevitable injuries by those too groggy or too ornery to pay attention. He ended the hubbub by announcing loudly over the ship's intercom, "Stand to, stand to. Battle stations, battle stations."

Like preprogrammed androids, the crew prepared for battle, donning their battle suits and arming themselves. Officers began hustling onto the command bridge, very confused; and when they realized that the *Predator* was now in deep space, it only added to the confusion. As they brought their workstations up and apprised themselves of the situation, they started entering commands to ready the ship for battle. The exterior weapons platforms emerged from the hull, altering the ship's configuration, and there was a reverberating double thump as Alec launched two T-Star mines in the direction of the leading elements of the englobing pirate fleet.

In the midst of the confusion, a fight broke out in Alexa's quarters, triggering a different alarm to the command bridge. Alec sent one of the battle androids to take care of it, ordering it to stun anyone fighting and to guard them. *Maybe it's our traitor or traitors*, Alec mused, as questioning voices from his senior officers filled his earbug. He answered each with a calm voice, assuring them that a full explanation would soon follow.

Throughout all this, Alec remained locked inside the CBR. Francis and Lieutenant Brown, their faces taut with concern, stationed themselves in the seats in the adjacent chamber, where a thick viewport allowed them to see into the CBR itself. Alec ignored them.

Moments later, two enormous explosions ravished the jewel-scattered dark, turning it so bright that anyone who looked at it unprotected was instantly blinded. Sixteen smaller explosions followed as the missiles of the two mines went to work against the *Predator*'s nearest pursuers, tearing huge holes in the pirate formations. The devastation gave the other ship captains, both in the main and independent columns, pause, and most held off a moment. A few of the faster ships flashed past the *Predator* at near-Galactic speed, expending a few attacks uselessly against its shields; they made the ship jerk and vibrate, but that was all.

"They could have blown us out of space just then," Behl snarled. "They're trying to incapacitate us." He tapped a command code and took over navigation from Alec, who was glad of the respite.

"Wants to capture us alive," Zlo agreed.

"Where the hell did all of them come from, and what are we doing in space?" Brown shouted over the controls.

"Focus on your job, Lieutenant, and I'll let you know what's going on as I can," Alec ordered over the command frequency. His voice was calm, and oddly comforting to those who heard it on the bridge. "We're jumping in five seconds."

Soon thereafter, the *Predator* entered the natural wormhole that Alec had found and plotted hours before, dropping a few standard mines in its wake. The mines should hold off their pursuers for an hour or two, Alec reasoned; hopefully they could find help, or at least another jumpgate to dive into, before pursuit became a problem again.

The *Predator* made its jump, following by a horde of pirate ships, all thirsty for the little frigate's blood.

SEVEN

THE destruction filled the holoimager on Ogstafa's command bridge, and she observed it with a hateful stare. But whatever her emotions, she did not let them show as she calmly ordered every ship to advance and capture the frigate. She knew now, with a cold certainty, that this was the same ship Horsa was looking for. The very moment her intelligence officers had picked up a message in a code known only to a very few select members of her clan, she knew that this was the prize so great that Horsa, her biggest nemesis, would risk his entire clan attacking New Frontier.

She had almost one thousand ships under her command, the united forces of her own Night-Hunters and two more clans: the Black Sun, and the Red Rays. A third clan, the Sunrays, had withdrawn from the alliance after sustaining too many losses to proceed. Besides, the cargo rooms of their surviving ships were already filled to the ceilings with loot and prisoners.

Ogstafa had ignored Horsa when he hailed her, demanding to know where she was taking her column. She hoped he would come to the conclusion that she was simply pulling away from the fight, having had enough.

But while she had suffered substantial losses during the Battle of New Frontier, her fleet was still a force to be reckoned with. In ordinary circumstances, a force of more than 100 Predator ships following close in her wake would send chills down her spines, and doubly so for her colleagues; but as long as she had the numeric advantage, not even their close proximity caused any major concern.

Ogstafa had no idea why Horsa had devoted all his energy to finding and capturing the little frigate, given that they had captured more loot in the last month than they normally would have netted in a year. But the battle had had its price: half her clan was gone, and her worries about a rebellion in their ranks were greater than ever before. Ogstafa quietly hoped that whatever she was chasing was worth it, or she could kiss her ass goodbye.

As her ship came within sensor range of the moon, she noted the destruction enumerated in one corner of the holoimager. One cruiser and two destroyers with all their crews gone; another flat loss. The thought of searching for survivors never occurred to her; she was far too busy for that, and any pirate knew that he or she would be written off rather than rescued if need be. She mused that the captain on the frigate must be very lucky or extremely talented. From now on, she decided, she would approach him more cautiously.

A warning shout from one of her crew draw her attention towards another sector of the monitor. A long, straggly line of bright dots, indicating ships far away, nearly out of sensor range, altered their course towards her location as she watched. "Horsa and his scum," she snarled under her breath. He must have suspected something, or he probably wouldn't have followed. By now, his sensors would have detected the explosions from the mines, confirming his suspicions.

More ships joined the formation, the number of dots quickly growing into the hundreds. "Bloody vultures!" Ogstafa shouted out loud, ignoring the fact that Horsa was doing exactly what she would have done in his situation. Several officers turned their heads toward her, questioningly, but she ignored them, too.

THE first thing that came to Alexa's mind was that she should bite hard. The snapping sound of her teeth coming together echoed inside her head; there was nothing to bite on. For an instant, she felt confused as she floated inside the room with fifteen other people, most of them naked. Liquids from several bottles, mixed uneasily with bodily fluids, drifted in slow-motion globules through the air. She heard the moans and snorts of a number of other people waking up, followed by groggy questions.

Alexa's head was jerked around; she felt pain lancing down her spine when someone grabbed her hair and pulled it from behind. Her instinct told her to curl up like a ball in a defensive position, and so Lieutenant Beck's fist hit her hard on her thigh instead of her stomach. "C'mere, you little whore, I'm not finished with you yet."

Beck had no chance against Alexa as her anger exploded and she turned into a raging fury of kicks, punches, head butts and bites. Her experience in close-quarter weightless combat was second to none; she'd had to develop her skills to a high level just to survive in pirate society. Beck hadn't even realized he'd lost the fight until the pain from his shattered jaw and crushed testicles hit at the same time. He crashed into a clot of drifting crewmen, screaming and not knowing which hurt to clutch first; Alexa slammed back against a bulkhead and bounced off into another man, whom she cold-cocked when she recognized him as one of the crew who had been cheering Beck on. It didn't take long before everyone in the room was fighting each other.

Most had no idea why they were fighting, though it seemed necessary. Some of the officers made futile attempts to stop the brawl and commotion, but were themselves pulled into the fray. No one heard the warning over the intercom about the gravity change—and they all hit the deck hard, some with bone-breaking force. People cursed and screamed, and more fights broke out.

That commotion ended abruptly when the space-black battle andy loomed in the doorway and, after intoning the required warning, fired several stun bolts into the crowd. Their recipients fell to the deck, and most of the other combatants immediately ceased fighting and lifted their hands in the air. The android ignored them, firing until everyone in the room had been subdued.

An hour later, the entire crew of the *Predator* was gathered inside the largest docking bay. Each person stood with their respective platoons—except for the fifteen who sat on the floor, guarded by one battle andy and four hovering guard droids.

Alec and his staff officers entered the cargo room, and the various conversations cut off immediately as the crew members turned their worried expressions toward their commander. Alec glared at his staff and crew while they straightened their lines, ignoring the prisoners.

When he spoke, his icy message was short and to the point: "We have one or more traitors aboard the ship."

A rumble filled the room, and Alec waited patiently for silence before he continued. "We will be in safe space, hopefully, in a week or two. Once we're there, we'll split up. I expect everyone to perform his or her duty without question during this time. About the fight among a number of my crew and officers, and the accusations of striking a superior officer versus a rape..." Alec looked over the prisoners with a disgusted expression, carefully avoiding Alexa's stare.

"As soon as we have time," he continued, "we will review the surveillance records and take the appropriate actions. I will not tolerate any insubordination or any crimes of violence on my ship. Both of the accusations are serious, and to prevent any further problems from any of you, all of you will be held in detention for now. Pier, Wolf: secure the prisoners in Cargo Bay Five. That android there will be their guard." Alec pointed at the battle andy, and noticed the protests that were about to interrupt him. "And gag all of them," he added.

Lieutenant Beck snarled, "I'm an officer, and I demand the respect that comes with my rank! I'm sure as hell not going to be put inside a..."

The guard android aimed one of its many weapons at Beck, who had nothing more to add.

"Anything else?" Alec ignored the few questions from the crew and snapped, "Very good! Captain Zlo, take command of the crew and have them to stand to. Oh, and by the way, this is not a drill."

There was some commotion as the crew hurried to their battle stations, alarms sounding in the background. Wolf intercepted Alec as he was just about to get in a lift. "Sir, the prisoners want to get dressed," he said in a low voice. "Um, most of them are half-naked, and we might need them next time we engage someone..."

"Put them in the blocks as they are, and turn down the Gull-damned heat in the cargo bay. That'll give the hotheads some time to cool off. I'm well aware that we might need them, but for now just do as I said."

"Yes sir. May I put their battle suits outside the bay at least?"

Alec nodded sharply.

The *Predator* headed off into deep space, its engines pushed to their limits as it piled on acceleration. Sending out several decoy drones prepped with his ship's transponder signals and electronic configuration, and passing through three more jumpgates, Alec took his crew deep into uncharted space over the next week. The mood among the crew was at its lowest ebb—and it didn't get any better when they were forced to avoid detection from ships on several occasions, requiring Alec to re-plot and plan a new course of action each time. They traveled without any obvious destination, and the crew's impatience begun to take its toll as they ventured farther from any known system.

Eventually, Pier informed Alec that they were running low on food, and Frances reported that there were problems with the crew, which had formed up into three factions. The former pirates formed one alliance, while one cadre had united around Lieutenant Beck and were making demands for his release. A third group was still loyal to Alec and staff officers; most were them regular Nastasturan troops from the *Crusher Five*, though there were several mercenaries hired on NF-16 among them...and of course there were the Grisamm monks. Alec finally ordered a long-overdue staff meeting.

When they had convened, he looked around at his staff and noticed the dark shadows under everyone's eyes. He was sure he looked about as lovely. After a brief welcome and a short status report from each officer, Alec announced, "I must leave you for three days."

Everyone in the room stared at him in disbelief.

"I have plotted a course to the location where you will pick me up. If I don't return within two days after you arrive, then the ship's command and ownership will devolve to you, Captain Zlo. The relevant legal papers are in my safe."

"May I ask where you are going?" Captain Zlo asked.

"You may not. Just know that I will do what I must, and I do it so I can save the lives of everyone aboard the *Predator*, and that's all I have to say." He made a gesture against any protest. "Now, about the prisoners. What do you have, Frances?"

Frances was still shaking his head from the earlier announcement. "The surveillance cameras don't show much that supports either accusation," he rumbled. "Alexa entered the room, and it appears that she tried to leave right away. Someone, perhaps her friend Nina, pushed her. It appears she fell, and then there were several people blocking the pickups, so it's impossible to see what happened next. Have you seen the recording?"

"Actually, no. I never looked at it," Alec replied.

"The recording was then interrupted by static interference, and after investigating I figured out why. Zicci had built some sort of sex toy. Its electronics caused the interference and eventually wiped the rest of the recording—so we'll probably never know what really happened in there. We have no advanced lie detectors onboard the ship, and I doubt one would help. The people involved are real hardcases, and most of them were drunk and don't remember much anyway."

Alec thought aloud, "That party was a very bad idea."

Captain Zlo shook his head. "Alec, you know as well the rest of us that all ships in space—yours, Nastasturus', Florencia's, private, pirates or whomever—have these types of functions to make it easier on the crew."

"Of course I know, but this was a case of very bad timing. Now, does anyone have any suggestions about what we should do with the prisoners?"

"Frances and I talked about that. Since the majority of them have no memory of what happened, I say we let them loose and put them back to work."

"Well, Zlo, that sounds reasonable. What about Beck and Alexa?"

"I'm afraid that choice falls on you."

"Great. Well, let's release all of them with a warning for now, and make sure they're kept busy—too busy to cause trouble, and too busy to think."

The meeting moved on to other topics. Alec's officers made several futile attempts to find out what had really happened while they were out, and why they had passed out in the first place, and were curious about why he had to leave them for a few days. However, he had no answers for them. He never told them or anyone else about the battle on the asteroid; no one would have believed him anyhow.

Alec realized that he couldn't afford to trust anyone at the moment, so he deliberately kept most of what had happened a secret. Some parts of what had happened the officers and crew knew; it was recorded in the ship's public log, which any crewman could access. Otherwise, Alec had to leave the entire crew guessing, something that he realized might be very dangerous if the crew lost faith in their leader.

―――――――――-oOo-―――――――――

THE first thing that hit Alec as he entered Cargo Bay Five was the stink of bodily wastes. He had difficulty hiding his disgust when he looked on half of the wretched prisoners sitting in two slave blocks, staring back at him; the rest were locked up behind them. Alec was grateful that Alexa was not one of the prisoners staring at him so balefully.

At Alec's direction, Wolf and several crewmen released the prisoners, and several medical andies ushered most of the group to the infirmary.

"Not them!" Alec gestured to the medics who helped Alexa and Beck. "Any more problems from either one of you, and you'll both spend the rest of the trip down here. Wolf, have the two of them clean up this shithole as soon as they can stand on their own feet."

"Clean up your own shit," Beck hissed threateningly.

Alec, who stood with his back towards Beck, turned around. Alexa struggled to her knees, got up on her feet, and using the last of her last strength, darted between Alec and Beck. The excrement intended for Alec's head struck Alexa in the mouth, and when she slammed down on the floor, she emptied her stomach of its contents. Two gunshots followed in quick succession—and Lieutenant Beck screamed in agony as his arms became just so much charred meat. Alec holstered his magma blaster and looked expressionlessly at Beck, who was whispering in shock as he writhed against a crate, staring at the cauterized stumps he held before him.

Except for Beck, the room was dead silent.

"I don't think Crewman Beck will be throwing shit at anyone again," Alec said calmly. "Take him to Doc."

Wolf gestured to a medical andy. "And his arms?"

"Have her fit him with some scraps from android maintenance, if she finds any."

"No cloning?"

"No, Wolf, no cloning, and no stim. Not yet, anyway."

Wolf gestured to Alexa, who was on her hands and knees, spitting and coughing. She was filthier than ever. The once-beautiful vixen looked more like a used wreck. Swallowing hard, holding her tears back, she started to clean the floor with her hands, looking away from Alec.

Alec sighed. "Wolf, let her go to her friends, and have a few maintenance andies clean up in here." He turned and left.

Alec never thanked her for protecting him from Beck, and indeed he never would. All he wanted to do was get away from her and never see her again. He didn't believe a word she'd said in her defense to Frances and Captain Zlo; he'd viewed several surveillance tapes from before, during and after the party, and he had made up his mind. He didn't have time to bother with her anymore, no matter that he felt that his heart had been ripped right from his chest; at the moment, he had bigger fish to fry.

He hurried down to the shuttle launch bay, where he found two battle androids waiting; Bax had convinced Alec to take them with him at least. Zuzack's former shuttle was prepped and ready for launch, one of the ship's single-man fighters mated to the top.

THOUSANDS of ships were hunting the frigate now. Hundreds of rumors were spreading about it, and several were actually close to the mark, in that they related to a certain old treasure map. Whatever the rumors were, they were enough to engage the imaginations of all types of gold-diggers, who then increased their efforts to find the ship. It wasn't just the pirates who were looking for the *Predator*, but also powerful civilians, merchants, and military factions and fleets from numerous worlds.

HORSA had scattered his remaining fleet in an attempt to escape from the continuing Nastasturan onslaught. Currently he was pursuing Ogstafa's column. There were no difficulties in intercepting communication between so many ships and thus determining out what was going on. In addition, hundreds of media ships had also joined in the chase, desperate to find a catchy news story and attract high ratings.

Admiral Hadrian Cook had regrouped his remnant force of the Nastasturan 11th Galactic Fleet, some seventy-five ships; they included some of the faster vessels in the pursuit of the *Predator*. Admiral Nass, second in command of the Florencian 9th Galactic Fleet, was once more in charge, and was taking the remaining ships to spacedock for repairs. Admiral Rimez had returned to Handover to answer to his Government as to why over half his fleet had been lost—on orders from his own father, Chancellor and President Rock Belim.

The Commercial Traders and the Federated Merchants were also interested in finding Alec. Their main reason, however, was because of the enormous wealth he had on deposit; it was already earning a substantial amount of interest. They were more concerned with discussing future business relationships than in taking him prisoner. The warrant from the Commercial Traders, which cited Alec Horn for stealing property (in this case, a slave from one of their wealthier members, Lady Zoris af Sun) could easily be solved with a little financial compensation and a fine; or so the Brakks thought, knowing nothing about either Zoris' plans or Alec's.

The media had begun spreading Alec's picture across the galaxy, and it wasn't long before everyone knew who he really was... or who they *thought* he was. The commotion surrounding the House of Hornet's headquarters, Alec's home, was soon outrageous, with reporters and news media camping out on the grounds and pestering everyone who approached. Stories and rumors were soon floated suggesting that the Marshall was using his son for cloak- and-dagger games. The situation demanded a scapegoat, and apparently Alec himself was to be held responsible for the millions of casualties at the Battle of the New Frontier. Any insurance company with contracts and claims in the New Frontier 16 cluster encouraged this particular rumor, and soon a third bounty was placed on Alec's head.

Rumors of a pending invasion from Florencia didn't help. Over half of Nastasturus' military might had been mobilized to various strategic positions, and the situation had destabilized the economic markets. Some were tanking, even as others took off for the stratosphere. When part of the true story was released to the media in a press conference held by President Alexander and Marshal von Hornet, explaining what had happened to Alec and his friends and that they knew nothing about any treasure, the media didn't buy it. That kind of story didn't generate enough ratings, and therefore was quickly dismissed.

The media soon came to a consensus on their own version of the truth, because the story sold better: it decided that Alec had a twin brother, or better, a bastard brother who hated his father and was the "Black Prince," an infamous pirate that the media knew everything about. The Black Prince, not Alec, had now returned to claim his rightful place in the House of Hornet. His father had therefore illegally sent an entire Galactic Fleet to intercept and stop him. In a desperate attempt to throw his bastard son off course, the Marshal had kidnapped his pirate queen and kept her hostage onboard the New Frontier 16. This led to the battle. This was the perfect explanation as to why thousands of ships were massing at a certain point in the universe right now. The fact that reality was never that neat was completely ignored.

The Florencian government seized upon the media's invention as an ideal way to quash the rumor that they had been preparing an invasion of Nastasturus; in fact, they accused the corrupt Nastasturan government of being the driving force behind it all. This was just another case of delusional propaganda on the part of capitalistic pigs, they said; the pirate clans, in fact, were the Nastasturan regime's own creation, evidence that their economic structure didn't work. Ultimately, they claimed, this was the prize anyone should expect when they lacked a proper God to worship. Indeed, this was God's way of punishing the horrid capitalistic non-believers.

Three colonial worlds held by Nastasturus, populated mostly by Fourth and Fifth class citizens, saw their opportunity to rebel; and immediately terrorist attacks increased throughout the Federation. Again Florencia saw an opportunity, and began—in secret, of course—to assist the rebels with funds and weapons.

During the months immediately after the Battle of New Frontier, the known universe was a roil of uproar and chaos. This escalated far enough that a number of independent worlds, facing financial ruin, were forced to band together in a new, unofficial alliance. Soon they, too, had sent out military ships to put an end to the menace posed by the fictional Black Prince. This time, new images of the prince and his princess began to emerge—pictures of Horsa and Ogstafa.

When His Imperial Majesty Salla XII, absolute ruler of Marengo and the Greater Sun Empire, heard this rumor, he immediately sent half of his mighty space fleet to assist his son, Zanches, in the search for "his" hero. This information eventually leaked out, and it soon seemed that all hell was going to break loose. Anyone with any sense of history was well aware of Marengo's bloody past—and those in power started mobilizing their own armed forces.

The rumors kept chasing their own tails and gobbling themselves up, and it wasn't long before a new one emerged that would, ultimately, change the universe for all time: that the Black Prince's father was the Emperor Salla himself, and his princess was the former wife of Nastasturus' President Alexander, a woman who had vanished without a trace over eight years earlier. The rumor held that this was just the beginning of a Marengan incursion; that the Emperor of Marengo was in cahoots with Marshall Guss von Hornet and the entire Nastasturan military clan; and that combined, they would take over the entire Nastasturan Federation before moving on to conquer Florencia. Once the last of the two large Federations had met its demise, then of course Marengo would conquer the rest of the universe, one piece at a time.

When Salla XII heard this particular rumor, he and his government panicked—and immediately ordered a major mobilization of all the entire Marengan armed forces. This was soon followed by a mandate to manufacture more ships and war materiel, and thus increase their military might as a whole. All this did was throw more fuel on the bonfire.

By then, the three bounties on Alec von Hornet's head had inflated to ridiculous amounts, and bets were placed at casinos throughout the galaxies regarding the likelihood of the young prince's survival, and how long it would take before he was captured in the first place. This widespread interest in the fate of the young Nastasturan, now certainly the biggest celebrity in the universe, caused something new and strange to happen: several independent military contractors, which were making a fortune helping all the major powers arm for war, saw the bounties as threats to their economic well-being. So they placed bounties on the *bounties* in an effort to ensure that Alec would make it back to Nastasturus safely. If anyone tried to collect one or more of the bounties on Alec, the merchant bounties would ensure that person died.

ALEXA sat on her bed with her knees folded, quietly sewing a torn garment. She ignored her friends' attempts to cheer her up; sometimes she smiled at them in response, but she was dead inside these days. She attended her classes and did all her chores as if nothing had happened...but she had become suddenly, deadly dull. Her friends, worried over this radical change, decided to leave her alone as much as possible, a practice Alexa encouraged. When Nadia tried to speak to her more personally, she excused herself and left.

She wasn't the only crewman acting that way. Many among the crew were similarly quiet and well-behaved. A hostile silence begun to creep over the ship. It was with great relief to all when Alec finally returned from his "secret" trip. The officers had managed to keep quiet about his hasty departure, not wanting to worry the crew, but everyone knew he'd left.

Alec himself was prouder than ever, after having returned from a dangerous flight all alone in uncharted territory, with only the fighter for protection and having hidden his shuttle.

One of the first things Alec checked when he returned was whether the traitor had sent any new messages. To his satisfaction, he found that one more had been posted. Alec started reviewing the relevant surveillance tapes—and smiled as he found the person he was looking for. "Once a pirate, always a pirate," he muttered, as he loaded a datastick with all the information pertaining to the traitor, and hid it in the secret compartment under his bed. "Fucking ingrate."

The day after his return, just as he had foreseen, the chase began anew. This time the *Predator* made a jump through a 'gate that would lead them toward the center of Nastasturan space, hoping things had calmed enough for them to find a safe (or at least neutral) port. They hadn't followed the news traffic; that had been nearly impossible. So they were surprised when, after exiting the gate and setting course toward a spacedock that called itself "The Iceteroids," they were intercepted by a media ship. The ship's captain had been ordered to locate any vessels with the *Predator's* configuration, and the captain was happy as a whore in Paradise when he saw the sigil of three lines and an eye on the frigate dead ahead. It wasn't long afterward that the first transmission was sent: *Have found the Black Prince.*

For the *Predator*, the first sign of a problem was when the media ship laid a shot across the *Predator*'s bow with a laser cannon, which was ordinarily used to clear away any incoming debris. If Alec and his crew had been twitchier—and less principled—that would have been tantamount to suicide. But they knew that they couldn't safely open fire on a civilian ship in Nastasturan space, else they might be declared law-breakers or, worst, pirates. So they did what any normal ship's crew would do: they calmly hailed the media ship, wondering what they wanted and why they had opened fire.

The ship's lead reporter, a male exotic with a very large mouth and even larger ears, demanded that they cut their engines and heave to so that they could board the ship for an interview. "It's the people's right and they demand it!" the creature squeaked.

Captain Zlo answered reasonably that they were on a preset course, and didn't want to have anything to do with the reporter's questions anyway. Incensed by this answer, the media ship fired off a few more rounds across the *Predator*'s bow, putting them dangerously close to the category of "enemy combatant."

By then, another media ship had closed on *Predator*, having intercepted the exchange between Zlo and their colleague. This ship's key reporter saw her opportunity to scoop the other reporter, and ordered her ship's captain to ram the *Predator*.

This time Captain Zlo looked at Alec, who immediately got on the intercom and ordered the entire crew to stand to battle stations. By then, the first ship had joined the first in her rush at the *Predator*, and the two media ships were firing upon each other sporadically. Instead of firing back at the two ships, Alec sent the *Predator* into evasive actions and did what anyone should do in such a situation: he called the police.

The *Predator*'s entire crew laughed themselves to tears when two police corvettes intercepted and boarded the media ships. The corvettes were followed by several border guard ships, which had already been pursuing the *Predator* for questioning.

But the joy didn't last long onboard the *Predator*. Soon, over five hundreds ships were trailing the *Predator*; and once again, all they could do was run.

Alec and his staff ignored most of the hails—until a red light started to flash, indicating that a Nastasturan military vessel was hailing them. Alec had the officer at the communications workstation put the hail up on the main holoimager. He and several others smiled when they recognized Captain Copola. "There you are! The Black Prince himself, ha ha ha."

Alec looked at him, dumbfounded. "What's that mean?" he asked.

"Don't you worry, whippersnapper, old Cap'n Copola is here to escort you and your crew back home!"

The bridge crew cheered raggedly...only to break off as the ship rocked under a massive concussion. "Enemy ship to starboard, three degrees Galactic South," Captain Zlo snapped. "Standing by to engage." Zlo's voice was calm, but his facial expression told another story.

OGSTAFA wasn't about to let anyone come between her and the ultimate prize, so she had her weapons crew fire off several broadsides against both *Crusher Five* and *Predator*. They were deflected by both ships' screens, of course; but now that she was in position, very little could keep her beam weapons and missiles from eventually eating through those shields, military-grade or not. She had used the cluster of ships trailing the *Predator* to her advantage, and she would continue to press that advantage as long as she could.

Crusher Five opened up with all its guns against the much smaller cruiser, just as it came under attack from dozens of other pirate ships. A number of police corvettes and border patrol ships—all destroyer or frigate class—joined in on the fight... as well as they could, at least, with the civilian ships crowding close. It wasn't long before more Nastasturan navy ships winged in from elsewhere in the system, and soon Ogstafa's ships and the Nastasturus Navy were engaged in a huge, snarled melee. The *Predator* led the way, receiving less than its fair share of fire; by then, their pursuers were all too busy fighting each other.

Shaking his head, Alec regarded the thousand or so blue dots scattered across the holoimager, each representing a Nastasturan ship at least as large as *Predator*. Almost a thousand other dots of many colors were intermingled with the blue, and Alec could no longer conceal his concern and frustration.

By now they were bottled up, so he had his crew open up with every weapon they had, except for the Triple-X missiles and the T-Star mines. None of the weapons were targeted at any of the ships—their intention was to scare them out of the way—but several ships collided in their haste, and chaos ensued.

All this, of course, was captured live by the media ships, and sent to their respective news agencies.

"Receiving a priority hail, Master Horn!" Brown shouted from her station. "It's coded so that only you can access it!"

Alec was just about to put his hand on an identifier pad on his console when a soft female voice declared, "Horsa. It's Horsa." He glanced to the side, and saw Alexa standing next to his command chair. He was about to upbraid her for leaving her battle station, but his annoyance drained away as she continued, "Horsa is Zuzack's brother, the head of the Wulsatures clan. I saw their clan markings onscreen at my station, and came to warn you in person." Alexa took a deep breath to gather her courage. "I love you, Alec, and if we should die here today, then I want to be by your side."

She stood proudly and glared at him, and Alec noticed the thin black cord looped around her head.

"Horsa's the most feared pirate in the universe," she said flatly. "I believe you civilians refer to him as the Shadow-Slayer."

"*He's* the Shadow?" Frances gasped.

Alexa looked straight ahead, nodding.

"The lead Wulsatures ship is hailing us," Lieutenant Brown announced.

"Let's see what he wants." Alec pressed a button, and the holoimager filled with Horsa's terrifying image. He looked at Alec with a friendly smile, and bowed slightly towards Alexa. "My brother's daughter! Let me guess: you are the brains behind all this? Ha! I always liked you, and I warned my brother about you over and over again."

"I'm not Zuzack's bloody daughter."

"Daughter, perhaps not; bloody, certainly. Consider yourself adopted, if it makes you feel any better."

Alec interrupted their dispute. "What can I do for the infamous Shadow-Slayer? I doubt all this," he made a wide gesture with his arm, "was undertaken so that you could chat with your niece."

Horsa let out a strange, loud bray—Alec decided it was a kind of laugh—before replying, "Young master Hornet, I shall give you one and only one piece of advice: once a pirate, always a pirate. But by all means, keep Alexa—*after* you comply with an honest trader's request."

Alec glanced at Alexa; the waves of pure hatred radiating from her towards the creature on the monitor were all but palpable.

"Return what you stole from my brother and me," Horsa continued. "Oh, you can keep the loot you took from the shuttle, and of course the shuttle itself, but return the map, my friend, and we can call it a day. I will transfer the coordinates of a neutral location where we can meet. As you might have noticed, my ships aren't firing on yours, and I've proven I can find you anytime, anywhere. I fear you have no choice."

Alec rolled his eyes dramatically. "Go to hell, pirate—or follow me there. I will *never* meet any of the treacherous terms offered by your kind. Look, Horsa, upon the Black Prince and his future bride: we who have crushed your clan, and will continue until it is ground into the dust and forgotten by history. Be witness to our true love, and know that we shall live out our lives in pleasure—spending all your treasure on our children and on ourselves, while depriving you of the ability to locate the rest." Alec wrapped his arm around Alexa's shoulders, and pulled her firmly to his side. She gazed at him, mesmerized, and slipped her arm around his waist. Both stared at Horsa.

Horsa no longer smiled; his expression was dead and skull-like as he answered, "To hell it is, then," and returned their stare with cold eyes as the image blanked.

Apparently unperturbed, Alec ordered Lieutenant Brown to locate the nearest jumpgate. A moment later, as the ship shuddered through an impact on its aft shields, Brown shouted, "I've got a commercial wormhole about 10,000 kilometers away, bearing Red 10, Blue 281, Green 97!"

"Let's thread the needle, then, Captain Zlo!" Alec shouted over blaring alarms.

The crested Marengan's eyes widened. "Sir, another ship has just sent a probe ahead, announcing its intention to enter the wormhole—and you know the dangers of making a simultaneous transit! There's no telling where we might come out!"

"We're running out of options, Captain! Make the jump!"

Nikko Behl met Zlo's horrified expression with a casual wave. "Better possible death rather than certain!" he shouted over the din. Zlo made it clear from his expression that he thought Behl and his erstwhile general were insane, and made no attempts to conceal his fear. Threading a jumpgate, especially one as small as a wormhole, in company with a ship the size of the massive passenger liner bearing down on them...well, it wasn't quite suicide, but it was damned close. If they weren't smashed into the bigger ship by the gravitational flux, they might exit the wormhole just about anywhere in the universe—or out of it.

Alec wasn't worried about Zlo's concern. He clutched Alexa tightly and glared into the main holoimager at the thousands of ship-traces visible within just a few light-seconds of their location.

History would record, based on Alec's personal log, that in the less than six hours since their arrival at the Iceteroids system, well over 7,000 spacecraft had pursued and fought over *Predator*. None who analyzed the situation later questioned his order, made while looking down upon the most beautiful eyes in the universe, to escape into the wormhole in what historians would relate as "The Incident at the Gate."

The *Predator* vanished into the tortured space of the commercial wormhole accompanied by the passenger liner, which would later be identified as the *Athena Ascendant* out of Tierre. Normally a jumpgate could be stretched only so wide without technical assistance, allowing the passage of only a few ships at a time; otherwise, entering the space fissure *en masse* was extraordinarily dangerous. Some of the pursuers nearest the *Predator* were able to bypass the jumpgate, but hundreds of others were less fortunate, plunging into the wormhole's throat as it swallowed the *Predator* and the liner. The actual traversable throat of the wormhole was relatively narrow, unfortunately for the ships that followed; almost all were inhaled and crushed to atoms by the singularity, increasing the wormhole's mass and event horizon significantly. The result was a runaway feedback effect that sucked in a thousand more ships before they could escape. Like the natural phenomenon it was based on, the jumpgate swelled into a vast sink of matter and energy.

And even when the ships stopped entering the event horizon, the region of warped spacetime continued to grow.

Captain Copola observed the entire event with as much suspicion as concern, as he watched the blot in space swell. He immediately ordered all the Nastasturan ships to cease pursuit and retreat to a safe distance with all the speed they could muster. Once his orders had been complied with, he continued to watch the image of the nascent black hole on his holomonitor, setting it to scale up and down the electromagnetic scale. There was something wrong here; he could feel it. Yes, the wormhole had swallowed over a thousand ships…but even so, it shouldn't have expanded so far or so fast. Something was wrong, far beyond the simple natural wrongness of a black hole…

After long thought, he ordered his intelligence officers to find out whether any Nastasturan fleet was about to make a major jump into this system, as Admiral Cook had done earlier with the 11th Galactic. Within moments came the answer he half-dreaded, half-anticipated: "No fleet on the approaching vector."

Captain Copola knew all too well what was about to happen, right before his eyes. The crumpled vortex of spacetime was flickering now, emitting radiation in the visual range, and in gamma the circular event horizon was expanding rapidly. This could only mean one thing, this far inside Nastasturan space: invasion. Face grim, he typed a quick message into the console before him, ensured that it had been accepted, then broke a thin glass shield and hit the large button beneath. Several probes immediately launched into space in all directions, screaming their distress:

> *Space is lit up!*
>
> *Large exit gate forming these coordinates:*
>
> *23-4.67.552-3.*
>
> *Suspected invasion*
>
> *Regrouping*
>
> *Copola, Commanding Officer* Crusher Five
> *11th Galactic Fleet*
> *Nastasturus Federation*

As fate would have it, Hadrian Cook's fleet, more than 100,000 kilometers toward Galactic North, was the first to intercept the message. Admiral Cook had earlier transferred his flag to another Omega-class cruiser, the *Colquin*, during regrouping maneuvers so that Copola could continue the search for Alec unhindered by a fleet admiral's needs. Having followed the event on his monitors, he was also aware of what was about to happen, and transmitted a back-up order with Copola's in the event that there might be a few hot-heads among the captains in the Nastasturan fleet group pursuing the pirates. Every available ship, he ordered, should regroup towards his location.

The military and police ships in the vicinity obeyed instantly, hurrying towards Cook's position; and once the message had pulsed through the local transit points, several Galactic fleets left their stations in neighboring systems and also hurried to his aid. The Predator ships in the pursuit group also pulled out of the swarm and converged on Cook's position.

Meanwhile, very few of the surviving civilian, media, pirate ships were aware of what was about to happen. By then, the jump-gate appeared to have stabilized somewhat, so the masters of most of those ships made the ill-fated decision to follow the *Predator* and the *Athena Ascendant* into the new black hole. After all, there were billions of credits at stake. Even a few of the ships that had sheared off and avoided the jumpgate in the first place reversed course and straggled in.

None of the ships had launched any advance probes before they entered the jumpgate, and none realized what its continued expansion meant, if they even noticed it at all...though they should have.

EIGHT

"**ORDER** the scout division to launch as soon as the probe transmits the all-clear," Admiral Hunemon Panmada snapped, and lay back on the crash couch, smoothing down the fur on a midleg. She grinned, honored to be among the senior staff officers of the Florencian Navy who would soon be actively making history.

"What does it smile for?" The hissing voice from behind sent chills down Panmada's spine. "We are months delayed from awakening our children, and it appears to celebrate before they have had their supper."

Marquessa De La Hoff did not wait for the Admiral's answer; she was far too absorbed, by then, in inspecting the enormous column of over ten thousand capital ships and their support vessels, all of which were preparing to enter the jumpgate along with the three Triton stations arrayed around them. One of the stations was located very near the expanded wormhole, prepared to launch in the first wave.

Alarms blared in sudden warning in the cadence for approaching enemy ships. Panmada leaned forward, stunned, and gawked as a frigate leaped out of the wormhole, straight toward the waiting armada, arrowing toward the *Gall*'s command bridge.

De La Hoff's high-pitched cry filled the bridge. The spidery woman-thing clutched her temples as she screamed out her pain and horror, before falling to the deckplates and convulsing in an agonized spray of acidic saliva.

"WHAT a view," Alec whispered to Alexa, as he looked down at the love of his life and kissed her gently, squeezing her shoulders hard.

"Sir, should I ask the war fleet in front of us to wait until you're finished before attacking?" Behl asked acerbically.

Alec looked at him; Behl rolled his eyes toward the holoimager. He whistled and stood. "We *are* popular." He pushed Alexa back into his command chair and said, "Just sit here and strap yourself in. Be back when I can." Alec hurried into the CBR and started shrugging into the command suit.

Captain Zlo's voice echoed over the intercom. "They're charging weapons, sir."

"Evasive maneuvers. And open fire with everything we have," Alec ordered. "And I mean everything."

By the time Alec had finished donning the command suit, Frances had arrived and parked himself at the command console inside the adjacent room, and Bax had arrived in time to help him fit the cyber gloves and slide in both the Florencian and Nastasturan command cards. With a thought, Alec pulled up the current shield configurations for the Florencian Navy, and shunted a command signal toward the waiting fleet. He realized that this would help them only for a few moments, but it was a start.

Before the command signal had reached the Florencian ships, Alec launched all the remaining T-Stars, followed by the last of the Triple-X missiles. Meanwhile, hundreds of unmanned interceptors emerged from the jumpgate, followed by thousands of smaller scout ships and shuttles.

At the *Predator*'s helm were Captains Behl and Zlo, working smoothly in concert. Together they took the ship on a rollercoaster ride from hell, while the crew opened fire with everything else the little ship had.

THE enormous armada's officers were supreme in their confidence, given their vastly superior numbers—but they were taken completely off-guard as the Triple-X missiles sprinted in from far too close a range for point defense, finding their targets in a vast matter/antimatter conflagration that effectively removed them from the universe. A round score of capital ships ceased to exist, and lesser explosions rocked space as the T-Star mines interpenetrated the Florencian front and spat their own deadly little missiles.

When the Supreme Commander passed out, Admiral Panmada was more than happy to take over the entire command. She shouted out orders to attack the little frigate and smash it like a bug. She already saw herself as the next Marquis of Florencia, appointed by the one true God—so she barely heard the warning from a captain that more ships were approaching at flank speed. She ordered the first attack wave to advance, not overly concerned about the little bug that surely must have been squashed by now.

The first five hundred supercruisers entered the jumpgate to implement "Operation Final Solution," marking the beginning of the end for the non-believers. Thousands of smaller ships followed.

A handful of minutes later, Admiral Panmada stared in horrified disbelief as the jumpgate suddenly swelled and ships in their thousands poured out, belying the promise of their surprise attack. She vividly pictured her own execution for being the worst-performing Admiral in Florencia's history; the Powers That Be did not take kindly to failure. In desperation, she ordered the entire armada to advance and attack. Due to a foul-up in communications, however, her order was misunderstood by most of the subordinate Admirals and ship captain at the end of the communications chain, almost half a light-minute back. None of those in the rear had any clue of what was really happening at the leading edge of the advance.

As a result, half the Florencian ships set course through the jumpgate, while the other half formed up to battle the incoming ships. The melee that ensued made both the Battle at the New Frontier and the battle that had recently erupted at the other end of the jumpgate seem like irresolute child's play.

———o○o———

STEADY amidst the confusion, Nikko Behl threaded the *Predator* through the swarms of missiles and beam-fire almost as if by instinct. A particularly close call came when they veered close to a Florencia cruiser as it left a Triton battle station's enormous docking bay. The *Predator* flew straight through station's shields, firing off several broadsides into the guts of the Triton and dropping off a T-star mine and dove straight through it, into one cavernous bay and out another. A tractor beam from the battle station easily captured the frigate as it exited after conducting its bold move, and begun pulling the *Predator* back—only to cut off when the T-star emptied its ZZ missiles into the exiting cruiser point-blank, causing it to explode while still half inside the station. A chain reaction of explosions followed, and the station began to tumble, dead in space.

The *Predator* was free again, taking off at maximum speed into open space like a cat with its tail on fire. Thousands of ships were still engaged in battle all around it, and already hundreds were either glowing hulks or fine debris scattered across the spacelanes.

Nearly half the surviving ships were engulfed in a nova-like explosion when the containment fields in the damaged Triton's matter/antimatter reactors failed.

———o○o———

ON the other side of the gate, the few hundred Nastasturan ships that had responded to the distress call from the *Crusher Five* had lined up in formation 500 kilometers away from the enlarged event horizon. Every crewman upon those ships waited with bated breath to see what the 'gate would belch forth.

Unexpectedly, nothing much happened.

Admiral Cook watched, perplexed, as the jumpgate settled down, the expanded exit irising shut without producing anything more than a multicolored spray of atomized metal and gases, which immediately began to be sucked back in by the hidden singularity. He breathed a deep sigh of relief, and looked around at the nervous faces on his command bridge. They were all as aware as he was that the now-ragged auroric display surrounding the black hole represented the remains of thousands of ships and millions of individuals. "Should we...send a SAR mission to look for survivors, sir?" a commander asked doubtfully.

Admiral Cook shook his head. "No, son, there's nothing out there to be rescued."

He stared at the dust cloud on the monitor for a long time as it dissipated, then turned and walked off the bridge, his hands clenched behind his back in an effort keep anyone from realizing they were shaking.

The probes they had sent through the exit after the other ships had darted through had confirmed Captain Copola's suspicion about the invasion—and explained all the dust particles that emerged from the exit. Apparently, that dust was what little remained of the ships from either side that had interpenetrated and annihilated each other as they attempted to transit the wormhole from opposite directions.

Hadrian Cook af Hornet prayed, as he had never prayed before, that his nephew's remains weren't included in that scattering of stardust.

———oOo———

WHAT had been intended as an inauguration of a new era, the beginning of the end for the Nastasturan non-believers, had ended an unmitigated disaster for the Florencian Federation. Thousands of the ships comprising the Grand Fleet had been lost, including one of the "invincible" Tritons, and thousands more were crippled. Worse, having expected to stabilize their economy and tighten their hold on their population by conquering the Nastasturus Federation, Florencia now faced an even more epic problem: revolution.

The many curious civilians, bounty hunters and scum in general that had survived and been captured would be enslaved and sold, of course. Some lucky few would be ransomed back to their families or organizations, assuming the funds were available. Needless to say, the pirates would either be killed outright or sent to work camps to strive for the greater glory of Florencia until their bodies failed. Even those that had worked for Florencia from time to time would be shown no leniency.

The few media ships that managed to survive the battle were eventually released. After all, Florencia needed some positive propaganda as they tried to convince the public that they had destroyed most of the pirates in the universe in one fell swoop. Why there'd been a huge fleet camped in front of the wormhole in the first place was never explained.

In the weeks to come, the two governments blamed each other for the debacle, repeating their previous, well-established patterns. Florencian spokesmen claimed that they had sent out a military fleet to intercept the pirates and nothing else. Any suggestion that the jumpgate had been vastly expanded to allow the transition of that fleet into Nastasturan space was vigorously denied. The enormous loss of civilian life was unfortunate, they explained, but not their fault; they had never invited those ships into Florencian space. The masters of those ships were responsible for placing themselves in harm's way by chasing after the pirates. But that was to be expected, since most of those ships came from capitalistic and democratic worlds, where the leadership failed to exercise the control necessary to keep the undesirable elements of their populations in check, especially when it came to space travel.

The Nastasturan government, on the other hand, was convinced that the entire pirate invasion was only a front—a diversion before the launch of the true invasion. The latter story was the one the media and the people of both Federations bought, especially when information leaked out that one of the key persons involved was neither a pirate nor a relative of Nastasturan Marshal von Hornet—

but a secret operative working for Florencia. He had even been awarded a medal before the disaster.

For a time, people forgot about Alec and his followers. The media didn't feel the story generated enough ratings. That over 75% of all the known pirates in that part of the universe had been eliminated and an invasion had been stopped was also something that quickly faded from everyone's mind, since after all there really wasn't any compelling physical evidence supporting either claim.

The primary response to all the troubles in the weeks and months that followed was an increase of trade. The truth was, over three-quarters of the pirates really were gone, and the remainder decided to maintain a low profile, at least for a while. Business was booming on all fronts...especially among the defense contractors, to their delight and joy. Of course, all the Nastasturan worlds began mobilizing, as no one with a lick of sense believed the Florencian lies. The Nastasturus Federation itself also expanded its already massive military, and all the independent worlds and the member worlds of the Federated Merchants similarly beefed up their respective military might.

Every free democratic world suspended its much hated "annual humanitarian support" to Florencia for the first time in over five centuries. In truth, it was more a bribe or tribute than support, something Florencia had long demanded lest they saw fit to just take what they needed. The planetary governments hated the very idea, and they hid it from their populations, but paying the Florencian thugs their protection money was much cheaper than a war.

This was, according to the Florencia elite and their "charitable relief organizations," a conspiracy against God and His followers, and it only added fuel to the fire. The only support Florencia had now was from the Commercial Traders, but even that support begun to falter. Many of their representatives and insurance agents complained that the contractors captured during the battles were honest traders, and demanded for their release.

Ultimately, when the Florencia government realized that they wouldn't receive their annual tribute and would, therefore, be unable to feed their people, they too began to remobilize.

DURING the course of one long, tense day, the *Predator* managed to make four jumpgate passages. Meanwhile, Alec kept the crew busy constructing and attaching to the ship another radar decoy, smaller than the first but hopefully just as effective. The exterior work was difficult and dangerous, so Behl reprogrammed the autopilots on six of the single-man fighters and stationed them above, below, behind and in front of the Predator, to act as flankers. With their warning radars combined with the *Predator*'s, he managed to increase the resolution of that warning system significantly. The small fighters couldn't be seen with the naked eye from the frigate, but each ship was followed via separate monitors on the command bridge, and operated remotely as necessary. Alexa, Nina, Tara, Zicci, Kirra, Miska, and Mohama took turns with Behl operating the fighters, two at a time. If worse came to worst, the fighters would also serve as a first line of defense.

A third of the crew worked on repairs, while another third ran the ship itself. The remainder remained at battle stations. The crew's mood was tense and nervous. Their casualties so far had been minimal, thank Gull, and the more seriously injured crew were healing just fine in the infirmary.

Hours turned into days, and as the time slithered past, the crew's bad mood morphed into a more spirited demeanor; it had taken time to soak in, but they had realized that their chances of surviving had increased, and that each of them had just made history. Stories of the various events and perspectives they had experienced were exchanged, and one of the larger briefing rooms became a gathering place were the crew came together to watch the video and sensor recordings of the various engagements. There was always an eerie silence when they watched the moon-sized Florencian battle station explode.

Alec finally confronted Frances and Captain Zlo about the secret message that had been sent before the battle, and both men opined that it would be best to arrest the individual responsible for treason moments before they docked at a safe location. In the meantime, they would follow the traitor round the clock with help of the ship's surveillance equipment. Frances volunteered to take charge of this task; after all, he was the chief of security. Both Zlo and Frances understood why Alec had used the "Captain's Privilege" when he'd put everyone to sleep back on the asteroid; but when he finally let them view the recording of the ensuing battle, they were disturbed when they realized that Alec had taken on three enemy ships alone. When they asked Alec what he had done during the three days he was gone shortly thereafter, he just answered that it was private and laughed it off.

Captain Zlo brought up the subject of Lieutenant Beck's insubordination, and insisted that Alec have his arms cloned back and remand him to Zlo's custody. Zlo knew the lieutenant's parents, and had hired him for the original mission with Lady Fuzza—and he didn't want the young officer to end up in a prison back on Marengo. Frances didn't like the idea, insisting that once a mutineer, always a mutineer, and that Beck could never be trusted again. It wouldn't be right if he got away with his actions; it could erode the discipline and morale among the rest of the crew if they saw how easily they could turn against their officers.

"I'll make an official report of his actions in my personal log," Alec decided, after thinking it over. "If he returns to work on the lower decks and behaves, then I might consider not reporting his actions to the ship's log. But he will never set foot on the bridge again, and you're responsible for him at all times."

Captain Zlo seemed relieved, nodding in understanding. Frances peered suspiciously at Zlo. "We'll be in a safe port any day now, hopefully," Alec commented when he noticed the monk's reaction.

"What will happen to my ship then?" Zlo asked.

"It's all yours again, Captain, once we've finished out the contract."

"You want to run the full year?"

"Not anymore. Well, at least not with this crew; there's too much tension. I'll pay everyone off according to the contract, and give the crew a generous bonus. Well...except for the traitor. That's the main reason I called this meeting, actually." Alec nodded toward

HUNTED | 249

the traitor's image on the viewscreen. "And as for you, Frances, and your fellow Grisamm: I've had my doubts, but I must admit that I'm very impressed with your services, and will give you and your troops whatever you want if it's within my grasp."

Frances gave Alec an interested look and said simply, "All we ask for is some of your time, someday."

Alec nodded and said, "I'll still throw in a nice monetary bonus for all of you, though."

After the meeting, Alec returned to the bridge with Captain Zlo. Zlo was just about seat himself in the main command chair—normally Alec's place—when he stopped and looked over at Alec questioningly. Alexa was curled up on the chair, fast asleep. Smirking, Alec walked up to her and lifted her gently. She whispered something unheard in his ear as she let him carry her away.

He took her to his suite. He was tired of thinking about her. He didn't know if he still loved her, or hated her; maybe both at once, it was very confusing. Once inside, he lay her down on the bed and put a blanket over her. He removed first her boots and his own, then lay down next to her, spooning her as he fell into a sound asleep.

―――――◦○◦―――――

THE loud bray of the General Quarters alarm sounded, coupled with the synthetic voice urging the *Predator*'s crew to stand to, followed by Captain Zlo's voice warning, "We are under attack. Stand to all battle stations."

A series of shudders and a distant explosion jerked them both to their feet. Alec gave Alexa a quick pat on her cheek before they dashed into the corridor and ran to the command bridge. Alexa hurried over to the area behind Behl, where the other girls had gathered and taken control of the remote-controlled fighters. Zlo had already left the command chair and sat next to Behl; be initiated evasive maneuvers, the ship's hull groaning with stress. Alec stifled his initial response, which was to head for the CBR; but the truth was, they had none of the illegal weapons left, neither Nastasturan nor Florencian. He strapped himself to the command seat and immersed himself in the situation.

He recognized the attacking ship. It was the *Bitch*.

The destroyer opened up with all her weapons, attacking the *Predator* from below, achieving several good hits on the frigate's shields as it passed. When it reached a safe distance above, it spun on its gyros and attacked again, falling down towards the top of the *Predator*. This time the *Predator* turned away from *Bitch* and fired a broadside with all its available weapons; it then made a fast turn to starboard, rolling on its long axis, and fired another broadside.

When the *Bitch* came back for another hit-and-run attack, the *Predator* was waiting. Alec sent a dozen sprinter missiles at the *Bitch*, point-blank; the *Bitch* responded in kind. Both ships took damage, some severe; debris and crew spewed from gaping holes in both ships as atmosphere blasted into space. Hordes of maintenance droids converged on the damage, and many were themselves damaged and destroyed as they attempted to make repairs. Force shields flickered in the gaps in the hulls, except in those cases where the systems for creating those fields had themselves been destroyed.

The *Bitch* launched three shuttles from one of its bays, and sent an army of two hundred armored fighters armed with jetpacks and weapons toward the *Predator* as it rushed the frigate. The pirate captain didn't give a damn how many were lost as the *Predator* picked them off, one by one; he had crew to spare, and their lives meant little to him. They were followed by as many battle andies. A battering ram, crowded with hundreds more pirates, unfolded from the *Bitch*'s bow, ready to penetrate the *Predator* and start the rape.

The half-dozen fighters controlled from the *Predator*'s bridge darted into the attacking swarm of astronauts and androids, cutting many to pieces with their blaster fire. They were met by twice as many fighters launched from the *Bitch*. The fighting intensified, and the primary weapons of both ships stopped firing as they closed on one another.

"MOVE it, you bastards!" Myra bellowed. Clad in battle gear, she ran down her gun deck, shouting out orders and instructions; and from time to time, she let out a horrible laugh.

"Time to earn your pay, lads," Wolf encouraged. He stood on the opposite gun deck, making sure all his gun crews maintained their rate of fire.

Finally, the words everyone expected but dreaded echoed from the intercom system: "Stand by to repel boarders! Level four, section fifteen!"

"What are you waiting for, my lovelies? Let's join the fun!" Nadia shouted, ordering every third gun crew to follow.

Back on the command bridge, Behl gestured at the girls and growled, "This is shit. You vixens follow me. Let's go."

They looked hesitantly at Alec, waiting for his consent. "Where are you going?" he asked the captain.

"General, we've lost all our remote fighters, all right? We didn't stand a chance against theirs, remote-controlled or not. But we still have eight fighters left. The vixens and I can easily take out their remote fighters and assist you better out there," he pointed toward the battle, "than we can in here—unless you want us down there?" Behl pointed at the crew who were preparing to meet the borders.

Alec looked at Alexa, noting her calm behavior and excited eyes. All her friends, "the Vixens," had similar strange expressions, like dangerous animals ready to be unleashed on their prey. *I'm not going to lose you,* he thought, then looked away from Alexa and stared at Behl. He nodded, and the girls took off like they were about to go shopping with no spending limit.

Alec motioned for Behl to approach, and whispered, "Should we not do well here today, gather the Vixens together and head off in some random direction. That way, they'll have a chance at a normal life. Promise me that." Behl looked at Alec and nodded, expressionless. "Here, take this." Alec handed him a debit card, and Behl started to protest. "Just in case, Nikko. There's enough there to set you and them up for generations...as long as they don't go shopping too often. Now go and give 'em hell."

He flinched at the shuddering crash of the *Bitch*'s boarding arm, the familiarity of it sending chills down his spine.

Frances led a large group of his fellow monks and former pirates toward the location where the *Bitch*'s boarding arm was battering its way through the hull. He and his crew were dressed in battle armor, helmets already affixed. Fighting in space between ships was one thing; close combat melees, in a ship that might lose atmosphere at any time, was another.

Displaying a frightening calm while inspecting the troops, Frances mused over the command frequency, "They expect us to fight with desperation, people. Ha! Just remain calm, and wait for the pressure change as the boarding arm penetrates. Remember the drill: they will not expect what we'll do, so take advantage of their surprise and destroy anyone who doesn't belong here."

"Hurry up, lassies and bastards, hurry up!" another voice ground out over the command freq.

"There you are, Myra. I thought you had forgotten about us."

Myra's voice echoed in Frances' earpiece, "Forgot, my ass! I have a couple of legs to collect from my former ship's master, and I intend to get them with interest. Maybe an arm or two."

"Why not just the head?" Pier muttered, as he checked his weapons. The crew looked at their commanders in astonishment at their cruel jokes; some of them even tried to laugh.

EIGHT single-person fighters exited the *Predator* from a bay astern, and formed up in preparation for entering the fight. Captain Zlo's voice echoed through their earbugs. "Brown, are you ready?" he asked.

"Standing by, Cap, standing by."

"Crew commanders, match freqs with your crews and stand by. Report when ready." Zlo listened as the reports came in; and when the last crew commander sent her signal, he looked over at Alec. "We are ready, sir."

Alec leaned forward and gave his final order: "By the numbers, people. No prisoners."

His orders were met with cheers, and he felt a surge of pride at having gathered such a splendid crew. Then he dismissed any extraneous thoughts and peered into the holomonitor before him; it displayed the locations of his seven remaining battle andies. On an adjoining monitor were the traces of over thirty smaller battle droids. He looked up and nodded towards Zlo, and the two officers in charge over the androids.

Alec knew the pirates probably had far more experience overall in space fighting, but they were also used to easy prey who surrendered immediately or, at best, after a brief resistance. Not this time; the pirates would have to earn their booty. The information Myra and Alexa had provided about Zuzack's tactics gave Alec and his crew some advantage, if not much.

The three pirate shuttles approached from different directions, two heading for docking bays and one for the largest cargo bay. One of the smaller battle droids managed to get inside one shuttle's defenses; another followed, both slamming into the shuttle in a one-two punch that left a drifting, lifeless hulk, spewing atmosphere and body parts.

"That's one," Nikko Behl called over the fighter command freq. "Two more to go. Get to work, Vixens, and stay in formation." Behl and his Vixens roared off into the fight and began engaging the *Bitch*'s unmanned fighters, destroying them one by satisfying one.

———————o○o———————

THE boarding arm finally breached the *Predator*'s armor, making short work of the hull itself. The pointed end spread open like a blooming flower, and out poured hundreds of pirates, firing in every direction.

Alec was observing the situation from a large holomonitor on the bridge. "Now," he ordered, as the stream of pirates exiting the boarding arm slowed to a trickle. "Destroy the boarding arm."

Zlo shot Alec a dry smile, nodding.

The pirates were taken by surprise when they encountered two hundred of the *Predator*'s crew, who immediately began mowing them down with laser and blaster fire. There was a sudden pressure drop as gravity let loose and a number of redeployed pressor fields twisted the boarding arm into scrap metal, crushing anyone left inside. The few hundred pirates that had been allowed into the *Predator* were killed one by one by the *Predator*'s crew, efficiently and relentlessly. Myra charged into battle with a huge blade, slicing off body parts as her payment; Wolf emptied his blaster and shifted to his battle-ax, the traditional weapon of his people. Frances worked like a skilled surgeon as he killed pirate after pirate; with two other Grisamm monks by his side, they set a perfect example for the entire crew.

"Duck!"

Frances heard Myra's warning immediately before an explosion behind him sent him crashing into a wall. Behind him were two parts of a large exotic, both still twitching as they floated in zero-g. A warning signal sounded from the speakers, and the gravity came back. The *Predator*'s crew had attached themselves to various holdfasts, but the pirates—those who were left—hit the deck hard in a grisly shower of blood and body parts. The melee turned fierce as the desperate pirates tried to fight their way out of the ambush.

Metal shrieked as a second boarding arm penetrated the hull, sucking several pirates and crew out into space as it ripped open the bulkheads. Thick foam splashed out onto the edges of the gaping hole and immediately hardened, sealing in the atmosphere. A new flood of pirates poured into the *Predator*, and the melee turned into a true slaughter. Two of the larger battle andies joined the fighting; but their discrimination circuits were not of the highest quality, and they killed several of the *Predator*'s crew members along with a slew of pirates.

The surviving pirates with jetpacks who had initiated the melee in space arrived, attaching themselves to the *Predator*'s hull. After a few moments of frenzied effort, they managed to blast open several hatches, and some of them followed one of the surviving shuttles into a landing bay. Hundreds more pirates poured out of the shuttle and into the fray. Unexpectedly, the gravity in the bays increased a hundredfold, crushing them into flat smears on the deck. The shuttle was smashed like a tin can stepped on by a giant; as gravity normalized, pressor fields grabbed it and hurled it contemptuously into space. The remains slammed into the *Bitch* amidships.

The third shuttle latched onto a docking arm next to the smaller docking bay, its commander either being smarter or luckier than his predecessors. The pirates that spilled out into the *Predator*, however, were met by two large battle androids—and very few of them could be described as lucky at all.

Nina's and Tara's fighter flashed past the docked shuttle, raking it with light blaster fire but avoiding the engines; it wouldn't do for the shuttle to explode this close to the frigate. Several pressure-suited pirates returned fire as they came back around, but Alexa arrived on the scene to blow most of them to organic slag with her magma gun. The handful who survived beat a hasty retreat. Behl ordered his Vixens to form up in diamond formation, and then they accelerated at full throttle against the smaller cannons on the *Bitch*.

Meanwhile, Brown and fifty-odd crewmembers in battle armor and jetpacks exited the *Predator* and began engaging individual pirates.

———————oOo———————

"**SHIT!** They have one more ram," Alec muttered.

"Myra and the others assured us he only had one main battle ram, with two minor backups," Captain Zlo protested, but he couldn't deny the evidence of his own eyes.

"Yes. Myra. Well, Captain, take the conn for now." He gestured at a squad of crewmembers who waited nearby. "Bax, leave thirty reliable people secure the bridge. You and the rest, come with me."

"Aye, sir." In moments, Bax had his troops sorted out, and he and twenty other crew were dashing through the passages of the ship behind Alec. Wisps of smoke had begun filling those passages, never a good sign. Along the way, they encountered several groups of pirates engaged with their own crew and the smaller, hovering battle droids. They assisted them, and made short work of the pirates. They merged the groups of surviving *Predator* crew with theirs, and their numbers increased steadily as they proceeded. Two battle andies took up the lead, and two followed behind; but by the time reached the area where the second battle ram was expected to come through, it was too late to stop it. The hull was already pierced, and the pirates were pouring through the arm in their scores and hundreds.

The hovering battle droids up front were immediately cut to pieces by several of the pirates' own droids; those, in turn, were dispatched in moments by one of the larger Nastasturan andies, which emerged from a hatch overhead like some gargantuan metallic black spider. It happened so fast that when the android dropped down amidst the pirates, they didn't quite understand what had happened yet, and were caught entirely off guard. It went to work on its grisly task.

Alec had heard that once, early in the history of his species, there had been laws built into robots and androids to keep them from harming Omans...but those days were long past, thank Gull.

Alec, Bax, and their surviving fighters found themselves outside the galley, where it was clear that a pitched battle was already underway. Chef Latoff was outraged by the sacrilege of pirates raiding her kitchen, and she and her crew were fighting a score of the heretics with everything at hand. Latoff herself swung an enormous meat cleaver as effectively as any battle ax, and her curses were more terrible even than the multicolored blood that dripped from her makeshift weapon. The big exotic had taken several serious wounds that oozed dark red ichor.

Alec shouted wordlessly as he emptied the last of his blaster charge at two pirates nearly as large as Zuzack. He crunched the now-useless weapon into the skull of another pirate, then yanked his side blasters out of their holsters and dropped the pirates as fast as he could pull the triggers. They'd told him at the Academy that it was almost impossible to use two guns effectively, but he'd proved them wrong before, and here he was doing it again. When one of the guns was emptied, he holstered it—no time to reload now—and pulled out a knife, slashing with one hand as he shot pirates with the other.

Something struck him and slammed him up against a bulkhead, and Alec was horrified to realize that he'd been immobilized by the sticky web of a Tilter dog. Bax ran to his aid; when another Tilter fired off its web, the big Grisamm responded with a cloud of moist smoke from a small gun in his left hand. The sticky web dissolved in midair and splattered to the deck as coin-sized drops, a mess that would surely piss Latoff off even more when she learned of it. The Tilter was smart enough to realize that its primary weapon had been nullified; it jumped at Bax, fang-filled mouth spread wide. Bax cut it in half with a magma blast, then dissolved the web that held Alec in place. By then, it was all over: the pirates had all died or retreated, and Latoff was already howling her outrage at the incredible mess they'd left behind.

———————○O○———————

"WE'RE all done here," Frances reported to Captain Zlo from the outer passageway, after mopping up the remaining pirates from the failed first shuttle landing.

"Assist in the galley section," Zlo ordered. "They had two boarding rams penetrate the hull in that region. Hurry."

Frances acknowledged and turned his attention to his troops. "Nadia, you and your squad remain here with a couple of them." Frances pointed at the hovering battle androids. "Wolf, you will take your group and attack from the back of the galley, while Myra and I get the main entrance. Brown, take your group and those two," he pointed at two of the large andies, "and hunt down any pirate that might have made it through."

With a chorus of "Yessirs" and "Aye ayes," the groups took off in their various directions.

When Frances and his group reached the melee at the second battering ram, they joined in with a raging appetite. By then, the battle was taking an ugly turn toward the worse as more and more pirates entered the *Predator*...including a hulking form in a gray battle-suit. "I have you in my sight, thief!" Zuzack bellowed, pointing his long sword at Alec as the young man exited the galley.

"And I have your *face*!" Alec shouted back.

Insane hatred filled Zuzack's eyes, and he charged Alec like the berserker he was. Alec met him halfway, swinging the cutlass he'd taken off a dead pirate to replace his broken knife. He realized that without an energy or projectile weapon, he was no match for the enormous exotic facing him, so he looked around hurriedly for a better position to fight him from.

They crashed together, blades throwing sparks, and bounced apart. Zuzack took advantage of the respite to flip up the visor of his battlesuit, revealing his scarred and battered visage. "Uglier than ever, I see," Alec taunted.

Zuzack's fury was nearly incandescent. He leaped at Alec, bellowing incoherently—only to be intercepted by a massive fist belonging to Myra.

"You!" Zuzack roared. "You're here, too?"

"You bet!" she shouted merrily.

Myra then screamed an eerie battle cry as her group and Frances' reinforced Alec's, and the odd cry gave them all a new surge of energy. They howled like mad in response as they cut the pirates down. Zuzack, overwhelmed, slipped on the slick deck as he went at Alec, who took the opportunity to slice at Zuzack's chest with all his strength. Zuzack rolled away from Alec's attack, but the blade lopped off his left arm at the elbow. Screeching in horrified pain, Zuzack barely managed to block with a blade that snicked out from the sleeve of his bloody half-arm. With the unexpected strength of pain and fear, he managed to roll onto his feet as a pair of fellow pirates covered his retreat, clutching his stump with his right hand as dark blood gushed through his fingers.

Alec picked up Zuzack's left hand and held it high over his head as blood dribbled down onto his face. Looking the perfect picture of a madman, he screamed, "First I took your face, and now I have your hand! Come back, Zuzack, so that I can add to my collection!"

Myra thought that was one of the funniest things she'd ever heard; laughing her head off, she joined with Alec as they hacked a bloody path through the pirates. When the pirates saw their injured captain escorted away through the ramming arm, their courage began to falter...and soon enough, most of them decided that discretion was the better part of valor, and began a sloppy withdrawal.

Wolf and his group finally arrived, and started picking off and killing any stragglers they could find.

"Zlo! Intensify the galley deck hull shield!" Alec ordered, when he realized that the ram was being pulled back into the *Bitch*'s hull. But it was too late; Alec slammed down his visor and most of his crew did the same as they activated the magnets on their boots, but not everyone could react so fast. Nearly twenty of his crew were sucked out into space before they could drop their own visors, and most of those were dead of explosive decompression in seconds.

An orange glow flashed into place over the gaping hole as a pressure door slammed shut behind them, protecting the rest of the ship from loss of atmosphere. Alec looked sadly at the body of Latoff, her face a crystalline blue from the lack of oxygen that had killed her. Damn, she'd been a good person.

Captain Zlo's voice came through his earbug: "They're retreating, sir. Shall we pursue?"

"No," Alec said tiredly. "Not today. We need to launch a SAR mission into near space, to see if any of our crew are alive out there. Call back our fighters, have them re-arm, and maintain a close watch while we start doing repairs—just in case the bastard returns."

"We have only three fighters left," Zlo said quietly.

Alec felt as though a mailed fist had crushed his heart when he heard that news, and all he could think was, *Alexa*. He came to himself when Frances shook him and shouted, "Wake up, sir! Your orders?"

He shook his head to clear it and snapped, "Follow standard protocol and secure the ship. Tend to the injured and get them to sickbay. Bax, make sure none of these shitheads are still aboard, and if you find any, don't bother taking prisoners. I'll be on the bridge."

Bax made as if to follow Alec. Alec looked at him, eyes hard, and said, "I can make it myself, dammit. Just take ten soldiers and a few androids and sweep the ship for intruders."

As he stalked through the ship, heart in his throat, Alec realized that the *Predator*'s interior décor had changed rather thoroughly. There wasn't a passageway, it seemed, that wasn't stained with blood or decorated with body parts or corpses. Bulkheads were scored, scorched, and smashed; hatches were blown all over the ship, both interior and exterior, and broken furniture littered the way. The olfactory landscape was worse: the stink of blood, spilled viscera and burnt flesh filled the entire ship.

He encountered damage control teams fighting several small fires with the help of maintenance droids. One fire proved too large to handle; he ordered the area evacuated and sealed off, then opened to space to kill the flames. Teams were already suiting up to repair the hold from outside, while others picked up the pieces on the inside. He found the sick bay to be overcrowded, and ordered two adjacent storage rooms converted to medical facilities.

He was absurdly relieved when he finally entered the bridge and heard his Alexa's laughter echoing over an intercom as she brought the surviving fighters in for a landing at the rearmost bay. Somehow, despite the loss of their fighters, she and all the other Vixens had managed to survive: on the monitor feed, he saw disabled fighters containing Nina, Mohama, Miska, Tara and Zicci being dragged inside by tractor beams from Alexa's ship, while Behl and Kirra flew nearby as their escorts.

The Chief's report drew away his attention, and it couldn't have come at a worse time, as far as Alec was concerned. "The ship has had enough," the exotic reported. "Either we dock on an asteroid or moon somewhere and piece this jigsaw back together ourselves, General, or we'll have to find some friendly world with a spacedock to do it for us. I'd recommend a colonial world. Most of them are neutral or unaligned."

"Is it as bad as all that?"

Chief glared at Alec and rolled her eyes. "Aye, sir, it's that bad. We have to do some major repairs or we'll not make it more than another dozen parsecs."

"I'd hate for us to be stranded on some world while the repairs are carried out." He glanced at Zlo, who nodded his agreement. "Can we make her somewhat operational, and..."

"Sir, if she holds on for another three days, I'll be damned surprised. We can cruise at an average speed with our shields at minimum, but if we get into another fight, we've had it. It's as simple as that. We need to put down somewhere and use the two larger shuttles to go out and find us some spare parts and raw materials."

"That's an option," Alec agreed, "but we only have one that's functional. I'm afraid the other is toast, unless you can repair it."

The Chief said tiredly, "I'll see what I can do."

"*If* we can find a place to hide," Frances reminded everyone.

"Let's see what Stellar Cartography can offer us. Captain Zlo, with me; the rest of you return to your stations."

―――――⸺oOo⸺―――――

FRANCES and Doctor Phalaxor both looked grave as they sat down at the conference table an hour later. Alec knew what they were about to report, and he dreaded having to ask, "What are the casualties?"

Frances looked at Phalaxor, who only nodded. He faced Alec and said, "Two hundred and eighty three dead, and 75 wounded."

"You can add another 30 dead by the end of the day," Phalaxor said dryly.

There was silence in the room for a long moment, then: "That's over half our crew!" Captain Zlo burst out.

"It is indeed," said Frances. "But they acquitted themselves well. We have counted 597 dead pirates onboard, more or less, but I would estimate they lost twice that number or more."

Alec turned his chair and looked at Alexa, who sat behind him. "How many pirates did you say he had?"

"Standard crew is four to six hundred, and the soldiers can number anywhere from one to three thousand."

"Isn't that a bit much for a ship like that?" Zlo asked, looking puzzled.

"No, I'm afraid not."

Alec tapped his fingers on the conference table. "Will he attack us again?"

Alexa thought for a while before replying, "Well...yes and no. He *will* eventually attack, but not until he's licked his wounds and replenished his forces. And when that happens, he'll attack us himself. Zuzack will never let someone else lead any engagement. He doesn't trust anyone enough."

Alec looked at Phalaxor and asked, "How long will it take him to either clone or stim his hand and forearm?"

"It depends. If his ship is equipped with the latest medical equipment, it'll take a week or two. If he has some cloned body parts on hand already, less than that." He glanced at Alexa.

"He doesn't have any spare parts that I know of," she said. "Most pirates accept their battle scars with pride. But he does have the resources to clone parts, so I think he'll clone his hand and have the new one attached before he tries again."

"How long will that be?" Frances wanted to know.

"Sir, I don't know. Perhaps a standard week if he can force-grow a cloned arm, or maybe ten days. Less if he has cloned body parts on hand; he might even not bother with replacing the hand if he can be reinforced immediately." The room went silent, and Alexa cleared her throat before continuing. "However, he's suffered unusually high casualties, and I doubt he'll return soon. If he tries, his crew will demand an explanation of why they should engage us again, when there are so many easier targets out there."

Captain Zlo looked at Alec. "Interesting point. Why *are* he and the rest of the universe so interested in us?"

Alec pretended he hadn't heard the question, and Alexa came to the rescue: "Revenge, I think. Zuzack never forgets or forgives."

"All this for revenge? I highly doubt that." Captain Zlo didn't bother to hide his frustration and disbelief.

"Well, Alec did take the guy's face," Alexa pointed out.

Captain Zlo looked baffled. "He *what*?"

"After he escaped and rescued Captain Behl, Alec caught Zuzack and, well, peeled off his entire face and scalp before they took off."

Frances smiled grimly, but the doctor and Zlo stared at Alec and Behl, aghast. Behl rolled his eyes and studied his nails. "Don't look at me," he muttered.

"Souvenir," Alec said flatly.

"Made good decorations for your boots, though," Behl observed.

Alec nodded. "Pretty good belt, too."

Frances lay his head down on the table, cushioned on his forearms, but his shaking shoulders betrayed his effort not to laugh. Captain Zlo demanded, "You're telling me that all this is because you *scalped* him?"

"Well, Captain, I don't know about all this other crap with the New Frontier colony," he said, neatly avoiding the truth. "I don't know what that was all about." True, he didn't know for a *fact* why all the fighting had taken place…whether it was because his actions, or something bigger he had taken away when he'd escaped. A certain map, for example. "I do think this pirate wants revenge," he continued, "and frankly, so do I. He's the bastard we were supposed to find in the first place. He found us instead—that's just what Tota and I had planned in the beginning, and I'm sorry as hell we can't go after him."

Frances sat up and said, "Well, at least we gave him a good licking. Perhaps we should move on to something more urgent." Most people in the room agreed, though some of them looked hesitant and doubtful after having heard this latest information.

Alec, Zlo, Behl and Frances adjourned to the Stellar Cartography lab, where they stood on a platform next a computer counsel and looked over a three-dimensional image of the local galactic sector. Each held a wireless joystick device, occasionally tweaking the image as they went over different options.

"As I see it, we have few choices here. Captain Behl, which do you see as the best?"

"This one is the best of a bad lot," he said, zooming in on a hot yellow star and then a particular planet, a blue-white water world. "This is the Colar system. One inhabited colonial world, completely non-allied. Just two jumpgates away…but normally, I wouldn't go there if my life depended on it."

"Why not?"

"Well, Zlo, it's a safe haven for criminals and pirates. We've had enough of both, haven't we?"

"Only two 'gates away? They could be all over us in no time."

"Relax. The nearest jumpgate is a one-way transit. It would take over a week for anyone in that system to get here from there." Behl made a few adjustments with his joystick, displaying a new system. "Gentlar. This system is Florencian. No go."

"What else do we have?" Alec asked.

"There's a medium-sized trading station located at Tyndall Forge, a small moon in Tyndall system. About thirty thousand inhabitants, but I think that's where our hairless buddy went. You can follow his trail here." Behl pointed at the map, which showed a diffuse hydrogen ion trail headed toward the Tyndall jumpgate. "We must have damaged his fuel cells, and pretty good at that...maybe we don't have to worry so much about Zuzack."

"Unless it's just a decoy," Frances suggested.

"You're right; it could very well be a decoy. But still, the trail leads to the nearest spacedock." Alec made paused briefly and looked over the three-dimensional holographic map. "What about this system? It's uncharted, but..."

"No, not that system," Frances interrupted.

"Why not?"

Frances looked at Captain Zlo, who obviously agreed with Frances, and then on to Behl. He nodded. "What?" Alec demanded.

"If you had a few more years under your belt, General, you'd know that there several systems no one ever enters. They're not forbidden, but they *are* more or less taboo."

Frances' explanation made Alec more curious. "Why?"

"To make a long story short, sir, no one ever comes back when they do. They might be home to extremely advanced societies that don't like being bothered, or home to some natural phenomena that destroy the ships that enter the systems."

"Well, what about this one, the Labosk system?"

"That's an option," Zlo said. "They're a colony world inhabited by many different species, including the ones all of us here belong to. What do you think, Nikko?"

"You're right; I didn't count that one in. It'll take two weeks to get there, maybe longer."

Captain Zlo looked eager. "Yes, but only a few days to get back, given the jumpgate configuration."

"I can go."

Every one turned around, and saw Alexa standing behind them. "This is a closed meeting."

Alexa disregarded Frances' protest and continued. "I can go to the Sakyyr system and get help. It's only a few days there and back, and I'll bet it's where Zuzack went. It's also a colony world, mostly farmers and service companies. They're non-allied, or so I think."

"Never heard of a system called Sakyyr," Behl muttered he worked the computer.

Alexa stepped up next to him, and gently took Behl's joystick. She worked it with a fast and steady hand, and within a few seconds had homed in on a binary system. "Here it is."

"How did you know about it, from where we are now?" Alec asked.

"I've been in these parts before, and I happen to know that there are several jumpgates nearby that you don't even have on your charts. Use this instead." Alexa gave Alec a memory stick, and after checking it for viruses with his wristcomp, he slid it into a receptacle on the holoimager. The image flickered, and several additional jumpgates appeared.

"Where did you get that?" he asked suspiciously.

"From under our bed," she said innocently. "Didn't you know it was among the loot you took from Zuzack?" Alec looked at her, eyes wide, inwardly terrified—not because she'd found his secret compartment, but for the trap that had been activated in the event someone tried to access the computer. Apparently, she had managed to evade it.

He blinked, and felt a wave of admiration for the woman standing next to him.

"Wonderful!" Captain Zlo said enthusiastically. "We can be there and back in less than a week!"

"All we need to do now is figure out a way to hide the ship," Alec agreed.

Alexa moved the joystick with an experienced hand, and every man in the room grinned.

"What are you... Assholes! *Men!*" Her lips curled in a smirk. "At least this one has buttons."

Alec tapped a cloud of dots in the outer Sakyyr system. "If we can get to this asteroid belt, we can easily hide the *Predator*."

Captain Zlo said, "Ha! That's where I would look for us first."

Alec shrugged. "Zuzack doesn't know about our predicament, and he surely won't tell anyone—he wants us to himself. Even if he followed us there it might take him forever to find us, and even if he were to find us, he would never engage us inside the asteroid belt. It's much denser than most. The people we select to get the spare parts can also send a message to Tota while they're in the system. It won't be suspicious if we send one to him from there, and he can get a ship out here within another week or two."

"And he will do this?" Behl asked.

Frances nodded. "There is more to little Tota than you think, my friend. He will probably fly out here himself. Alec has made a lasting impression on him, or my crew and I wouldn't be here."

Alec smiled and ordered, "Let's do it."

―――――oOo―――――

BEHL sat at navigation, Alexa next to him; they were laughing and whispering over something. At the back sat Alec and Frances; six more Grisamm monks were spread out throughout the shuttle, which Frances had christened *Dargu*. One fighter flew in escort, with Nina at the helm. As necessary, the fighter could dock atop or below the shuttle.

Alec listened intently to Frances as he lectured about his order. After the battle against the pirates, Alec finally felt closer to and more trusting of his crew, especially the Grisamm members of it; they had proven themselves.

The shuttle accelerated at full throttle, leaving the *Predator* in its wake. The *Predator*, in turn, cruised towards the asteroid belt in the far distance.

Little did Alec know that he would never see the *Predator* again.

NINE

"**UNDER** Galactic and Intergalactic law, I, Captain ik-lin Zlo heffar, hereby arrest you for treason against the ship's owner and conspiracy to take over this ship. Take her away."

Zlo wiped a droplet of blood from his forehead, and he looked sadly on the three dead crewmembers. If it hadn't been for the two Grisamm monks, he would be dead.

With help from a battle android and three security guards, Myra was hauled down to Cargo Bay F. She was too big for either of the slave blocks, so a special electromagnetic field enclosure had been erected. The guards and the androids placed her inside and shackled her wrist and ankles to the wall. Myra, who was unconscious, slept like a baby through the whole process.

A few hours later, Captain Zlo visited Myra to begin her interrogation. When he entered the bay and stood outside her enclosure, the large woman rolled her eyes and observed him with little or no interest. She tapped the shield surrounding her, and cursed as it sizzled, burning her fingers. "This is how you reward your crew, is it?" she snarled.

"Give it up, Myra, you got caught in the act. We've got records of you transmitting."

She shrugged. "Girl gotta do what a girl gotta do."

"I bet you do. Does that include getting half your fellow crew members killed?"

Myra looked puzzled for a moment; then she raised her eyebrows. "Oh, you mean our last little fight. I had nothing to do with that."

"Bullshit you didn't. You told Zuzack exactly where to find us."

"He may have intercepted my transmission," she replied evenly, "but it was never meant for him." She lifted her head proudly. "Is there any point in me trying to justify my actions? I'm still doomed, aren't I?"

"No one will judge you here. You did help defend the ship during the pirate attack, and Alec is also very grateful that you saved his life."

"Saved his life? Hardly. I was just making sure he didn't take the pleasure of killing my old nemesis away from me. I have a score to settle with the ugly bastard. By the way, where *is* young master Alec?"

Captain Zlo tried to get himself comfortable as he sat down on a crate. He put a clipcomp and light pen on his lap, ready to take notes. "He couldn't make it. Perhaps he'll drop by later. So: if you didn't betray us so that Zuzack might find and capture us, then what?"

Myra looked at Captain Zlo tiredly, "Oh, come now. Don't be a fool. You and Alec have been talking about all of us gaining our freedom, and moving on with our lives after we're done here. What freedom would that be, pray? There are too many warrants and bounties out on me, pretty much everywhere. I will never be forgiven or forgotten. I doubt even young master Alec, with all his connections, could get me off the hook."

Zlo nodded. "I suspect you're right. We were going to let you go anyway, and give you a chance to take off."

"To do what? Find a mating partner and have babies and grow old?"

"Something like that, perhaps."

"Captain, we're both mature, experienced people of the universe. You know as well as I do that it would never happened. We two are just alike; the call of the universe is too strong. This is where I belong—well, perhaps not locked up, but definitely in space."

"We are nothing alike, you and I," Zlo snapped. "You plunder and steal, while I work for my living. But enough of that: if you weren't contacting Zuzack, then who?"

"Ogstafa is a fellow sister. All I wanted to do was take an escape pod and have her pick me up."

Captain Zlo noticed something in Myra's eyes. He had expected to hear only lies...but somehow he knew she had told the truth. Part of it, at least. But she had kept something out; perhaps she was lying about something. He interrupted: "Ogstafa is your sister?"

"Ha! No, not like a family sister, but a fellow pirate sister. We share some of the same bloodlines, perhaps, be we're not closely related. Yet we do belong to the same sisterhood, if you will. I had no idea anyone had intercepted the message, if that was in fact the case. Had I known that could happen, then I would have been more careful. I don't want to die in this tin can any more than you do."

Zlo scowled. "What were you doing with Zuzack in the first place, if you despise him so much?"

"I was supposed to get close to Ogstafa's biggest adversary and kill him."

"Zuzack?"

She snorted. "That pig? No, his brother Horsa—but what's it to you? He probably died when that Triton station blew. Ha, I'll bet you and Alec have pissed off the Florencian Federation. Good on you."

Captain Zlo was beginning to believe Myra...and the lie detector app on his clipcomp indicated that she was telling the truth, at least as she knew it. He made several notes, and began speaking to Myra in a friendlier tone. His intention was to milk her of as much information as he possible could, and from time to time he was surprised just how cooperative the big exotic was.

He had to be honest, though, when she asked him what was likely to become of her, now that her plans lay in ruins. "Personally I believe you should be locked up for life," he said stiffly, "but that is not for me to decide. That burden falls on Alec alone. He might just let you go. That all depends on him now."

"You'll need me if we're attacked again."

"Well, that depends on who's doing the attacking, doesn't it?"

Myra blew him a kiss and laughed. Rolling his eyes, Captain Zlo stood, walked over to the hovering guard andy, and checked its programming. He then moved out to the hallway and checked on the battle android standing guard. He glanced at the crewman standing guard nearby. "Is it programmed as I ordered?"

Crewman Beck—formerly Lieutenant Beck—answered, "Yes, Captain, no one comes in but you."

"Good work, crewman. Now, walk with me and let's discuss your future. I've vouched for you to the ship's commander, and I expect you to perform accordingly. After all, your behavior as a ship's officer has been... questionable at best."

SAKYUR was a small colonial world with fewer than five million inhabitants, and about the same number of visitors annually. Its primary sources of income were mining and maintenance service to spaceships passing through or near the system. The entire planet was more or less a service station for other space travelers. There was no regular government and its attendant laws: each town (there were no cities) was managed by its citizens.

Alec and friends chose to visit Diablac, a town with some 50,000 inhabitants: not too big, not too small. The shuttle landed on a dusty landing grid west of town; immediately they were mobbed by a swarm of vehicles and maintenance androids. A customs vehicle glided up to the shuttle's main hatch, and three officers stepped out. Alec talked to the custom officers while Frances instructed the maintenance personnel about what they needed done. He also ordered two of the Grisamm to guard the ship, along with two battle andies. He then left the shuttle proper to inspect the fighter mated to the top.

Later, Alec, Alexa, Frances and Bax, escorted by four Grisamm monks, walked toward a nearby terminal, leaving Nikko Behl and Nina behind with the other guards— Oman and android—to direct and assist with repairs and the purchase of new fuel cells. Alec noticed idly that Alexa wore her hair up, and that she was dressed in a new outfit under her cloak. The cloak was similar to the ones the Grisamm wore, but her odd new outfit was cobbled together from battle gear and a pressure suit. It was tailored perfectly to her shape, reminded him vaguely of a suit of armor from the ancient pre-Space days. He grinned fondly.

Neither Alexa nor Alec had brought up their differences, deciding instead to bury the past and move forward.

Once they reached a communication station, Frances, Alec and one Grisamm monk, Mikka, went inside to send a cryptic message to Tota. Alexa and the other monks waited outside, making sure they were not being followed or otherwise gathering too much attention. When the message was sent, they all proceed to the local markets and made several purchases. They mostly met friendly traders and merchants, who were all eager to comply with their requests.

Alexa saw the perfect opportunity to make sure Alec kept one of his promises, and soon she was a favorite among the storeowners. She attacked the shops like a vulture attacking carrion.

When they finally returned to the shuttle, they saw a major change. It had been cleaned up and neatly repaired; several maintenance droids and a few people were finishing as they arrived. Dozens of large hover trucks were lined up nearby, and Nina and a Grisamm monk were directing the loading of supplies and spare parts, going over the merchandise with scanners. Behl greeted Alec with a friendly smile, and reported that most of the equipment and gear had been received already. He also mentioned that there had been several people asking questions, but he thought that most of them just wanted to sell something. There had been a couple of requests to purchase space onboard both for cargo and travelers. He had denied them all.

Behl confessed, "I'm surprised it's only taken one day. They're very well equipped down here."

"Must be used to this," Frances suggested.

Alec reminded everyone, "Remember, we'll have to pick up the large stuff from one of the stations in orbit, and that will take several hours. We need to hurry."

"Well, when will it be ready?"

"Not until early tomorrow, Captain."

"Then what say we find a local cantina and get shitfaced?" the old spacer Behl suggested.

Alec shot him an irritated expression and, without answering, walked away to inspect the shuttle.

Meanwhile, Alexa went to find Nina. She wanted to show her friend some of her "useless junk," as Alec called it. A poor Grisamm monk followed after her, weighted down with bags and boxes, muttering about being a soldier and not a bloody servant. Alexa heard this, and turned to give the old monk a soft kiss on his forehead. He turned red and smiled, embarrassed and not really knowing why.

"WHERE the hell is he?" Alec demanded.

"He said he was going to show Nina some of the local sights." The monk's voice was cut short as Alec slapped off his wristcomp.

"Shit, and we're just about ready to leave! Frances, we need to find them right away."

Frances replied, "I'll take a couple of men and start looking."

"Can we scan for them?" Alexa suggested.

"Hmmm, maybe. Well, Frances?"

Frances rolled his eyes at his own obtuseness. "Yes, of course we can."

They soon located two small blue dots on a 3-D map of the area, inside a building downtown.

"It's probably a cantina," Francis said, exasperated. "I'll go and get them."

"No, Frances, you stay here and secure and prepare the ship for launch, while Bax and I go and get them."

"And me!" Alexa shouted.

Alec was about to stop her, but changed his mind. She'd already armed herself with a small machine pistol; Bax helped her attach the straps on her shoulder holster and handed her a couple of spare power magazines.

"Wait for us. We'll be right back."

Frances then barked some instructions. Soon the rest of them were armed to the teeth.

"We need to hurry," Alec stated, as he, Alexa, and Bax hurried toward the terminal. "Behl can get pretty wild when he gets drunk."

"So can Nina," Alexa added dryly.

"The last thing we need is a problem with the local authorities," Bax insisted, as he tried to wave down a hover cab.

The cantina was typical for both Behl and Nina—it was the kind where unsavory characters hung around, and the quality of the food and beverages was questionable at best. One giant bar stretched along one wall, facing twenty tables packed with drunken guests. A dozen erotic dancers of various species danced on the tabletops to ear-scraping music from a particularly bad band. Several small scuffles and fights enhanced the dull crowd.

Alec saw Nina on one table, half-naked, dancing and flirting with two female and three male exotics (apparently). One of them appeared to be the owner or manager, given the stained apron. Behl, for his part, was at the bar drinking himself senseless.

Alec shook his head. "I'll take her, and you take him," he said to Bax, "while you wait here and guard our backs, Alexa."

Bax had no problem extracting Captain Behl's bottle and tossing him over his shoulder, considering he was twice Behl's size. Despite the old man's loud protests denouncing Bax as a bloody pirate and mutineer, no one moved a hand to help him. The people near them had noticed Bax's infamous uniform, recognizing him as Grisamm, and happily gave Bax all the space he needed, and then some.

Alec, meanwhile, walked up to Nina and extended his left hand toward her. She peered at him, confused, radiating attitude and more than a little fright. Her new fan club urged her to keep dancing, and loudly told Alec where he could go. Alec ignored their threats, yanking Nina from the tabletop. From the corner of his eye he saw a blade flash in the dim light—and a loud shot rang out.

One of the female exotics lay on the ground screaming, holding a bloody stump where her hand once had been. Alexa had done a fine job of guarding him, he decided. He tossed a very intoxicated and very angry little Oman vixen over his shoulder, like Bax ignoring all the furious words hurled at him while she pounded him in the back.

The owner-cum-manager took exception to Alec's attitude, and lunged at them; he, Alec, and Nina tumbled to the ground in a spitting, flailing knot, and seconds later everyone in the bar was involved in a free-for-all brawl. Meanwhile, the owner plopped his 200-kilo weight down on top of Alec and Nina, and raised a large butcher knife over his head. Before he could do more than that, a disk blade sliced into his forehead, sending the top of his skull flying like fleshy bowl through the air, splattering blood and brains over all and sundry.

"Hurry!" Alexa shouted, discharging two more disk blades and a couple of knives from her sleeves of her uniform, cutting down bullies threatening Bax and Alec.

When Alec joined Alexa, still carrying Nina over his shoulder, he noticed several blades sticking out of various spots on Alexa's uniform, warning everyone not to get too close. The six long, down-pointing blades on her back were already slicked with blood. It was easy to see where it had come from: behind her was one of the cantina's enormous bouncers, lying on his back with several cuts along his chest and belly. The cuts were perfectly aligned.

"And I paid the bastard to wait," complained Bax, when they got outside and saw that their cab was gone.

Behl was practicing his vocal cords still, providing the three bouncers outside with his personal opinion about their entire DNA structure and their true professions, even as he hung upside down over Bax's shoulder. Nina, meanwhile, was still struggling for her newly-earned freedom. Alexa followed behind, covering them; which was just as well, for the bouncers saw a perfect opportunity to teach some foreigners a lesson. They launched themselves at Bax and Behl, and the Grisamm found himself fighting a big transgenic and two large exotics with the old man singing from his back, cheering everyone on.

As Alexa lined up a shot that would have killed the transgenic, Alec snatched his own gun from its holster and discharged a few rounds into the air. The fight stopped abruptly, and he motioned for the bouncers to get inside. One made the stupid mistake of lunging at Alec's gun; Alexa sliced off his legs below the knees with a pair of disk blades. The other two bouncers saw the light; they ran back inside the cantina shouting for help, and locked the door behind them.

Two black hover limos darted straight at them just then; the first one hit Bax, who vaulted through the air to one side, while Behl went down hard on the other side, flapping his arms along the way. In the background they could hear the sound of several police vehicles approaching, both hover and groundcars alike. Six exotics and four Omans, all of them large, spilled out of the first limo and attacked Alec and Alexa, who had to fight for their lives. Two Omans grabbed Nina, and beat her until she stopped moving. They hauled her toward the trunk of the aircar.

"Shit, Grisamm!" one of the Omans growled, just before his face was crushed by Bax's strong fist. The other thug got as far as, "No one told us about Gri..." before a huge boot was inserted between his eyes. They dropped Nina to the ground. She was still too confused and drunk to understand what was happening.

Thanks to her newly-made outfit, Alexa handled herself better than Alec did. One exotic grabbed her from behind while his two friends tried to help him, at the same time trying to avoiding the two long, flashing blades extending from the toes of her boots. Both of them already had several cuts from the blades, and they were getting steadily more pissed off. As one fingered his blaster, a voice from the nearest car shouted, "No! We must deliver them alive!"

Oh really, Alec thought, as he was pinned down by several large bodies. A fist struck him dead center on the nose, and then someone shoved a stunner into his belly, shutting off the lights.

Alexa immediately went ballistic. The exotic holding her from behind screamed at the top of his lungs, and her other two assailants backed away with stunned expressions as their comrade let go of Alexa and grabbed at his belly. Oddly enough, she just hung there for a second; then, with a weird swishing sound, she dropped to the ground. A long line of six sharp knives were folded back along her spinal column and the man behind her fell down on his knees, screaming as entrails and blood poured out of the cuts in his torso.

With surgical precision, Alexa put him out of his misery, slicing through the meat and cartilage of his neck with her suddenly-deployed right elbow knife. She brought it back around and jabbed it into the heart of the man on her right, then round-kicked the other assailant twice in his upper body and twice more in his legs. He fell to the ground in pieces, gray with shock.

Bax was all over the other attackers, who were dragging Alec towards one of the limousines. A short firefight between them resulted in two more attackers slipping and falling in their own blood. A third hovercraft appeared on the scene, this one a smaller and sportier model; one Oman and an exotic that looked like a pile of orange bricks got out and started firing, hitting Bax several times. One of their compatriots saw her opportunity, and fired a stun bolt at Alexa that sent her crashing to the ground. The two new arrivals walked cockily towards the injured Bax, taunting and laughing.

That stopped when Behl and Nina loosed a hail of laser bolts at them, leaving the orange exotic sprawled dead on the permacrete.

"Let's go!" shouted one of the Omans, who appeared to be the leader. He spat orders for his colleagues to take the prisoners and take off, firing several magma blasts at Behl and Nina. Both of them, still a bit wasted, were forced to take cover behind the bodies of their dead attackers; they watched helplessly as the ringleader got into the driver's side of one limo, while Alec and Alexa were tossed into the trunk.

The limousine took off into the sky just as two police vehicles slid to a stop in front of the cantina, and four police officers emerged with weapons drawn. Nina and Behl, bowing to the inevitable, dropped their weapons and knelt with their hands on top of their heads. Two of the police officers covered their partners as they approached Behl and Nina, restraints ready.

They never knew what hit them.

Bax leaped into the air, landed among them, and went to work. Within seconds, the four police officers lay unconscious on the pavement. Behl and Nina applauded his performance, but Bax's expression sobered the two immediately. "Idiots!" he snarled. "If not for your iniquity, none of this would have happened! Now, get back to the ship and tell Frances that Alec and Alexa have been kidnapped. I'll go after them in *that*." Bax pointed at the sporty red hovercraft.

"Are you hurt?"

"From those peashooters? My body armor absorbed the blasts. Now hurry."

Behl and Nina ran toward the landing field, passing through a small crowd of curious onlookers. Bax, meanwhile, searched the bodies for any clues. But when the bouncers came back, and the street grew too crowded even as more police vehicles were heard to approach, he gave it up as a bad cause and dove into the little hovercar, bouncing one of the bouncers aside as he took off.

THE two Omans who reported to Frances were a poor sight indeed. Frances calmed them down, explaining that Bax had already called him on his communicator.

"Captain Behl," he gritted, somehow retaining his patience, "get this shuttle ready to take off. Mikka, take this message to the communication center in the terminal. Send it, and wait for Bax to contact you there. When he does, you will assist him."

"Can't we just send the message from here?" Behl asks, Nina injected him with Sober-Up.

"Too likely to be intercepted. That's why we sent the other messages to Tota from the same place," Francis told him. "Now, we have to take off before the local authorities learn more about us."

"I know, Frances, but we can't leave anyone behind."

"We're not leaving anyone behind, but we have to make the rendezvous with the service station and get to the *Predator* to get more help. That's what Alec wanted us to do if something like this happened. The crew are sitting ducks out there."

"I...thought you would insist on rescuing Alec and Alexa."

"I want to, and we will eventually. But let's face facts: if the authorities catch us, any authorities, we're all screwed. We'll be taken off to Gull knows where, and it could take weeks before Tota or someone else could bail us out—if they ever could." Frances gave Behl a stern look: end of discussion.

Behl refused to take the hint. "Dammit, we can leave the fighter with Bax and her." Behl tilted his head towards Mikka.

"It only takes one person."

"Yes, Frances, I *know*, but it's better than nothing— and it might increase our chances of finding them."

Nina interrupted, "I'll fly it."

"No, Nina, I need you as my co-pilot and that's that," Behl replied.

Exasperated, Frances said, "*I'll* stay behind with Mikka and Bax. The rest of you will take off immediately for a rendezvous with the station. Mikka, get the message send to Bull. I'll take the fighter and coordinate with you and Bax."

Behl looked at him, unaccustomed fear on his face. "You just said...Bull? You mean Bull the Butcher, one of the most feared Grisamm monks in the entire universe? What's going on here, Frances?"

Face grim, France replied, "He is not a monk, Nikko Behl, but an actual Knight of the Order Grisamm. He is my master instructor, and I am his shield bearer. Something very big is happening here—and we don't have the time to chat about it now."

They made their hasty farewells, and then Frances and Mikka dug out some spare equipment and gear, including several emergency-healing bags. Meanwhile, Nina got the fighter down from its perch, showing some frustration as she handed Frances the fighter's pin-key. "Take care of my little slut," she whispered with teary eyes... and she didn't mean the fighter.

They stuffed all the weapons and extra gear inside a compartment aft of the cockpit, and Frances took it up while Mikka hurried away. Behl, Nina and the rest of the monks got onboard the shuttle and, after a long wait, finally received permission from the flight controller to lift off.

TEN

THE dense, cold air, heavy with the musty smell of something long dead and rotten, made Alec cough. He couldn't move his legs or arms, and the rough stone floor made him shiver. Dim light filtered down in from a small hole far up on the wall. He tried to get his bearings, but his head was pounding and he couldn't think. He was stripped naked except for his undergarments, with his hands tied behind his back. He felt a strange pain along his legs, and noticed that his ankles had also been shackled and pulled back with a rope to his hands.

Alexa lay on her stomach, and like her paramour, she had been hog-tied. She only wore a thin, torn shirt and her underpants; dried blood covered her face, and she wasn't moving. Alec started to slide towards her, whispering her name, scraping his skin on the rough stone surface. The blood trail he left behind went unnoticed. All he cared about was saving his damsel in distress, not thinking that he might need some saving too. When he finally reached her, he snuggled his head up to hers and kissed her gently, murmuring her name, trying in vain to awaken her.

To his horror, he noticed that she had bruises all over her body. The leather cords around her wrists and ankles had been tied too tight, leaving her hands and feet distended and discolored an evil, dark purple. His own bonds had been tied with as much care, he soon realized, and his muscles had started to cramp; the pain was excruciating.

When the cramps passed, he started to inch toward a nearby wall, where water was pouring down the rough stonework. He licked at some of it and made sure it was drinkable, then swallowed as much as he could. His thick, dry tongue eventually regained its normal size and shape. He filled his mouth to the brim, and crawled back to Alexa. He moved her head to the side with his, and tried to trickle some water into her mouth. He repeated this over and over again, and was nearly exhausted when she opened her eyes at last.

Alexa mumbled something and coughed. "Finally tied me up, did you? Ha!" She cleared her throat. "I knew you were kinky. Tied me hard, too, didn't you? 'Salright, I like that."

Laughing dryly, he rasped, "Did they hit you too hard, or did you just lose it?" He kissed her, and she responded, and soon they were both on their sides facing each other. After a moment, Alec stopped and shook his head.

"Why did you stop?" she pouted.

"Oh, maybe we should try to get out of these restraints and find a way out of here...you know, before they kill us or something."

Alexa rolled around and looked over the dark room. "Can't see any door."

She yelped as Alec bit her. "Sorry, didn't mean for that to happen." He started chewing on the tough, wet leather binding her wrists, and it wasn't long before the cord was slicked with blood. He spat and cursed as a front tooth chipped.

"Wait, let me try it on you. After all, I'm more used to using my mouth than you are."

Again they laughed, and Alec rolled over, as Alexa crawled up, positioned herself by his waist, and started chewing on the rope attaching his hands to his feet. "Nice ass," she whispered, and Alec cried out as Alexa bit him for real. "Sorry, dear, couldn't resist. They're so firm and perfect."

"Holy Gull! You must be a nymphomaniac, if you're thinking about sex at a time like this!"

"Are you complaining?" Alexa asked, and went back to chewing on Alec's cords.

"Well, no, but I think we should get back to what we were doing..."

"Turn around!" she ordered suddenly.

Rolling his eyes, he turned toward her. Alexa looked down towards his groin and frowned. "You can't tell me you weren't thinking the same. I can see better."

Alec blushed, but there was now use trying to hide the bulge in his pants. He rose toward her, lips pursed for a kiss.

"Down, boy, down," she muttered, and motioned for him to turn over on his stomach again. She went back to biting and chewing on the leather cords with skilled teeth, but after a while her own mouth was filled with blood. She took a break, spat out some blood, and crawled up next to Alec. Despite their exercise, they were both trembling from the cold. He noticed the blood on her lips, and he felt a jolt of pain inside.

She smirked and, her lips pursed, tried to blow her hair out of her face. That triggered it for Alex. She noticed his pride growing, and the agony in his eyes. "Men!" she hissed.

She moved closer and kissed him. She tried to move her back towards him, and he gave her a helping "hand", digging his chin over her shoulder and helping her tilt herself with her back towards him. He moved closer and could sense by her breathing that she was as ready for him as he was for her. But to Alec and Alexa's frustration, being hogtied limited their options.

"Wait, let me," she mumbled, as she fumbled with her hands in an attempt to grab his hard shaft. His panted moans were evidence that he was close. Finally, she could feel it, and she grabbed it hard. She guided it towards her hot, aching center. She moved her wrists and ankles to the side, and the moment she felt the head of his penis by the entrance of her jade gate, she moved backwards and he pushed forward, filling her up. It wasn't long before they exploded together, leaving them gasping for air. They were sweating and laughing, forgetting about the cold damp air in this primitive dungeon.

The culmination of their lovemaking was met by laconic applause.

To their embarrassment, they saw that that cell had grown brighter, and that they'd been joined by four Omans and two exotics. The six stood at the base of a stone staircase that spiraled upward to a round opening in the ceiling.

One Oman walked towards them and said, "Mind if we join you lovebirds?"

Before Alexa knew it, the ropes securing her hands and feet were cut away, and the Oman was forcing her legs apart and back. She let out a short cry.

"Give us a hand here, will you?" the Oman snapped. The others eagerly came to his aid, dragging Alexa along the rough floor on her knees while Alexa shouted and writhed, helpless. They slammed her body over a large squared-off rock, with her hands and feet still tied up.

"I'll do her from the back, while you can get warmed up at the front," the Oman in charge declared.

They all laughed, even as Alec screamed at the top of his lungs, threatening them with bloody death. The more he screamed, the more they laughed.

One Oman unlimbered his member and stood before Alexa, brandishing his erection...but when he looked at her eyes, he hesitated. The man behind her could read his thoughts, and ordered his friends to bring up Alec. They forced him to his knees next to Alexa's face.

"You bite, bitch, and we cut his throat."

With that, he penetrated her roughly from the rear, while his friends at the front told her to be very good or they would cut her tits off. Alec fought desperately against his bonds as he witnessed his love being violated. As he collapsed from exhaustion, another couple of guards stepped up as the two first finished, and went to work on Alexa.

Alexa's face was clenched in pain, her eyes filled with tears; but her anguish didn't come from being raped. That was something she'd experienced countless of times since childhood; it was the price a woman had to pay in a pirate clan. She had taught herself to accept the degradation and move on. No, the pain was from the forlorn, despairing expression on her knight's face.

"Don't you want some?" the head guard asked the two exotics, which stood watching with amusement.

"Not from that skank," one said. "Him."

"Me too," one of the hulking Omans chimed in.

"Yeah, I wouldn't mind some of him either," said another. "Think I can get it up again."

They cut the ropes securing Alec's hands and feet, and this time Alec was taken from behind while Alexa was forced to watch. One Oman forced his erection into Alec's mouth and hit him several times. When the knife moved against Alexa's throat, drawing a line of blood, Alec was forced to give head or let her die. He did it without hesitation. He was totally overwhelmed, in shock; but he knew, at least, that he couldn't let her die that way.

When he first saw the knife at his love's throat, he emitted a strange cry, childish and weird. The sound would not leave Alexa's memory for the rest of her life. Alec looked confused and in agony; in a life of horror and bloodshed, it was the most horrible thing Alexa had ever witnessed. When the first couple had finished, the exotics walked up and raped Alec, while their Oman friends were all over Alexa, violating her again.

Eventually, their rapists left, laughing as they wiped their former erections clean of blood and more disgusting fluids. Alec and Alexa were left on the hard, cold floor, still tied up; only this time, their captors hadn't bothered to reattach their ankles to their wrists.

Alexa crawled up next to Alec, who lay on the floor trembling, curled up in a fetal position. "Alec. Alec, listen to me. Look at me."

His body and face was covered with blood and white grue, and a puddle of blood around his backside gradually spread. He didn't look at her. He wasn't there.

After several failed attempt to make contact, she gave up and started to cry. She knew what must have happened to him. She'd seen it before with first-time rape victims, especially men and boys. It was never the physical act that ruined them; it was always their psyches refusing to accept what had happened. She knew then that she might have lost him forever.

The days passed, glacially slow, and every night a dozen or more men and women came down to the stone cellar and had their ways with the prisoners. Alexa and Alec received nothing to eat or drink; the only thing available for them was the cold, rank water dripping down the walls. But Alec never drank or said anything; he only lay on the ground, curled up and trembling. The only time he uttered any sound whatsoever was whenever he was being raped, and it was that same strange childish sound he'd made before. Their kidnappers didn't even bother keeping them tied up. Alexa brought him water in her mouth, as he had for her. She kept saying comforting words, assuring him that they would get free, planning out their future. She did everything she could to make contact with Alec, but Alec was elsewhere.

Both of them were bruised and dirty, and the stink in the room increased with every moment. Alexa realized that if they didn't get help soon, Alec would die. That she too faced the same predicament did not cross her mind. Every time Alec was raped, he lost more blood. Alexa managed to gather some of their garments from the filth around them, and crawled up behind Alec to do what she could to stop the bleeding. She pushed up the dirty garment toward him in a desperate attempt to stop the rectal bleeding. Her lover was fading away, mentally and physically, with each day that passed.

On the fifth day, both of them were left on the cold, wet stone floor after the rape session. Alexa noticed that Alec's lips had changed color from purplish-blue to white. She used all her strength to crawl over to him. His bleeding had stopped, and his breath was faint. A rasping sound came from his throat, and Alexa knew he would die before sunrise.

She was too exhausted to do anything for either of them, so she just sat up, held Alec in her lap like a child, and stroked his head. She was too tired to cry; she had reached her limit. She looked around the room for something she could use on herself, to end her life after she had ended Alec's.

BAX peered through the binocs at the small estate at the end of the road. It was an old road, probably built to service the hovercraft hangar nearby. He lay on a forested mountain ledge, under the cover of darkness; Mikka lay next to him, silently prepared the equipment for their assault.

A fighter was silhouetted against the patchy clouds above them.

The voice of Frances came through their earbugs. "Normally, we'd blow the entire building—but since the local authorities are after us, we have to keep it as quiet as we can. Now, on my mark: go."

The two Grisamm acknowledged and swung into action, rappelling down the cliff face to the ground below. They advanced in one-by-one formation, each providing cover for the other. "They're in some kind of cellar or basement at the far side of the estate," Frances whispered in their ears. "The entrance should be on the mountainside."

When Mikka and Bax reached the near vicinity of the main target Frances ordered them to stop. "Someone coming."

Several people stepped out of a door in the wall, walking confidently toward a small wooden structure. Bax and Mikka glanced at each other, concerned, as they could make out some of the conversation. "Disregard them and proceed towards the primary target," Frances ordered.

Frances too had heard the conversation, and his expression was cold, filled with an odd mixture of hate and sorrow.

ALEXA heard a skittering faint sound echoing down from the small opening on the far side of the wall. *They're coming back*, she thought despairingly. She looked down on her dying love, and she made her final decision. She was going to fight to her death. She struggled to her feet and moved slowly towards the staircase…and fell down, hard, before she'd taken half a dozen steps. She had no strength left. When she looked up, she saw someone in black standing a few steps above her; her vision darkened then and her hailing failed, drowned in the susurrus of her own heartbeat and despair.

A short jolt of pain came, and then another, from her left leg. Her spine fired electric shocks into her body, and she felt her muscles spasm. She woke up abruptly, and could see, somewhat, and think more clearly. The hunger was still there...but part of her strength was back.

"We must hurry," a rough voice said quietly. "Sit down and put your head between your knees, and let the medication take effect."

Alexa thought she recognized the voice, but her vision was still too blurry in this dimness to be sure. "Alec. Save him," she whispered. After a few very long moments, Alexa finally felt her strength returning. She looked up, her vision clearing, and saw Bax kneeling next to Alec. There were two empty general first-aid ampoules next to her, and four next to Alec. As she watched, Bax injected him with a fifth.

"You can't give him more than three or he'll die!"

"Relax, Alexa, I know what I'm doing. He was already very close to death. A couple too many is better than too few." Bax looked her and asked, "Can you walk?"

"Give me a moment."

He nodded, then touched his earpiece and whispered, "Out of time—they're returning. There's a convoy of vehicles heading up the mountain...could have something to do with you guys. Here, take this, and I'll carry him." Bax handed Alexa his machine pistol and picked up Alec gently. "Let's go. Mikka's outside."

Face grim, Alexa tied the torn remnants of her garments around her waist and cleared her throat. She looked at Bax's water bottle, and he smiled, gesturing for Alexa to take it. She grabbed it and emptied it. She made as if to toss the bottle away, and Bax shook his head sharply, not wanting to leave any clues behind. He took the bottle and put it away, motioned to Alexa to hurry. When Alexa passed him in the staircase, she grabbed Bax's machete from the sheath strapped to his left hip, and led the way, pistol in one hand and the large knife in the other.

Mikka waited outside; she smiled at Alexa and gestured for her to join her. As she noticed Alec's condition, her eyes became shadowed with concern. "Alexa, I'll take the front; you watch the rear," she suggested.

Alexa nodded, and they headed away like stealthy shadows. Not stealthy enough: a guard android warbled in the distance and then zapped each with a stunbeam. As he tumbled to the ground, Bax growled, "Where the hell did that one come from?"

He snapped off a few laser rounds from a pistol in his left hand as he marched up to where the others writhed on the ground with cramps. Cursing, Bax fumbled a first aid pen from a pocket in his robes and jabbed the needle into his thigh, excoriating himself for being so incompetent as to have been dropped by a stunner, of all things.

Then he grabbed his machine pistol from Alexa and put a half-dozen rounds into the andy's main processor; its head exploded into shrapnel as both he and Mikka rose, his fellow monk with a syringe pen hanging from her own leg. She picked up Alexa and dashed away. Bax followed with Alec over his shoulder.

Lights flickered, and the entire yard was lit up as alarms began to yammer. Half a dozen bokka—vicious three-legged creatures with two bone-tipped tails—sprinted towards them. "Have to take them head on," Bax ordered Mikka. He looked at her and smiled, and they carefully lay the two fragile bodies next to each other on the ground. The first bokka was cut down by Mikka's machete, while Bax punched the second bokka hard in the skull as he brought up the handgun; two more crashed into him, bearing him to the ground. He blew one's ugly head off, as he emptied the laser pistol's charge into the other's chest. He dropped it and put a bullet into the brain of the bokka he'd stunned with his punch. Mikka cut down one more, and Alexa, who had managed to stop shaking from the stunbeam, brought Bax's machete down on the neck of the last bokka, half severing it.

"I see you're back, lazy one," Mikka taunted, handing Alexa a spare handgun and magazine.

"Let's move it, people!" Frances shouted into Bax's and Mikka's earbugs.

A score of guards emerged from the main estate building, firing, it seemed, in all directions. Alexa wondered briefly why they were wasting their fire in directions other than towards the refugees, but her question was soon answered: explosions marched among the mercenaries, sending them flying through the air, some in pieces. The fighter thundered past overhead, passing very low and very fast. "Frances," Bax explained.

Frances had bought them some time. They took advantage of it, hurrying into the darkness as fast as they could move. But soon, they heard shouts close behind them, and magma blasts and bullets began to speed past. Worse, a cluster of five civilians hovercrafts crunched down into the brush ahead of them, cutting off their escape; a crowd of thugs emerged and began laying down withering suppressive fire. Frances brought the fighter alongside them, protecting them from the fire with its armored fuselage and shields. "Get on the wings, get on the wings!" he shouted, mowing down their attackers with his mini-guns, hovering near the ground.

"Alec can't!" Bax shouted over the racket of the firefight.

The enemy closed in, and a decision had to be made. It was the hardest and most difficult order he had ever given, and yet Frances never hesitated. "Leave him behind. We'll come back for him later." To himself, Frances whispered, "I swear to you, my friend, I *will* come back for you."

Bax set down Alec, kissed his forehead, and whispered in his ear, "I'll be back, Alec von Hornet, my liege. I swear by my soul I will be back."

Alexa began protesting—but she was too weak to put up a fight as Mikka grabbed her. She aimed her weapon at Alec—she'd rather he died than go through that horror again—but Mikka knocked the gun aside and snapped, "Get on the bloody wing."

Mikka took Alexa's weapon and used it to cover their retreat as they climbed up on one of the fighter's wings. Moving carefully to compensate for their weight, Frances moved the small ship gently into the air, holding it between them and the enemy fire as he covered them with his mini-guns and a pair of well-placed missiles, being sure he avoided Alec's position. Then he released a pair of smoke grenades, choking the area with dense black vapor. Alexa, Bax and Mikka held on for their very lives as Frances took them up and away over the mountaintops, staying as near to the surface as dared.

He couldn't help but glance repeatedly at the forlorn, lifeless body on the ground where they'd left him, surrounded now by a crowd of thugs.

THE small fighter landed in a remote grain field, and Frances immediately disembarked and helped his friends down from the wing. Cursing, Mikka yanked open the storage compartment aft of the cockpit, snatched out a few boxes, and tossed Alexa a jumpsuit and a pair of boots.

"Wait, wait, I want to clean myself up over there," Alexa said, pointing at a small stream.

Mikka followed Alexa, and watched as she walked into the cold water until it covered her and began scrubbing away all the dirt and filth, using the clean sand from the streambed as an abrasive. Because she was turned away, Mikka never saw the tears that fell as Alexa scrubbed herself clean.

Afterward, they sat in silence and ate some rations. Frances handed Alexa his share; he had no appetite.

As they finished their meal, a series of floodlights lit up their position. "Great, the police," Frances muttered.

"Shall we fight them?"

"No, Mikka, we will let them take us into custody, and pray for Tota or Captain Zlo to get us out. We're in no condition to take them on. Besides, they have the high ground, moral and otherwise. Just remember, don't say anything. If Zlo or Tota can't make it, then I know Bull can."

Neither said anything more. Two of the police craft landed, and the police approached with caution.

ON a large, comfortable bed, at the center of a spacious, well-decorated room, lay Marquessa De La Hoff. She was pale and motionless, and appeared dead. By some measures, perhaps she was.

Her fellow Florencian Marquessa, Nosassa De La Peck, stood on a balcony overlooking a beautiful terrace decorated with fountains, stone sculptures, and an enormous garden. A physician, a man belonging to her own "exotic" race—as Omans styled any species but their own—joined her. Behind him hovered an Admiral, waiting nervously. A dozen Silver Guards stood like statues along the walls.

"Marquessa, there is nothing more that I or anyone else can do for Marquessa De La Hoff."

"Is she dying?"

"No, my lady, she has no physical injuries. Her injuries must be psychological in nature. The only medicine that will work for her, I fear, is time. Perhaps it is some sort of auto-hypnosis, a trance, or even some sort of healing coma, thought I doubt the latter. I would like to run a few more tests if I may…"

Nosassa motioned for him to be silent, and nodded towards an Admiral who stood nervously by the door. "You. Take some of the monst—um, the guards and bring me the old witch doctor."

"Yes, madam."

"And Admiral, hurry. Time is of the essence."

The Admiral saluted and sprang into action, gesturing at the line of Silver Guards. Wordlessly, four joined him as he left the chamber.

The physician was discomfited, to say the least. "But my lady, I insist that I can find the problem yet, and that we—"

"Thank you, Doctor, that will be all for now. It's in God's hands now." She smiled at the upset physician in what she probably imagined was a friendly fashion, and motioned for him and his staff to leave.

When they were gone, she dropped the false smile and snapped, "You. How long before we can have a new invasion fleet and the troops for it ready?"

A skeletal exotic with a shock of reddish, wirelike hair stepped from behind a pillar. "Almost eight more years, my lady." He noticed her expression and corrected himself: "Perhaps six more years, unless of course we reassign forces from some of our provinces."

"Unacceptable. They will remain where they are. I'll give you five years, and I doubt Marquessa De La Hoff will give you half that time when she returns to duty."

"Five years is impossible," the advisor answered evenly. "We have neither the funds nor the resources, and wishing otherwise will not change that."

"We will be bankrupt and starving within five years unless we find more and better resources!" the Marquessa shouted. "God commands us to spread His Word, and unite the universe under his rule. You will comply! Five…four years!"

The man backed away, expressionless, bowing his head in acquiescence.

Marquessa De La Peck leaned on the railing, trying to calm down. This was just one of her six hundred palaces, but it was a jewel placed in exquisite setting, and the air was the cleanest she had ever tasted. In the far distance she could see the spires of a smaller palace, this one under construction; it would have more than two hundred rooms. Next to it were several small buildings, housing two hundred servants. The palace being built was for her favorite pet, something akin to a small dog.

De La Peck had never owned a pet before, and she couldn't wait for the new little pet-house to be ready so that her little toy could move in. *Life is wonderful*, she thought, *and soon, it will be much better.*

Now that the day's hard work was done, she began to focus on a personal dilemma that had concerned her ever since she had acquired her pet. Should she get one more? A male, this time, and have the two of them mate? Then she could have her own cute little kennel. "But where should I put their new homes?" she wondered-with a concerned expression, as she looked out over her million-hectare estate.

THE shuttle descended toward one of the fifty battle cruisers, slipped into the main docking bay, and began docking procedures.

Half an hour later, Frances, Alexa, Bax and Mikka emerged, greeted by Tota and a young man dressed smartly in the uniform of the Marengan navy. Tota greeted his friends as he always did: he bobbed up and down and jumped all over them, while his trunk slapped his poor victims' faces. "My precious little princes, and the goddess of all females!" Tota exclaimed, embracing Alexa's neck.

After a few awkward moments, the little alien finally managed to find a comforting place to sit—on Alexa's elbow. He burst out, "But why this sadness, my morning light that fills the dark universe with her crystalline laughter?"

Alexa fell to her knees, covered her eyes, and wept. Tota looked at her sad face, took her head in a firm embrace, and whispered to her, "Whatever saddens you, we must amend. We will find him. Look who is here." Tota lifted gently Alexa's head towards the young handsome man in uniform. "This is a son of an old friend of mine. Allow me to introduce to all of you the dredded Count Zanches of the house of Salla. He is the youngest son of the Emperor of Marengo."

Everyone but Alexa bowed his or her heads to the young man whose confidence was reflected in his body language. A svelte figure joined them. "And this is Lady Fuzza, a business partner to young Master Alec."

When Alexa heard Alec's name, she burst into tears again. Lady Fuzza walked over to her and helped her to her feet, speaking gently to her. She escorted Alexa away, while a medic came and assisted. They placed Alexa on a hovering medical bed and gave her a sedative; soon she was asleep, and the bed filled with a soothing gel. Consulting a control pad, the medics took Alexa away to the ship's infirmary.

"Let me guess," Frances said drily, "you actually know the Emperor himself."

"One of my best friends!" Tota smiled, winking at the young count.

"How did you manage to get us out, sir?"

"Well, Frances, when I received your message a month ago, I called my friend here," Tota glanced at Count Zanches, "who was already looking for you." Tota noticed the sudden change in Frances' expression and said quickly, "Relax. Master Alec himself sent a message of friendship to the Emperor himself through Lady Fuzza. The Emperor wishes to meet Alec, and thank him for his very thoughtful gift. With the help of Count Zanches' fleet, it didn't take long for the local administrators on this little planet to decide to release you. However, they refused to cooperate with us any further. So tell me: what is going on, and where is young Master Alec?"

"It's a long story."

"They always are. I've come a long way, so why don't you start from the beginning?"

"Before I do, there's something we must do first. Count Zanches, our ship, the *Predator*, should have been here long ago to help us in rescuing Alec."

"Rescuing Alec!" Tota blurted.

Frances motioned for Tota to be patient and continued, "Could you send one of your ships to investigate what has happened to them?"

The young count motioned to one of his officers, who joined them. "Give me their last coordinates, sir Grisamm. Perhaps some of your friends can follow Captain Jorik here." Zanches motioned toward Mikka and Bax.

"I will go after my blood brother alone," Bax protested. "I have given him my oath of honor. Just give me some supplies and a ship."

Mikka stepped forward, "Not alone. I'll go too."

Briefly, Frances informed the others about what had happened, leaving out the treatment that Alec and Alexa had received at the hands of their captors. The main question was, who had taken Alec—and where were they now? Zanches recommended that they send down a commando unit to the estate and abduct some people for interrogation. Frances insisted that he would lead the operation, since he had once before had the place under surveillance.

Tota motioned for Frances to turn around. Lined up behind him were five hundred Grisamm monks and fifteen hundred troops. "Bull sent them," Tota explained. "He will join us later. They arrived in their own destroyer..."

The Grisamm Commander, a hard-looking woman named Lafer, stepped up and joined them, clasping Frances' forearm in brotherhood. She smiled in a friendly way as she was introduced to the others, but her eyes could not conceal the fact that she was a professional killer. Once the introductions were out of the way, Lafer said, "The Grand Master Grisamm himself, Grimm, has ordered all of us to aid Tota during the pirate conflict."

Francis smiled grimly.

———————o○o———————

IT didn't take long for Frances and Lafer to organize and pull off a successful raid against the estate. But when he returned to Tota and the others, his report was not good: everyone left on the estate was dead, butchered where they stood. They were, however, able to turn over some boxes of material that might be of some use in the search for Alec.

It was then the first major clue was revealed. Tota was the one who recognized it: a simple patch on an otherwise plain gray uniform, sporting a bright multirayed sun against a dead black background. That drained him of most of his famous good cheer, and he delved deeper into the material they'd brought back. In one of Zanches' secure chambers, Tota compared some of the recorded transmissions with other potential evidence. He sent out messages to merchants among the Commercial Traders, and compared the many different bounties that were now pending on Alec and Alexa. Hundreds had been removed from the warranty and award list, and Tota's mood turned even sadder when he went over the long list of names.

"I think I knew who has young Master Alec," he told the assembled group two days later.

"Who, *who is it?*" Alexa demanded.

"A known art dealer, somewhat eccentric. She is known as Zoris af Sun."

"Are you sure about this?" Zanches asked.

"Several lines of evidence bring me to that conclusion. The first is the patch retrieved by Frances and his commandos, but the second is the most important. Her bounty on Alec has been paid in full. She has also increased the reward for the return of Alexa, who is considered her legal property throughout Florencia and the Neutral Zone."

Alexa looked worriedly at Zanches.

"Don't be concerned, my lady, Marengo is not one of those worlds. We do not hold with chattel slavery."

Alexa looked puzzled. "But...you have slaves on Marengo."

Zanches smirked. "Not at all; they are legally and gainfully employed individuals. Yes, they may be *called* slaves and sometimes treated as such, but all are paid very well and all may leave at any time. Yes, we used to have chattel slaves as part of our old culture—over a thousand years ago. Not anymore. Don't worry, Lady Alexa, you are very safe with us, all the more so because you are a friend to Alec."

Alexa let out a sigh of relief and sank back into her chair.

"Perhaps you would like a job as one of my slaves?" Zanches teased her.

"Doubt you can afford me," Alexa muttered.

"Name your price?"

Alexa looked angry at first, but she smiled sweetly and answered, "My lord Count, there is no price imaginable for something you can never hope to purchase or hire. I will marry Alec, and we will belong to each other to the end of our days. If he wants to sell me, then he can; *that* is how much I love him."

Zanches looked at Alexa silently for a long moment, then solemnly apologized. Then he insisted, "And that is why you will join Captain Jorik on his cruiser, and assist in the search for the *Predator*."

"Like hell I will! I'm going with Frances and Mikka!"

Frances cut in, "Alexa, we really do need your expertise. If they have fallen victim to Zuzack, then only you can help...or at least be our best advisor."

Alexa looked at Zanches. "What will you do?"

"I'll take two-thirds of the fleet and find this Zoris, while the remainder will go with Captain Jorik."

Alexa wanted to protest, but she saw the expressions on the faces of her compatriots, and capitulated as gracefully as she could. "Fine. I'll go, but if you fail, then I will be after you like a demon from Hell..." She blinked back tears. "Sorry. Forgive me. I was unjust, and had no right to release my anger on anyone here."

Zanches left his place at the table and walked up to Alexa, who stood up. He grabbed her shoulders and looked her in the eyes. "This 'young master Alec,' as Tota calls him, is the wealthiest man in the universe at the moment—and I don't mean moneywise. Perhaps someday, I too will find such wealth and marry her. I will find him for you, not because of my father's orders, or because of a desire to help my father's friend Tota, or because of you. Those are all valuable contributing reasons why I do this—but mostly I do so because something within me tells me that I must. Go now; and next time we meet, Alec will be by my side."

HE must have her, no matter what. For months, ever since he had first seen her and fallen so madly in love, he had been determined to make her his own. Nothing could stop him—and he would rather die or kill her than let someone else have her. The misunderstanding that had occurred after the party could easily be explained. After all, one of her best friends had carefully, if drunkenly, revealed that she liked it rough.

Once their misunderstandings were behind them, she would return with him to Marengo and marry him. They must have at least two sons, he decided, and she would always be his devoted wife.

He had made such plans more than once during his life, ever since he'd had his first girlfriend as a lad of 12. He was extremely jealous, and honestly believed his depth of emotion was simply evidence of his devotion and honesty toward the women he loved. No way in hell was he going to allow that incompetent snot to wed his Alexa. The rich ones always got the best of everything...but not this time. Hell no.

Lieutenant Andrei Beck examined his robotic arms, and hate filled him like pus in a gangrenous wound. *He could have at least let the ship's physician clone me a new pair.* Didn't matter; he'll have another pair cloned or stimmed as soon as he could return home. He sneered. *Zlo promised me that much, that traitor. So much for working with a family friend. That bastard will pay dearly.*

Beck looked up at Myra, who was arming herself. "Remember: no bloodbath."

Myra looked at the young fool in front of her and nodded. Then she looked over his shoulder at a couple of colleagues from her former ship, the *Bitch*. "Let's do it," she ordered, but stopped herself when she noticed the dislike in the young lieutenant's expression. "After you, of course, Captain."

"That's better. Stick to the plan, and get all the officers down here."

Beck looked at his two partners, Lieutenant Harris and Second Officer Dasbar. Both of them were the same age as Beck, both Oman, and they were all old friends from the same university on Marengo. They waited impatiently in the corridor near Cargo Bay Five, together with some fifty crewmen. All were fingering their weapons nervously.

"Is this all?" Myra burst out.

Beck answered, "We have almost another hundred troops waiting down by the small docking bay."

Myra rolled her eyes and frowned. "Lock and load! Let's go." She ordered, disregarding the young fool's expression. *At least he had the intelligence to take out the surveillance cameras on this section,* Myra thought, hurrying down the corridor. She paid no attention to the large battle android that stood like a statue next to the bulkhead, smoke curling up from its ventilation ports.

Beck followed at a run, grinding his teeth, biding his time. *Once we have the ship I'll have the bitch and her friends executed, and all the blame will fall on them. I'll be a hero when I get home, and Alexa will worship me for rescuing her from Alec.*

The mutineers spread out over the ship in squads of ten. When Beck and Myra reached the large docking bay they were met by Captain Zlo and a few crew; all of them looked surprised.

"Are we under attack?" Zlo demanded. "I have heard no alarm!" Then he noticed Myra. "What is she doing here?"

Two loud rounds echoed in the docking bay, and Captain Zlo's head vanished in red mist. Everyone looked with horror at Myra and her blaster barrel.

"I said no bloodbath!" Beck shouted hysterically.

Myra gave him a dry and evil smile. "No turning back now. Let's go!"

That was the beginning of the bloodbath.

A shuttle dodged asteroids as it approached the *Predator*, sending docking requests but receiving no signals in return. When it finally got a response, it closed in and started the docking procedures, entering the frigate's larger docking bay.

Behl, Nina and the two Grisamm monks were met by "Captain" Beck and several crew members, who immediately stunned them into immobility. "Put them with the others," Beck ordered, as he mused over being a captain for the very first time. He liked giving orders, and so far his plan was almost going perfectly. All he needed to do now was take care of that conniving bitch Myra.

SHE looked down on him and admired what she saw. "He is almost a perfect specimen," she said wonderingly, "if a bit scuffed. It will take a while before we can work with him, but it will be worth it. We shall be patient. Yes, we must be very patient." She touched his lips. "Soon I will have your beloved also, young man, and the two of you will be my masterpiece. I can't wait to see your expressions when you look upon each other while being..." she trailed off. "And then, oh yes... and then, the true work begins." Zoris af Sun trailed her long, thin fingers down Alec's chest, brushing aside the last of the healing gel.

She glared at her assistant. "Clean and shave him meticulously, Sebilla!"

"Yes, my lady."

"Is there any new information about the location of my rightful property, this young pirate princess Alexa?"

Zoris turned to a pair of bounty hunters, whom she knew only as Ballack and Giggi. Neither displayed any fear. They were husband and wife: he of the Crom species, she of the Nastyr. They'd been tracking down bounties as a couple for more than a century now, and their passion for each other was equaled only by their professionalism. They rarely failed to find anyone on their list, and their expertise was known throughout the occupied universe. "It is only a matter of time before Ballack and I have her," Giggi said now.

"Good, that's very good. Bring her back to me quickly, and your award will be larger than any you have ever known before."

Zoris looked back at her newly acquired property and thought, *It is dreaming...*

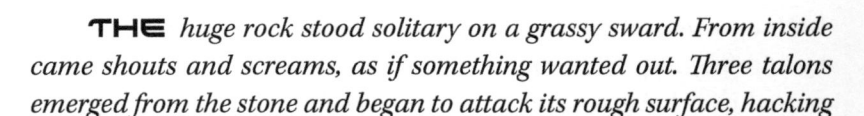

THE *huge rock stood solitary on a grassy sward. From inside came shouts and screams, as if something wanted out. Three talons emerged from the stone and began to attack its rough surface, hacking and chopping until a statue begun to emerge from the rock.*

"We are shaping you as we have shaped so many others; we are shaping you so that you can embrace your destiny. Accept it or die, as the others have died. Embrace us, and come and get us; we are waiting for you. Bring us back...bring us back."

The pain was excruciating as the talons hammered on, harder and harder, until blood poured out of the rock. The crudely-formed eyelids opened; the eyes stared, and blue beams emerged and joined. A bright light flashed, and an explosion thundered in the sky as a dark cloud grew to blot out the sunlight.

"Bring me back...bring me back, and I shall let you thunder by my side for all eternity. Hear me, hear me, the drums are my voice! Bring me back, and thunder!"

The dark cloud vanished; beneath it was a blood-soaked battlefield, where countless bodies of many species lay as they had fallen. The sky was black, and the ground was red, green, blue, yellow, milky white...all the colors of blood. From the horizon, in all directions, fire rushed in upon them, falling upon the corpses and devouring them.

On a central hill, surrounded by huge dead creatures with monstrous fanged heads, knelt an androgynous person in body armor. That person's eyes stared up into the universe as the firestorm rushed in. The figure extended its arms towards the universe and shouted angrily, in a voice more beautiful than any other in creation, "Mother, father, forgive them not, for they knew exactly what they did! Father, mother, I have spoken! I have thundered!"

The eye was black as a thundercloud, and from its center emerged three dark lines. The dark lines spun around the eye, forming a triangle; the center of the eye erupted in flames, and the three sides of the triangle parted from each other and formed up into three ragged lines in the shape of talons: two nails to the left, and one nail to the right of the eye. The talons gradually altered their appearance, turning into huge razor sharp fangs that were slowly hidden as the monstrous eye closed. It let out a roar; it was angry beyond mere anger, angry beyond rage. So very angry, and when it shut there came a thunder as of drums—many, many drums, pounding from within.

ALEC finally opened his eyes, surprised to discover that he was comfortable. He rolled over and hugged the pillow. All he wanted to do was to go back to sleep...

"No, not sleep!" He sat straight up. "Hell no, that was the worst nightmare ever..."

His voice trailed off as he realized that he lay inside a large room build on an open terrace; the breeze blew in his face, and he could hear birds singing. The sound of crashing waves breaking against something far below filled his ears, and he could smell what seemed to be hundreds of different types of flowers. He frowned, and realized that he was naked. He felt somewhat sore and stiff, but otherwise great—better than he had for months, in fact.

He slid out of the bed and looked for his clothes, but couldn't find them. For a second he blushed to think of his own nakedness, but decided to explore the place anyway.

He walked out onto a large balcony overlooking a steel-blue ocean several hundred paces below. Blinking the sleep out of his eyes, he stretched his arms in the air, taking several deep breaths. It had been a long time since he'd breathed fresh air, and he gulped it down as he might a nice bottle of wine.

"It is time for your morning bath," a woman said from behind him, as she clapped twice.

Alec spun around, blushing again, and found himself facing a middle-aged woman. Her face seemed younger than her body...or was that just the effect of her voice?

He lifted his eyebrows as ten half-naked male and female Omans entered the room.

"My name is Sebilla," the woman said, "and I am here to serve you. Now, which do you prefer; males, females or both? Should you desire a species other than Oman, then please inform me and I will comply."

Alec looked at the woman, puzzled. "What? What do you mean, and what are you talking about?"

"Your bathers, sir."

"My *bathers*?"

Alec didn't know what to think...but his eyes were drawn to the five beautiful women. Noticing this, Sebilla gestured for the males to leave.

The floor opened up, and from it emerged a large circular pool filled with bubbles. Two of the girls giggled as they grab his arms firmly and escorted him into the warm pool. The girls were young, perhaps seventeen standard years old, if that.

They washed him gently, while massaging his skin and feeding him tasty fruit and a pale greenish liquid that cranked all his senses up to one hundred percent. Chills tickled down his spine.

Given the effect of the drink, combined with the professional attention from the very attractive girls, it wasn't long before he had an erection. Whenever he tried to conceal it, the girls just moved his arms and began cleaning the areas around it.

Not one of them talked to him, but he didn't mind. After a while he leaned back into a particularly generous bosom and relaxed as several pairs of hands rubbed and massaged various parts of his body. He closed his eyes and a treacherous part of his brain thought, *Life is good.*

After the bath, five new girls escorted him into an adjacent room. He was still naked and couldn't hide his erection, but the new group of girls behaved identically to their colleagues. They dried him off and placed him on a table, and begun massaging him with warm, steamy oil. The oil smelled of natural perfume, and was applied liberally over and over again. When they turned him over on his backside, his erection stood high and proud, and the girls whispered soft and suggestive things about what they could do for him.

They teased and tickled him from time to time, but always without touching his little mutineer. He said nothing to them, deciding instead to simply enjoy himself. That treacherous bit thought, *Must be dead and in heaven...or maybe hell, if someone doesn't do something with the little bastard soon...*

Since none of the girls would, he decided to take matters into his own hands. But whenever he tried, one of the girls moved his hands away, firmly but gently, while moving one finger in the air, gesturing that this was a no-no. But they kept teasing him with vulgar suggestions. Alec was about to go nuts when one of the younger, darker complected girls happened to touch the head of his penis by mistake, as she reached for a bottle of oil. She looked down in horror and then lost her balance, falling onto him face first. He fired off a volley, but not everything. Disappointed, he demanded that someone relieve the pressure of his throbbing cock.

The girls stopped what they were doing and looked at Alec in horror, and at their friend in disbelief.

"No, no, no, you clumsy fool!" Sebilla shouted.

"I didn't mean for it to happen, it was an accident, please, I'm so sorry! It won't happen again!" the dark girl sobbed.

"You're precisely right: it won't happen again. Prepare her!" Sebilla ordered.

While the young girl begged for mercy, her four friends forced her down on the floor, cursing and screaming at their friend like beasts. They quickly removed silk scarves from their harem outfits and tied them around her ankles, which they then attached to a long stick. Two of the girls grabbed the stick, one at each end, and lifted it up, exposing the girl's feet. They tossed her slippers away while she cried, begging and straining at her restraints. She made several futile attempts to reach the rope around her ankles with her hands, but the two girls who held the stick held it too high. The young girl screamed aloud as the other girls whipped the soles of her feet with thin canes.

Sebilla looked on and assured them if they didn't put one hundred percent behind each and every stroke, they would all receive the same treatment. They kept striking until blood splattered all over, and not until then did Sebilla gesture for them to stop.

Alec looked on in disbelief...and for the first time since his wakening, began to remember something about a similar-looking girl with exotic, dark golden skin, but even more beautiful than this one...but who?

His natural warning system suddenly screamed out that all this was very wrong.

Four of the girls returned to Alec, as if nothing had happened. The punished fifth wept in silence as she removed the scarves around her ankles and pushed aside the long wood stick. She looked at the canes with her blood on them...and then she started to clean them with her clothes. She knelt and bowed her head as she handed them to Sebilla, holding back her tears.

"Go and take care of that." Sebilla motioned towards the girl's bloody feet. The young girl began crawling away on all fours. "When I said you should go," Sebilla snapped, "I meant walk, not crawl."

The girl looked at Sebilla in horror. Then she got up and stumbled away, leaving small bloody footprints on the white marble floor.

"When you are done, return and clean up your mess," Sebilla called after the girl.

Alec was no longer aroused, and didn't see how he could be ever again. He had lost interest, thank Gull, just as they started to beat the young girl. He knew this was all wrong, but until he could remember, he had to keep a low profile...so he allowed the other four girls to continue massaging him. None had changed their attitude towards him, treating him just as they had before, laughing, giggling and caressing him with professional skill.

Eventually, they wrapped him in a white toga and placed thin slippers on his feet, then left him, bowing their heads while backing away. Alec turned around and noticed a tall exotic dressed with white clothes and a thin cloak with a hood, which covered her face. It—she—was looking at him. He couldn't see her expression, but her ugly yellow eyes sent cold chills down his spine.

"And how is my patient doing this morning?" she asked in a breathy voice. "We are truly sorry for the clumsiness of our servant, and the trouble she has caused you."

"Who are you, and what am I doing here? Why can't I remember anything?" Alec demanded.

"Ah, so many questions at once. My, my, you really *are* strong. Walk with me, young master Alec, son of the house of Hornet of the Nastasturus Federation."

They walked through long hallways cooled by fresh breezes, bringing natural scents with them. They passed a gallery of tall marble pillars interspersed with statues of men and women, mostly Oman, which appeared to be made of different types of stone. Some marble pillars had green vegetation climbing on them in a race to reach the sun. A variety of birds and small animals were singing and making beautiful sounds; some birds, in fact, fluttered up and landed on the tall woman's shoulders. She whistled back to the birds, and held them with unconscious grace.

Alec found himself staring at her spidery pale fingers. The nails were long and black, and looked sharp. Some of the skin on her wrists was scaled. *She must be very nice, considering the birds' reac-*

tion, he thought, as he listened intently to the very old and apparently very wise woman walking next to him.

"Soon your memory will return in full, Master Alec," she murmured. "I must admit, you were a mess when I finally received you. But thanks to my healing skills, you are as good as new...and probably in better shape than ever. I had planned to give you a lecture on stealing other people's property, but I suppose there is not much point in that right now, is there, since your memory has not been restored yet?"

"Did I steal something from you?"

"Why yes, you bad little boy."

She pushed her long index finger into his side, and with skilled experience, she struck a nerve. Alec jumped high and laughed.

"What...I'm not ticklish!"

"You weren't. Well...no more than average. I changed that when I healed you. It will make it more interesting, later..."

"Later?"

"All in good time, Sir Hornet, all in good time. Come: let me show you some of my precious art collection. It is the best in the entire universe. Come, come." She sounded more and more excited as she mentioned her collection...and it didn't go unnoticed by Alec when she drooled a bit.

He tried to look through the thin white garment covering her face, but failed to make out her appearance. He did, however, notice that the saliva that hit the floor pitted the marble like acid, reminding him of something repugnant. *Some of my memory is returning,* he thought.

Inside the first gallery were contemporary paintings and art pieces of all types from many different worlds. In the second gallery was older art from many cultures and worlds. Some Alec recognized from books and films. Inside the third stood hundreds of beautiful sculptures and statues. Some made of stone, while others were crafted of precious metals. Alec was flabbergasted; his hostess loved his interest, and made sure that she answered all his questions satisfactorily. She found the young Oman very interesting and cultivated; it had been a long time since she could discuss her art collection with someone who really appreciated it. She almost regretted what she'd soon have to do with him.

A servant brought them refreshments. Once he had finished his drink, he handed the gold cup back to the uniformed servant, who stood waiting patiently with a gold tray. Impressive, but Alec had been served in such style before; he was, after all, the heir to the House of Hornet. Alec noticed that his hostess hadn't touched her own drink, however. The wind grew warm, and Alec was glad he didn't sweat.

"Are you not thirsty?" he wondered aloud.

"I seldom drink, but for my medication. I am very old, you see; please forgive me for not being a good hostess."

"You are an excellent hostess, my lady. I have no complaints."

"Good, that is good. One must always remain calm, or the treat will be spoiled."

Alec looked towards her, puzzled, and she glided away and opened up the doors to yet another of her art galleries.

"Now, this is a great honor to you, young Master Hornet," she breathed. "Not many people have ever seen this. This is true art, the art of life. Come, come, you must follow and see."

Alec felt strange, and wondered what had been in the drink. He started to sweat, and her words filled his brain with a strange echo.

Something told him he must follow her. He walked into the dark room, and slowly, as his eyes adjusted and the light became brighter, he remembered everything... and when he looked over the room, his face became a mask of horror.

It was filled with...abominations. There were no words for the vileness.

"For two months I have healed you, physically as well as mentally," his hostess said. "Though as to the latter, I must confess that I didn't have to do much. Your inner strength is far greater than that of anyone I have ever encountered, save for one. My servants will make sure you are ready. They will be by your side at all times, and will ensure that you are aroused at all times, without any further mishaps like this morning."

She turned toward him. "It will increase all your sensations for the main banquet, you see. In ten days, I shall begin my work with you. Oh, don't bother; the drug should have had its effect on you by now. Little servants, take him away—and if any more mistakes are made, then you will all be the course after him. Keep him aroused but do not let him climax at any time, not even when he is asleep; you know what to do."

A dozen beautiful girls, aged perhaps fifteen to twenty, escorted Alec away from the main gallery. The cold, clear laughter of his hostess, combined with the horrors decorating the floor and the walls in the large room, was the beginning of a new introduction to pure evil for young Alec. As he was escorted away, he looked at a strange painting on the wall, dully wondering what it was. It bore several strange features he couldn't quite make out... it seemed an odd but normal piece of somewhat contemporary art, except for the one eye staring out at him.

Just as he was dragged away by the friendly girls, Alec could have sworn the eye blinked.

THE battle shuttle moved cautiously towards the *Predator*. "I'm telling you, something's wrong," Mikka said as they approached the frigate.

"There's some kind of interference...I don't understand why we can't get any readings at all," the major piloting the shuttle contributed.

"I don't like this," Alexa mumbled, crossing her arms tightly over her chest. "What if life support is down or something, and they're all dead?"

"We will soon find out," Mikka noted sourly.

"I guess so."

The shuttle eased into place beside the *Predator*. Repeated hails and commands failed to get the frigate to open any of its docking bays, so after an hour or so, ten figures left the shuttle and jetted toward one of the larger ship's emergency hatches.

"I'll go first," Mikka said.

One by one, Alexa and eight Marengan soldiers clanged down onto the hull with their magnetic books, while Mikka jetted toward the hatch. Alexa waited until she was inside before following. As one of the Marengans followed her, the *Predator*'s security system powered suddenly, sounding an alarm in their suits—and slamming the outer hatch shut so quickly that the Marengan had no time to get out of the way. He was crushed and all but cut in half, dead before he could cry out.

The *Predator* came to life. Lights flickered on, and a missile flashed from a starboard launcher to the shuttle, converting it into an expanding ball of shrapnel and plasma that chewed the surviving Marengans on the hull into flash-burned, bloody paste.

Mikka and Alexa, unaware of what had just happened outside, were thrown to the deck as gravity returned to normal. The inner hatch opened, and before either could move, they were struck by a stun beam.

CAPTAIN Beck stared down on his prize, smiling happily. Alexa laid in her own bed onboard the *Predator*; Beck had taken possession of Alec's suite, while Myra had taken Captain Zlo's. His woman lay before him in all her nude glory; he had washed her with care, exploring her entire body in the process. Soon, once she awakened, she would be ready to welcome him to her bosom. Even if she were reluctant at first, it must surely be clear to her that he had done so much for her—and that only a real man worthy of her affection would make such sacrifices. And in any case, a real man was always in charge of his woman.

Beck too was naked, stimulating himself as he waited for her to awaken. He was too busy daydreaming to realize that his prize was only pretending to be unconscious. He became abruptly aware of it when both her feet landed squarely on his testicles with great force, all but driving them into his abdomen and assuring he would never have children without a great deal of medical help.

Alexa didn't know what had happened or why she'd ended up where she was, but her natural instinct for survival took care of her.

At first she thought she had woken up from some horrible nightmare, but when she saw the despised Beck standing by the foot of the bed, dreamily masturbating like some idiotic teen boy, she knew it was time to fight. Once she'd ruined his ability to reproduce, she lunged at him like a demon as he screamed and clutched himself. She hit him hard in his mouth with her left elbow and uppercut him with her right fist, feeling his nose crunch almost as satisfactorily as his balls had. Alexa leaped over him—and crashed into the bulkhead as she lost control of her muscles. She slid to the deck, convulsing.

Myra looked down at the two of them, shaking her head as she holstered her stunner. "Told him he couldn't take care of her alone. What an idiot." She glanced at the women accompanying her. "You two take care of your friend, and make sure you put her with the others. When he comes to, tell Beck I need to see him ASAP on the bridge."

She scuffed at a couple of teeth that lay on the deck, and smiled at Alexa. She stopped smiling when Alexa's eyes meet hers.

---oOo---

"IT appears she doesn't want you," Myra explained to Beck several hours later, after he'd been seen to by the medical andies. "And if you or anyone of the other males touch her or any of the other female crew or prisoners without their express permission, you'll have another mutiny to deal with."

Beck protested loudly, flapping his robotic arms. He looked like an idiot. "But she'll love me once I've made it clear it's in her best interest to do so!"

Wondering if he'd been born that stupid or if he'd had to work at it, Myra snapped, "Maybe she will, but not right now. Like I said, if you mess with Alexa again, I'll tear your balls off. We have more urgent matters to deal with. That Marengan cruiser will be on our trail soon enough." Myra spun the command chair around and issued some instructions to the bridge crew.

"I'm the captain of this ship, do you hear me, Myra?" Beck demanded.

"Why, of course you are," Myra agreed, without taking her eyes away from the holomonitor in front of her.

"YOU could at least have given me some clothes, you assholes!" Alexa screamed.

She slammed her foot into the bulkhead, swearing so vociferously that it was a wonder the paint didn't peel. She was inside a large storage closet. It was very cold and she shivered, her teeth clattering like a jackhammer.

Beck's voice filtered through the wall. "You will stay there until you realize it's for your own good," the sanctimonious prick intoned. "And you must apologize for hurting me. I know very well that love hurts, but you have to accept the fact that you love me. Don't deny it—I've seen it in your eyes. I've known it since the first time I saw you. I can understand playing hard to get, but I think you've gone a little too far. I want you to think about what you did to me. I have to spend a whole day in sickbay undergoing reconstructive surgery. I want you to think about how I'm the only real love in your life while you sit in there and freeze until I get back. Remember, Alexa, this hurts me more than it does you."

"I hope so!" she shouted. "And if you ever give me a chance, I'll make damned sure I *kill* you next time!"

She glared at the locked door in disbelief. She couldn't believe the nerve of this retard.

Alexa was jogging in place and hugging herself to keep warm when the door finally opened hours later. She stopped and stood in the center of the room, crouching with her hands extended, poised to jump at whoever was coming in if she got the chance. Her skin was a pale blue by then, her lips purplish, and her hair and eyebrows were frosted with a thin rime of ice. She was the cutest thing Captain Beck had ever seen.

He held a thick blanket in front of him, and Alexa ran into his open arms. Beck felt very satisfied as he embraced his one true love. He didn't care about Myra's warning; after all he was the captain.

Wrapping the blanket over her in a protective manner while talking to her comfortably, explaining all her errors and how he would show her the right way in life, he was tickled to death to know that she must really love him. After all, hadn't she run into his arms and embraced him?

Alexa held her clenched fist under her chin and didn't hear a word. The only thing she had in mind was Alec, and getting away from the cold. She didn't pay any attention to the blabbering idiot beside her.

She was too cold and exhausted to protest when Beck lifted her up and carried her to his quarters. Inside, there was a nice hot meal for two waiting, along with some mulled wine. He set her down gently on one of the chairs, and the two of them had their first, long-overdue meal together. More than once during the meal, he complained about her table manners, explaining that if Alec was any kind of a real man, he would have taught her proper manners. Alexa didn't give a damn; she was starving. She attacked all the vegan and bakery dishes, avoiding any meat products. This, however, was not acceptable to any carnivore, according to Beck, who insisted she should have some meat. "Good for our children!" he announced.

"Go to hell, dumbass," muttered Alexa, between bites of bread and cheese.

She didn't notice the sudden hate shining in Beck's eyes as she emptied her third cup of warm wine. She started to feel faint, and muttered, "Must have eaten too fast."

Her companion smiled superciliously. "No, my love, I prepared your wine—just to make sure."

Alexa looked up at Beck, who now stood next to her. He grabbed her head hard and forced it under his arm. Alexa struggled, but she was weak from the drugged wine. Beck explained that she must have her meats—and so he forcefed her as her future loving husband. After all, he knew what was best for her, since she was only a woman.

Alexa spat and screamed, coughed and cursed him. Even when she vowed to kill him slowly someday, he entertained her threats only as her playing hard to get. Beck convinced himself. But when she hurled up all the bloody meat he'd forced down her throat, he had had enough. He started to slap her, and couldn't stop; he hit her harder and harder, which just made him want to hit her harder and harder. He was soon using his fists, and when she slid to the floor, he kicked her in the face over and over again.

Beck smiled lovingly when he saw fragments of her teeth on the deck. By now, she lay on her stomach, with her right arm cocked up against the armrest on the living room couch. He couldn't stop himself: his heavy boot crashed mercilessly down on her elbow, and he laughed when he heard the sound of breaking bone. Alexa took the pain with little more than a short moan; by now, she was more dead than alive.

"Look what you've done!" Beck shouted. "Just look at this mess!" He leaning over her, grabbed her hair, and yanked back her head. "This is all your fault! This was supposed to be a perfect dinner for the two of us. *You are a lying, deceiving whore.* That does it!"

He calmed himself, and again surveyed the destruction in the suite. "You will clean all this up, or I swear to you that what just happened is nothing compared to what will come." He grabbed a pitcher of water from the table and poured it over Alexa. She woke up, spitting and cursing.

"Still won't apologize, eh?" He grabbed her hair and dragged her into the bedroom, tossing her on the bed on her stomach. He began to unbutton his trousers.

Alexa was disoriented at first, but quickly came to her senses. She disregarded the throbbing pain from her broken arm; that clean, pure agony had cut through the drugged haze that had enveloped her. She hurt like hell and knew she would probably die in the next few minutes, but she didn't care. No way in hell was she was going to be raped again, ever.

She felt him penetrating her—but for some reason, he never went all the way. Instead he felt soft, too soft. Beck started to curse, and slapped her across the back of her head. "This is your fault, you stupid bitch!" he screamed. "Now I can't perform because of all this violence!"

Alexa rolled off the bed and curled up into a little ball on the floor, trying to protect herself. "Wait, stop, stop!" she begged.

But Beck didn't listen. Instead he started kicking her again.

An odd gurgling arose from her, and it took a moment for him to realize that she was laughing. "My love," she gasped. "My love, thank you..."

He stopped kicking, peering down at his woman in bemusement.

"Thank you," she considered, "for teaching me how to be your future wife and what I should expect...and now, I beg, please allow me to reward you, my master." Her voice was slurred, given her broken teeth and busted lips, but it was clear that she was chagrined and broken. She lifted her left arm, and with her hand she caressed his inner thighs and his manhood with the grace of a goddess and the skills of a nymph.

"Finally," he sighed. With a satisfied expression, he looked down on her cutely bloodied little face. He used his thumb to wipe away a trickle of blood from the corner of her eye, and gently brushed her hair back from her black-and-blue face. It had swollen grotesquely, so that he could barely recognize her; but it didn't matter, because he wanted her to look like that anyway. That way, no one but him would ever desire her.

He nodded, and she smiled back at him. He felt a twinge of disgust when he realized there were only jagged gaps where her front and bottom teeth had been. But that was a minor thing, easily fixed; and the massage she gave his scrotum was the best he could remember, so he closed his eyes and bend his neck back. He could soon feel her warm breath on him, the exquisite sensations as her lips wrapped around his shaft and began to move. The slick, almost greasy slipperiness of her blood made it feel even better as her lips and mouth slide back and forth. *On her knees where she belongs,* he thought.

She stopped long enough to ask if he was close to orgasming, then went back to sucking him lusciously. Beck couldn't answer; he was in heaven. Alexa sensed that he was just about to explode...so she maneuvered his rock-hard erection between her broken, jagged teeth, and just as her "captain" was about to orgasm, she bit down hard.

His cock didn't come off in one easy snap, as she thought it might, and she was glad. She had to grind down hard, back and forth like a saw as his screams echoed through the suite, before it finally came free.

SCREAMS of unspeakable pain and horror filled the banquet room. Before she had begun, the lady Zoris had injected her captive with a chemical cocktail that she assured him would do three things: magnify his pain tenfold, ensure that he didn't pass out from the pain, and stabilize him mentally so that his mind wouldn't break. She wanted him awake, sane, and in agony for the entire proceedings.

It had begun when she had electrically stimulated him to erection—and then begun to slice off thin, bloody slabs of his penis, frying them up in clarified butter with garlic in a small skillet over an open flame. An assistant placed a wide cup under the dripping stub, collecting the blood. When the cup was filled, another servant applied something to the stub to stop the bleeding.

The guests applauded Zoris when she served them, one by one, small pieces of the butter-fried meat. They were all dressed in black, and wore masks covering half their faces. Each one of the twenty had two servants attending to their needs, and they sat around horseshoe-shaped table. Alec was at the center of their table, the focus of their attention. He was stretched backwards with his head attached to a sort of coronet covered with blinking lights. His left wrist and ankle were shackled to each other on one side, and his rights on the other. Small heavy weights were attached to all fingers and toes, forcing them to spread in an unnatural position. His six-pack abs were tight as his position forced his muscles to flex. He was impaled through his anus, and a small plate prevented him from sliding down too far, injuring any vital organs. His head was at the same level as it would have been if he would have been standing. If he looked down through his bent knees, he could see the floor a few feet below.

Several catheters and wires and electrical devices had been inserted into his body, some supplying him with medications while others kept track of his life readings. A computer behind him displayed a status report. Two physicians sat next to a monitor, hidden from the dinner guests behind a screen.

Alec's mouth was gagged with an instrument that forced his mouth wide open; his tongue moved desperately in a futile attempt to form words. His eyes were forced open by a similar device, and a small hovering android occasionally dropped precise little dabs of liquid into them.

Zoris turned around, and took a bite of his naked muscular chest with her horde of sharp teeth, tearing away a chunk of pectoral; the white glean of his ribcage was suddenly visible. Solicitously, she applied a clear spray to the gaping wound, and the blood stopped flowing. She smacked her lips and chewed his flesh with care, still facing him.

Zoris took her time. She paced in front of her guests, asking for their opinion and advice while drying her bloody lips daintily on a silk cloth. One woman gestured for Zoris to come closer, and whispered something to her.

Zoris smiled. "Why, of course you may have it. But I'll need to keep what is inside for...later."

Zoris walked over to Alec and threw him a kiss—then cut off his scrotum with a dull iron knife. Alec's scream then seemed beyond anything that a human throat could ever produce; he prayed for death, or at least unconsciousness, as Zoris removed his testicles from the ragged mess and carefully placed them in a chilled cryogenics flask. She then lay the scrotum on a small silver plate, walked it over to her guest, and made sure she was pleased.

"I'll have it prepared for you." She handed the plate to a servant and left a few instructions.

Zoris turned her attention back to Alec, and started slicing off his left breast with a surgical saw, handing it to her servitors to fry up. Then she selected a scalpel and, with consummate skill, moved down and removed half his six-pack, quickly applying a purplish gel to make sure his intestines remained viable. A servant had to assist her as she removed the right half the ribcage; by then, over an hour had passed.

Alec cried and whimpered, for all the good that did him. His tears were collected by an android. Periodically, the guests applauded him and their hostess. After the ribcage had marinated in sherry, it was placed on a large grill on the center of the floor while Zoris carefully removed Alec's right arm and the lower half of his leg, leaving them tied together around wrist and ankle. Humming under her breath, she then flayed his thigh until the bone was visible.

After the physicians had stopped the bleeding, Zoris removed Alec's gag. She squeezed his cheeks hard, preventing him from swallowing or damaging his own tongue. His breath came fast and hard, like his chest might explode, but of course it wouldn't; she was too careful for that. "Anything to say?" she asked sweetly.

"*Kill me...*" he rasped.

Zoris laughed. "Kill you? Why? The thought has never crossed my mind, young man. I'm no murderer. Once we are done here, I will keep enough of your organs and your spinal cord alive inside one of my specially-made frames to last for eternity, with your brain and all its wonderful sensation of almost reaching climax intact...but instead of climaxing, you will feel this pain forever. Look around you."

She released the lock holding Alec's head in place, and turned it towards the right wall of the room. A drape was pulled away, revealing dozens of elegant frames of silvery metal, all of different sizes and shapes, with human remains arranged in elegant designs within. They were covered with some clear gel...and he could see that some of the organs were pulsing and twitching. All of them had one or more intact eyes, and all were staring back at Alec. Next to them were a dozen trophy heads...all alive.

"Look: there is your frame, and over here is your Alexa's."

She moved his head to the left, and he saw that on the wall hung several similar pieces. One of them had Alexa's name engraved on it. "I thought that the two of you could look at each other for eternity," she cooed. "Now isn't that nice of me? At first I was going to make statues of the both of you, but then my friends and I would only have been able to nibble a little on some of your meat. That wouldn't do."

Alec stopped screaming. In a voice that was cold and hard as neutronium, he said to her quietly, in a voice so low only she could hear, "Kill me, Zoris af Sun, or one day I will come to you and kill you a centimeter at a time—until you beg for death. And then I will let you live, wondering when I will come back and finish the job." He had the cold satisfaction of seeing her mask slip a bare millimeter, then gave in to the agony and horror. Before it subsumed him, he screamed, "By my soul I swear, I will kill you and all your kind!"

His words were met by applause from the guests.

Zoris replaced the gag and returned to her work.

By then, nearly half his body had either been removed or eaten. Under the gel-like substance covering his torso, his right lung, liver and other viscera were readily visible. Zoris forced Alec's head forward so that he could see his half-eaten body, and an android brought up a large mirror so he could see it better. "It intensifies the moment when they can watch as they are eaten alive," Zoris explained to her hungry guests. "The meat is sweeter."

She made a gesture and the dinner marshal lowered the plate on the pole, impaling Alec further. He screamed again as he slowly slid down. Zoris motioned to the dinner marshal and he replaced the block on the pole, preventing from Alec sliding further down. At that moment, a uniformed guard appeared behind the two physicians. Zoris glared at him with disgust, and then turned to her dinner friends.

"I'll be just a moment."

The guests started talking among themselves, and from time to time they looked at Alec, who kept screaming incoherently, overwhelming the soft background music. Some of the guests took the opportunity walk up to him and touch his body gently. Of course, his body interpreted the sensation as pain, and he screamed even louder.

"What is it?" Zoris snapped to the guard.

"You have an important visitor, my lady," he said in a low tone. "I could not put him off."

Zoris turned to her friends. "Please excuse me for a moment, I won't be long."

She was furious as she entered her audience chamber—but that fury quickly soured into dread, and for the first time in over eight hundred years Zoris af Sun truly feared for her own life. Before her stood a calm Florencian officer with Admiral's stars. That would never frighten her, of course, but the presence of the four figures arrayed behind him, all of them undeniably Silver Guards reborn, did. It could only mean one thing: the rumors about the return of de la Hoff were true.

The admiral stated flatly, "Your presence is required immediately."

Zoris bowed her head, gesturing to one of her servants. She gave him lengthy instructions and then turned back to the Admiral. "Lead the way, good sir."

The servant hurried into the banquet room and whispered to the two physicians, who listened intently and nodded. Upon receiving his own instructions, the dinner marshal turned to the guests and struck the floor with a tall, decorated staff three times. He apologized for his Madame, and broke the news that the rest of the dinner must be postponed, due to the preparations that it had become obvious still needed to be performed. They would all be compensated within months, he vowed, when the Lady Zoris hoped that she could continue serving more of Mr. Hornet and perhaps the pirate princess Alexa at the same time. He assured them that no parts would be cloned back on Mr. Hornet.

"We serve only the real thing here," he said, with great professional pride. Whereupon he clapped his hands, and all the Gormé chefs and servants begun to clean up, as the guests were escorted away.

The woman who had requested Alec's scrotum as a souvenir walked up to him. Even though half her face was covered with a decorative mask, she looked distinctly amused. One servant cleared his throat for her to move on; she ignored the servant. She let out a short, friendly laugh and then she placed a wet kiss on Alec's forehead, leaving a smear of lipstick.

Alec stared at her, and then on his partial-eaten body, in horror and disbelief. The pain was like an unrelenting blanket of fire; what was left of him convulsed and trembled uncontrollably. Tears poured down like a stream, and the calm little hovering android continued to collect them as fast as it could.

TO BE CONTINUED...

ABOUT THE AUTHOR

Photo Credit: Marit Lasson

ERIK Martin Willén loves creating worlds of epic proportion and exploring those worlds in the stories he creates. He is the author of the science fiction series Nastragull (*Pirates*, *Hunted*, *Dawn Sets in Hell*, *Section Twenty-one*, and *The Beast*) and the suspense thriller *The Lumberjack*. He lives in a small village in south Sweden where he is currently working on his next novel.

Ingram Content Group UK Ltd.
Milton Keynes UK
UKHW011816110723
424957UK00005B/378